Cynnwys

Ceffylau ... ceffylau ... ceffylau

Mae dros filiwn (1,000,000) o geffylau ym Mhrydain.

Mae rhai ceffylau'n rasio.

Mae rhai ceffylau'n neidio.

Ble:

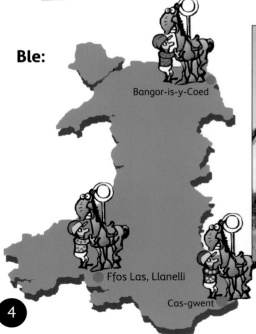

Bangor-is-y-Coed

Ffos Las, Llanelli

Cas-gwent

!

(ylau

@ebol

Cyfres Darllen Difyr

Hwyl! Briciau … briciau … briciau
Gwahanol! Chwaraeon gwahanol
Hapus! Hwyl a gŵyl ar draws y byd
Bach! Pryfed yr ardd

Anturus! Ydych chi'n barod am antur?
Cyffrous! Chwaraeon pêl gwahanol
Heini! Rasio gwahanol
Gweithgar! Ceffylau … ceffylau … ceffylau

Cyflym! Beth sy'n symud yn gyflym?
Talentog! Beth ydy'ch talent chi?
Peryglus! Anifeiliaid peryglus
Gofalus! Anifeiliaid peryglus yn y dŵr

Golygwyd gan Non ap Emlyn
Dyluniwyd gan stiwdio@ceri-talybont.com
Mapiau gan Alison Davies, www.themappingcompany.co.uk
Cartwnau gan Roger Bowles
Rheoli ac ymchwil lluniau gan Megan Lewis a Dafydd Saunders Jones

Aelodau'r Pwyllgor Monitro: Eleri Goldsmith (AdAS); Michelle Hutchings, Ysgol Pontyclun; James Jones, Ysgol Gynradd Victoria, Wrecsam; Petra Llywelyn; Pamela Morgan, Ysgol Gynradd Baglan, Port Talbot; Anthony Parker, Ysgol Gynradd Rogiet, Sir Fynwy; Laura Price, Ysgol Gynradd Llysweri, Casnewydd a Sara Tate, Ysgol Tanyfron, Wrecsam

Noddwyd gan Lywodraeth Cymru

Cydnabyddiaethau

Hoffai'r awdur a'r cyhoeddwr ddiolch i'r canlynol am eu caniatâd i atgynhyrchu'r lluniau a'r deunydd hawlfraint yn y llyfr hwn. Mae pob ymdrech wedi'i wneud i ganfod perchenogion hawlfraint y deunydd a ddefnyddiwyd yn y llyfr hwn. Bydd unrhyw ganiatâd hawlfraint sydd heb ei gynnwys gan y cyhoeddwr yn yr argraffiad hwn yn cael ei gydnabod mewn ail argraffiad.

Alamy: tud. 16 a thud. 17; Roger Bowles: tud. 7, tud. 18 a thud. 21; Canolfan Ceffylau Dolbadarn: tudalennau 12-15; Alison Davies: tud. 21; Getty Images: tud. 22, tud. 23 a thud. 24; Gwasg Carreg Gwalch: tud. 24 (clawr llyfr); Margo Harrison: tud. 4 (rhan isaf); Mary Evans Picture Library: tud. 19 (dau lun), tud. 20 (rhan uchaf); Photo Library Wales: tud. 5, tud. 6 (dau lun), tud. 7, tud. 18; S4C: tud. 20 a thud. 21; Yr Urdd: tud. 10 a thud. 11.

Mae rhai ceffylau'n gwneud "dressage".

Mae'r ceffylau'n symud yn smart iawn. Maen nhw'n dangos sgiliau arbennig.

Mae rhai ceffylau'n chwarae polo.

ffon

pêl polo

Trotian

Mae rhai ceffylau'n trotian. Edrychwch, mae'r ceffylau yma mewn rasys trotian. Maen nhw'n trotian yn gyflym iawn.

Ras trotian, Dyffryn Aman

Ras trotian, Aberystwyth

Ble:

Maen nhw'n trotian yn gyflym iawn!

Mae'n bosib ennill cwpan.

Ras trotian, Tir Prince, Towyn

Mwynhau

Mae rhai plant yn hoffi reidio ceffylau ... neu ... marchogaeth.

Mae'r plant yn dysgu sgiliau ac yn mwynhau. Mae'r ceffylau'n ffrindiau da i'r plant.

Mae rhai plant yn hoffi mynd i glwb marchogaeth.

Yn y clwb, maen nhw'n:
- marchogaeth
- cystadlu ar geffylau
- dysgu am geffylau
- gofalu am geffylau.

Mwynhau eto

Edrychwch - mae hi'n braf! Marchogaeth tu allan. Gwych!
Mae llawer o geffylau yn Llangrannog.

Mwynhau gyda'r ceffylau
yn Llangrannog

Rhaid gwisgo het reidio bob amser!

Mae hi'n bwrw glaw! … Dim problem!
Mae marchogaeth dan do yn hwyl.

Gwersyll yr Urdd
Llangrannog

Mwynhau gyda'r ceffylau dan do yn Llangrannog

Mae marchogaeth yn Llangrannog yn hwyl.

Ceffylau ar y teledu

Mae rhai ceffylau'n gweithio - ar y teledu ac mewn ffilmiau.
Edrychwch ar y ceffylau yma yn y rhaglen deledu *Merlin*.

Mae rhai o'r ceffylau ar y rhaglen *Merlin* yn dod o Lanberis. Mae rhai o'r ceffylau yn y ffilm *Robin Hood* yn dod o Lanberis, hefyd.

Ffilm *Robin Hood*

Wel! Wel!

Maen nhw'n gwneud rhannau o *Merlin* yng Nghymru - ger Caerdydd.
Roedden nhw'n gwneud rhannau o'r ffilm *Robin Hood* yn Sir Benfro.

13

Mae canolfan geffylau arbennig iawn yn Nolbadarn, Llanberis. Yn y ganolfan, mae'r ceffylau'n dysgu triciau a styntiau.

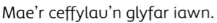

Dysgu i berfformio mewn joust

Mae'r ceffylau'n glyfar iawn.

Mae'r merched yma'n gwneud styntiau a thriciau ar geffylau.

Gweithio gyda'r heddlu

Mae ceffylau'n gweithio gyda'r heddlu hefyd.
Mae'r heddlu'n marchogaeth ceffylau yn y dref.

Edrychwch ar y ceffylau yma. Maen nhw'n helpu'r heddlu i reoli'r bobl mewn gêm bêl-droed.

Heddiw ...

Mae ceffylau'n gweithio ar y gamlas.

Mae'r cwch yn cario pobl. Mae'r cwch yn drwm.

Tynnu cwch camlas yn Llangollen heddiw

... Ddoe

Roedd ceffylau'n gweithio ar y gamlas yn yr hen amser hefyd.

Tynnu cwch camlas yn yr hen ddyddiau.

Roedd y cwch yn cario pethau - glo a haearn.
Roedd y cwch yn drwm.

Gweithio ar y ffordd

Yn yr hen amser, roedd ceffylau'n gweithio ar y ffordd. Dyma'r goets fawr.

Ceffylau'n tynnu'r goets fawr

Roedd y goets fawr yn cario
- pobl
- y post.

Roedd pobl yn eistedd:
- tu allan
- tu mewn.

Edrychwch ar y dillad smart.

Roedd y goets fawr yn mynd o Lundain … i Gaergybi.
Yna, roedd hi'n mynd o Gaergybi … i Lundain.

DW I'N MYND I LUNDAIN …WPS!

LUNDAIN

IWERDDON
Caergybi
Llundain

Ceffylau rhyfel

Yn yr hen amser, roedd ceffylau'n mynd i'r rhyfel.

Roedd ceffylau'n
- tynnu gynnau
- tynnu ambiwlans.

Gweithgar!

Roedd milwyr yn marchogaeth y ceffylau.

Dyma lyfr am geffyl rhyfel gan Michael Morpurgo.
Ceffyl Rhyfel ydy'r enw Cymraeg.
War Horse ydy'r enw Saesneg.

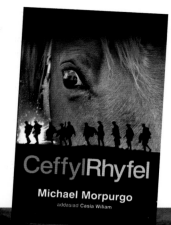

Yn y stori, mae ceffyl yn mynd i'r rhyfel.
Mae'n mynd o Loegr i ganol y rhyfel yn Ffrainc.

Mae'r stori mewn drama
a ffilm hefyd.

Drama *War Horse*
yn Llundain

24

Little
Monkey

An elephant, a lion and a giraffe
were having a sleep under a tree.
A little monkey was up in the tree.

The lion shouted out,
"Who hit me?"

"It wasn't me," said the giraffe.
"I was asleep."

"It wasn't me," said the elephant.
"I didn't hit you."

The little monkey looked down.
"Did I hit you?" she asked.
"Please don't be cross.
I want to be your friend."

"You want to be our friend!"
shouted the lion.

"We don't want a little monkey
to be our friend,"
said the elephant and the giraffe.

And they all laughed at
the little monkey.

"I'll go then," said the little monkey.
"I have lots of friends and
we have lots of fun.
We can swing from tree to tree and
you can't do that.
Look at us!"

And away went the little monkey
with her friends.

The elephant, the lion and the giraffe
were just going to sleep.

Then the giraffe said,
"Look across the river.
What's that thing there?"

"I think it's a tent," said the elephant.
"Can you see that man?
I think he wants to catch us and
put us in a zoo."

"What can we do?"
asked the giraffe.

"Let's eat him!"
said the lion.

"But how can we cross the river?"
said the elephant.
"We can't swim.
The crocodiles will eat us."

"We'll have to think," said the elephant.
So they all had a think.

"Got it!" said the elephant.
"Let's ask the monkeys to help us."

"How can **they** help?"
asked the lion.

"They may not want to help us,"
said the giraffe.
"We laughed at the little monkey.
We said we didn't want her
to be our friend."

"I think they will help us,"
said the elephant.

"Little monkey! Little monkey!"
shouted the lion.
"Come down here!"

"Say please," said the elephant.

"Please!" shouted the lion.

"Did you call me?"
said the little monkey.

"Yes, we did," said the elephant.
"How good of you to come.
Please will you help us?"

"What do you want me to do?"
asked the little monkey.

The elephant said,
"A man has come to catch us.
He wants to put us in a zoo.
We want to make him go away but
we can't cross the river.
Please will you help us?"

"I'll ask my friends,"
said the little monkey.
"We'll think about it."

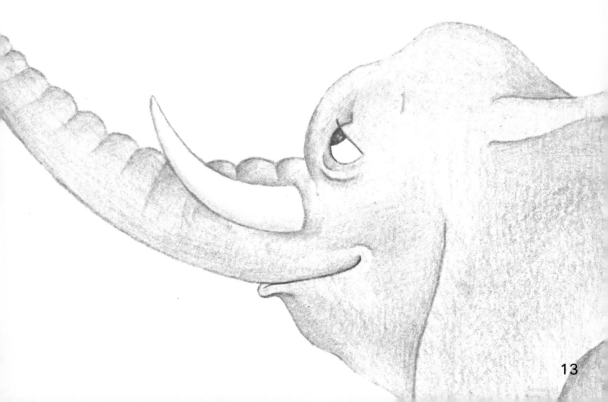

The little monkey called her friends and
they all came to the tree and
talked and talked.

"That is what we'll do then,"
said the little monkey.

The little monkey called
to her friend across the river.
"I am going to swing out
across the river," she shouted.
"You swing out and catch me."

And that is what she did.

Then all the monkeys went across the river.

The monkeys went up to the man's tent.
"Now let's take his tent,"
said the little monkey.

And that is what they did.

The monkeys took the man's tent.
They took all his food and
all his things.

The monkeys had lots of fun.
The man did not like it at all.

The monkeys came back across the river.

"That was fun," said a big monkey.
"Do you think the man will go now?"

"Yes," said the little monkey.
"Look! He's running away."

All the monkeys laughed and shouted.

"It was so good of you to help us.
Thank you, little monkey,"
said the elephant.

"Thank you, thank you,"
said the lion and the giraffe.

"We want you to be our friend now,"
said the elephant.

"No thank you," said the little monkey.
"We monkeys don't need you."

And off she went with her friends,
swinging from tree to tree.

RT HON HENRY MCLEISH began his political career in local government in 1974, and was leader of Fife Regional Council for five years. In 1987 he was elected to the UK parliament and became Minister for Devolution and Home Affairs from 1997 to 1999. In the first Scottish Parliament he was Minister for Enterprise and Lifelong Learning from 1999, and in 2000 he became First Minister of Scotland until 2001. Resigning from politics in 2003, he is now a consultant, adviser and academic.

TOM BROWN is one of Scotland's most respected and experienced political commentators. A former Fleet Street journalist, he was political editor of the *Daily Record* and contributes to a number of newspapers and broadcasts regularly. He has also written books on politics, biography and football.

ANNE ELLIS MSC CFCIPD is business woman, lecturer and Director of Psychology and founder of PeopleMaps which provides psychological profiling and psychometric testing applications for individuals and businesses. She has built several high-growth companies, was part of the team that introduced the first Master's in Business Psychology degree at a UK university and is a motivational speaker who has addressed audiences worldwide on positive thinking and self esteem.

Luath Press is an independently owned and managed book publishing company based in Scotland, and is not aligned to any political party or grouping.

Viewpoints is an occasional series exploring issues of current and future relevance.

By the same authors:

Scotland: The Road Divides (Luath Press, 2007)

Scotland

A Suitable Case for Treatment

TOM BROWN and HENRY McLEISH

with a special chapter by
Anne Ellis

Luath Press Limited

EDINBURGH

www.luath.co.uk

First Published 2009
Reprinted 2010
Reprinted 2013

ISBN: 978-1-906307-69-5

The paper used in this book is recyclable. It is made from
low chlorine pulps produced in a low energy, low emission manner
from renewable forests.

Printed and bound by Bell & Bain Ltd., Glasgow

Typeset in 10.5 point Sabon by 3btype.com

Contents

Acknowledgements

The authors would like to thank Anne Ellis of Peoplemaps, for whom a request for help on the Scottish psyche became a chapter, complete with penetrating psycho-profiles of our leading politicians; Michael Keating of Aberdeen and Florence Universities, whose work has been an inspiration and a source of ideas; John Millar, whose book *The Lithuanians in Scotland* is both a history of his own people and a reminder of the benefits Scotland has gained from giving sanctuary to immigrant communities; and *Holyrood* magazine in which some aspects of the material first appeared.

PART ONE

SYMPTOMS

Introduction

HEALTH WARNING: If you are a typical Scot, proud and patriotic but prickly and easily insulted, this book may offend. If you are a symptomatic Scot, with a low boiling-point and high blood pressure, it may cause apoplexy. And if you are a classic Scot, dour and depressive, it may send you into even deeper dejection.

None of these is our purpose. *Scotland: A Suitable Case For Treatment* is written from the best of motives: to make our country better and our fellow-Scots happier. That may seem idealistic and impracticable but that is another motive for writing this book – to tackle the pessimistic streak in the Scottish character and the granite-faced grimness which led a prominent psychologist to tell a lecture audience that Scots find a perverse pleasure in their dourness and resent being told to cheer up.

Scotland has a double image abroad: on the upside, acknowledgement of a rich history of world-leading achievements but on the downside, an exaggerated cartoon-like caricature of our more ridiculous characteristics. We make our own contribution to this parody with undue emphasis on what has been dismissively described as 'Tartanry, Kailyardism and Clydesideism'.

At a time of dramatic change confronting every aspect of our social, political, constitutional and economic life we still do not have the quality nor the intensity of debate in Scotland that our country deserves. Our book is a contribution to that debate.

The Enlightenment was a period in our history when there was an extraordinary outpouring of creative genius. Nothing was taken at face value. There were inquiring minds and a search for the truth. This approach was the key to the Enlightenment which allowed Scotland to imprint its achievements on the world, the benefits of which we see today: more questioning, more inquiry, more thinking.

Faced with a new era and unprecedented change, we need to create the conditions in which this innovative and intelligent approach becomes the hallmark of a modern Scotland. For this to happen, we need a new and different type of leadership at every level, to inspire, to enthuse, to enrich and to educate.

In turn, we need a forward-looking, inclusive and informed citizenship and this will require changes in our society from school to how our media operates. We are simply not meeting the challenges of a modern Scotland. We need to take ourselves more seriously. We have been credited with 'inventing the modern world' but the challenge now is to reinvent our own country. This requires a national conversation worthy of our past but, more importantly, of our demanding future.

The first part of the book asks us 'tae see ourselves as ithers see us' and the remainder deals with how Scotland should see itself. It asks the difficult question: Scotland – who are we?

Why is it we remain engrossed with the past but do not expend the same interest and enthusiasm about the future? Gerry Rice, who was born in the east end of Glasgow and rose to senior positions in the World Bank and IMF, has asked why Scots have more memories than dreams. Why are we more obsessed with our past than focused on our future?

Being proud of our history and achievements is one thing, but living in the past is the formula for complacency. It is all very well chanting about 'The Flower of Scotland', but the modern task is to release the Power of Scotland.

This should be a time of national reflection, made more urgent by the bewildering impact of global, European, Union and Scotland issues over the past few months where much of the confidence and faith of the public in our institutions and political system have been severely damaged. The direction we are going in now seems to lack certainty and purpose and signposts are nowhere to be seen.

Change means understanding our existing state of mind and recognising the common character faults and failings which hold us back. This is the hard bit, because Scots congenitally have 'a guid conceit of themselves': 'Here's tae us! Wha's like us?'

We fully appreciate the praiseworthy points of the Scottish character particularly the sense of national worth and togetherness, moral strength, creativeness, ingenuity, trustworthiness and humanity – but it would be self-defeating to ignore the negative traits which will handicap us in creating a viable and worthwhile 21st century Scotland.

Pessimism and defensiveness have already been mentioned, but the symptoms we examine also include an unexpected lack of confidence (why else do we have a government supported Centre for Confidence and Well-being?), a chip-on-the-shoulder attitude, a default grievance culture with a 'blame the English' tendency, addictive personality (shown at its worst in our chronic drink problem), bigotry, poverty, a growing dependency culture, violence and anti-social behaviour.

A major component of the New Scotland must be political and consti-tutional reform. Already, it is obvious that the next two elections (UK in 2010 and Scottish in 2011) could bring about a radical realignment of nations and parties. The public distrust of the political system (disgust would not be too strong a word), added to the election of a Scottish Nationalist government and an intensified debate about devolution and independence, all mean we have reached a 'no going back' stage.

The survival of the United Kingdom is at stake, yet the Unionist parties have failed both to provide effective opposition to the SNP and to advance a clear Scottish alternative to the 'slow march to independence'. It seems manifestly obvious that the Union will only be preserved by granting greater powers for the Scottish Parliament and devolution for England in some form of federal settlement; yet all we see is foot-dragging, vacillation and stalling at the Westminster level. As a result, it is increasingly possible that independence will not be won by the Nationalists but given away as a result of the negligence of Unionists.

We write as unashamed Unionists and as determinedly Scottish patriots (it *is* possible to be both) but not as blinkered Bravehearts. Indeed, Irvine Welsh – who has a clear-eyed view of his fellow-Scots – has pointed out that Scots are probably more faint-hearts than Bravehearts.

And before anyone else says it, we are typical Scots, conscious that we have our fair share of the flaws examined in this book. Recognising our failings is the first step ...

We have split the book into three sections; the **symptoms**, which deals with the initial signs of a problem, the **diagnosis** analyses the problem, and the **treatment** endeavours to suggest effective solutions. We warmly encourage readers – be they policymakers or otherwise – to engage in these issues. In this complex modern world there are no easy answers. But we have to keep asking the questions.

CHAPTER ONE

The McGlums

It is never difficult to distinguish between a Scotsman with a grievance and a ray of sunshine.

P. G. WODEHOUSE

SCOTLAND, IN THE EYES of the world, is a four-letter word. That word is D-O-U-R. When eminent psychologist Professor Ed Diener came to Scotland to lecture on happiness, he found he was talking to the wrong country. His professional diagnosis of Scots was: 'They like being dour.'

In other words, what is regarded as the international caricature of the gloomy Scot is true in reality. The professor was surprised (perhaps even depressed?) to discover that as a nation we are – in the words of the song – 'very glad to be unhappy'...

Professor of Psychology at the University of Illinois and editor of *The Journal of Happiness Studies,* Professor Diener has won international recognition for his studies in subjective well-being, temperament and personality and has perfected the 'index of happiness'. He explained to Members of the Scottish Parliament and business leaders the value of augmenting traditional measures of a country's wealth with an assessment of happiness, which could measure policies known to increase people's sense of well-being, such as democratic freedoms, access to healthcare and the rule of law.

He found the Scots are in favour of such things, but not because they make people happier. 'They said too much happiness might not be such a good thing,' he reported. 'They like being dour, and didn't appreciate being told they should be happier.'

Unfair it may be; but it is small wonder that when other nations are looking for an image of meanness and a miserable outlook, they lampoon the Scots.

Advertising campaigns the world over use Scottish stereotypes to reinforce messages of cheapness, equated with meanness. In March 2008, Europe's largest motoring group, the German ADAC (Automobil Club Deutscher Allgemeiner) was asked to apologise after it based a promotion for cheap petrol on a kilted Scot pushing his car rather than driving it. The Scottish protest that they were using a 'puerile' stereotype was met with surprise, since it was regarded as merely an extension of the common practice of

German firms advertising cut-price products as diverse as mobile phones and condoms with the label 'Schottenpreis', 'Scotsman's price'.

In Canada, the character typifying a belligerent beer drinker is (naturally) a constantly-outraged kilted figure and the epitome of thrift in a commercial for a financial firm is (inevitably) a tight-fisted Scottish uncle. As Dan Brown of CBC News commented: 'It's hard not to notice these characters for one simple reason: they yell a lot. In fact, they behave exactly as non-Scottish people expect the Scottish to behave: they're quick to anger and slow to spend money.'

In 2005, newspapers and news agencies on either side of the Atlantic carried reports of a Mr Alistair McGregor (the name should have been the giveaway), an expatriate Scot living in America, who was treated for depression and 'Pervasive Negative Anticipation', a belief that everything will turn out for the worst. The tale includes the telling quote from the pessimistic patient: 'I kept telling them this was all pointless, and they said that was exactly the sort of attitude that got me here in the first place.' This chronic defeatist was scheduled for Electrical Convulsive Therapy until at the last minute, doctors realised he was not suffering from serious clinical depression, but from the natural condition of being Scottish!

Was this an urban myth? In another version, 'Mr McGregor' was given another name, but it has entered into the pop-psychological culture and has even been used in teaching psychology – because the picture of a pathological pessimist is regarded as so typical of the Scottish character that it MUST be true ...

Such examples are infuriating (there we go again!) to Scots because they are laughably unfair, lazy stereotypes and clichéd caricatures of our national identity. But do we only have ourselves to blame? Should we not be more concerned about the image we present? No nation is more self-conscious and sensitive to slights than the Scots, yet we appear careless of the impression we create.

The 'Scottish psyche' has become a catch-all catchphrase used by everyone from psychologists to historians to politicians to bloggers to explain everything from Scottish culture, religion and entrepreneurship to family life, class attitudes and divisions, attitudes to immigrants, love of football, binge drinking and the so-called 'Scottish cringe'. It is generally accepted that Scotland is a state of mind as well as being a state of nationhood, yet it is vague and indefinable – as well as being contradictory.

A recent question in the Scottish Qualifications Authority's Advanced Higher English paper was: 'A comparative literary study of aspects of the Scottish psyche as represented both individually and collectively in *The House*

with the Green Shutters, Gillespie and *Greenvoe.* I intend to examine similar-
ities and contrasting features of the Scots personality and types of Scottish
community as represented through such techniques as setting, character, theme
and symbol.' If the pupils could do that for the elusive 'Scottish psyche',
they earned their marks.

The national character is so multi-faceted that Scots could be described as
schizophrenic, ferociously proud, yet strangely lacking in self-belief; possessing
a distinctive sense of humour, yet prickly and unable to laugh at themselves;
hard-headed yet prone to maudlin sentimentality; enterprising, adaptable
and ingenious, yet far too often content to leave leadership to others.

The boast is that Scots have given the world ideas, inventions and pioneers
in every sphere; yet we are quick to decry success (the 'kent his faither'
mentality) and are embarrassed about talking the language of competition.
Do Scots really want success? Or are we afraid of it, because of the changes
needed to achieve it? Others say 'can do' but, too often, ours is a 'canna dae
that' culture. Are we really satisfied to be 'The best small country in the world'?

Are we handicapped by history and traditionalism? Robert Louis
Stevenson wrote: 'The mark of the Scots of all classes is that he stands in an
attitude towards the past unthinkable to Englishmen ... there burns alive in
him a sense of identity with the dead even to the 20th generation.' Does living
in the past mean that Scotland will continue to be a 'never-never land'?

In view of these complexities, it may seem foolhardy to attempt to put
Scotland 'on the couch', diagnose its mental state and identify the personality
traits and faults which handicap the nation.

In a changing world where only modernised and confident nations will
survive, it is time Scots took control of their national identity to erase the
caricatures and put in place an image that other countries can respect.

However, if the nation is to change to meet the challenges of the new
era, we have to understand Scotland's mentality and how it impacts on our
enduring and deep-seated problems – economic, social, political and cultural.

We have to understand what is holding us back, whether it be national
character; external considerations; our form of government; our increasingly
fraught relationship with England and the UK; social problems like poverty,
crime and anti-social behaviour; dependency on the public sector; ambivalence
towards the private sector; lack of entrepreneurship; collectivism; top-down
state-sponsored egalitarianism and reservations about risk and success...

Change of character and attitude also has to be linked to a sense of
national ambition and determination of our place in the UK and the world.
Self-knowledge is essential for an honest assessment of what we want to be
and how we are falling short of our goals. In an increasingly complex

world, we need to plan to improve our position as a nation; there will be winners and losers in the new global order and we need to ensure we don't slip down the international league table.

Scots, collectively and individually, should be asking: Is our true potential being tapped? Are we deluding ourselves about the future? Have we become entrapped by national character and centuries of behaviour? Are we in danger of acting out a home-made caricature of ourselves – and allowing others to portray us in cartoon terms? What does 'changing for the better' mean in this context and how can it be measured?

Scotland has to prepare itself for a future where change will be the only constant and which will presents new challenges and threats, only some of which are emerging and visible. That must mean adapting, responding, innovating and exploiting and the choices will be to be leading or following; being truly international or insular; becoming global, European, UK or Scottish citizens.

Changing the national character will be a matter of individual action, communal purpose and national leadership.

In our previous book on the new post-devolution politics 'Scotland: The Road Divides' we wrote: 'It is essential that the Scottish state of mind should change ... the nation's mood is a key factor in adapting for the future.' We believe that split personality is holding Scotland back from becoming a truly 21st century country.

CASE NOTE: Scots have always had 'a guid conceit of themselves' but the arrogant 'wha's like us?' mentality conceals crippling self-doubt and pessimism. We KNOW we are better – but are we kidding ourselves? Scotland is, in fact, a suitable case for treatment?

CHAPTER TWO

Past, Present and Future

We look to Scotland for all our ideas of civilisation.

VOLTAIRE

OUR DIAGNOSIS IS that the Scottish character must change to survive, never mind succeed, in the increasingly competitive future. Only those nations sure of their identity and confident of their attributes will meet the challenges – and Scotland is neither of those.

Scotland's character is as strange a mix as the influences which have formed it: its often turbulent, yet richly intellectual history; its geography with clearly-defined territories within its borders, conjoined but separate from the larger nation to the south, on the edge of Europe yet always more closely-linked to the Continent than the rest of Britain; its religion, starkly contrasting Calvinism and Catholicism; and its politics, an inherently small 'c' conservativism, yet dominated by Socialism and with a burgeoning nationalist movement.

The 21st century Scotland that has resulted from these is complicated, contradictory, not easy to separate and dissect and highlight the significant against the trivial. Too often in Scotland, it is the trivial – typified by minor regional differences, sectarian pettiness and football rivalries – that becomes inflated in importance.

Yet Scotland clearly has a national spirit and, in the modern setting, there are core issues about its character, psyche, morale and the meaning of Scottishness.

Any report card on Scotland 2008 would struggle to give the nation pass marks. The boast of 'a smart, successful Scotland' conceals a people that may be too smart for its own good and the sometimes spectacular success of a few contributes to a complacency about the problems and the plight of many Scots. We take comfort from the past and have become comfortable with the way things are – and always have been. The result is a country that claims to be ambitious but actually has limited aspirations.

Scotland could continue happily in this vein, talking ourselves up on the back of selective successes but failing to make the extra effort requires for real across-the-board success and prosperity for all. Given Scotland's pre-occupation with football and the resulting disappointments, it is easy to make the comparison: individual brilliance does not equate with world-class achievement as a team ...

Another excuse for inertia could be that Scotland's enduring social problems are too deep-seated to be changed. It is easy to be defeatist about deprivation, urban rundown, alcohol, drugs and anti-social behaviour when they have been with us now for generations; are they beyond our ability to change them or do we lack the will?

Scotland has no choice but to change its attitudes for the all-too-obvious reason that the rest of the world is changing and modernising. When he was First Minister, Henry McLeish had the chance to discuss Scotland's future with one of the foremost original thinkers Francois Rischard, Vice-President of the World Bank for Europe and author of *High Noon: 20 global issues and 20 years to solve them*.

He suggested that countries which are small physically and in population terms can still deal with global issues by being smarter. A number of countries are not achieving their potential for a variety of reasons and these reasons have to be honestly and openly identified for each country.

He has said he considers the central challenge of our times to be that the world has been cut up into so many nation states: 'It's a recent phenomenon, roughly 350 years old, and does very well for internal management of countries. A nation state that is democratically organised is actually a very good machine for solving internal issues.

'But the problem at the international level is that nation states are by design territorial in their perspectives. They look out for the inhabitants of their own territories, first of all. And the politicians that run for elections in those countries run for elections every four or five years, so their horizon is maximum four or five years.

'The global issues like dangerous climate change, deforestation, bio-diversity losses, contagious diseases and so forth, are the opposite. They are not territorial issues; they are cross-border issues and they are long term issues. To solve the global warming issue, it takes a 150 year plan to start today to actually manage the 150 years to stabilize carbon dioxide concentrations.

'So you have this absolute clash between the territorial and short-term perspective of the nation states and the non-territorial, long term nature of these global problems. And that deadly clash is something we must get out of the way one way or the other.'

That wider world viewpoint should not be incompatible with the new post-devolution, self-determining Scotland. Self-government was needed because the United Kingdom and London will never be in a position to know what is best for Scotland, but it would be self-defeating if it lurched into narrow nationalism, limited horizons and merely defining ourselves against others, particularly our neighbours south of the border.

Over the centuries, Scots have developed a posture that will not make us too many friends in the modern world. Despite the achievements of some remarkable entrepreneurs, risk-takers and artists working in all forms of national and international culture, there is a lack of national self-confidence. And all of these spectacular one-off successes have experienced the unattractive eagerness of their Scottish compatriots to down-play the accomplishments of those who are successful, typified by the 'ah kent his faither' mentality.

The 'Braveheart' fantasy

Only the Scots could have forged a political movement from two unattractive characteristics: the arrogance of the 'wha's like us?' mentality combined with a victimhood complex. From these, the early Scottish National Party was not so much formed as fermented.

True Scots will claim to be small- 'n' nationalists, but the Nationalist political culture combines the swaggering bravado of 'Braveheart' (more of an emotional delusion than a response to genuine history) with the grudge culture which has become unfortunately endemic in Scottish society. For those who do not see Scotland as a partner-nation in the United Kingdom but as a subordinate supplicant-nation, it is easier to blame the UK, the Westminster Parliament and the English for Scotland's problems than to look at our own faults.

In fact, it could be said that the SNP's First Minister Alex Salmond is the absolutely typical and inevitable product of that brand of Scottish Nationalism – to his followers, charismatic; to others, infuriatingly cocky; and a past-master at the politics of grievance which he will exploit to drive an ever-widening wedge between Scotland and the Union.

Self-examination should lead to self-worth and self-esteem. A sense of nationhood is not about being 'anti' others but 'pro' the things which distinguish us from others. It is remarkable that throughout all of this runs a golden thread of progress and learning right from Reformation to the present day. Scotland's leadership in the Enlightenment and its part in the Industrial Revolution, the Age of Empire and the creation of a huge and amazing diaspora. When the American author and historian Arthur Herman coined the title *How Scots Invented The Modern World*, he was paying our nation a handsome tribute – but it also fed into the Scottish sense of complacency

Quite rightly, Herman asked: 'Who formed the first modern nation?

Who created the first literate society? Who invented our modern ideas of democracy and free market capitalism? The Scots.' His well-documented thesis was that in the 18th and 19th centuries Scotland earned the respect of the rest of the world for its crucial contributions to science, philosophy, literature, education, medicine, commerce, and politics—'contributions that have formed and nurtured the modern West ever since and 'made this small country facing on the North Atlantic an inspiration and driving force in world history'. It is also a romantic story and it is all-too-easy for Scots to wallow in Herman's warm-hearted account of 'how John Knox and the Church of Scotland laid the foundation for our modern idea of democracy; how the Scottish Enlightenment and, before that, the Declaration of Arbroath helped to inspire both the American Revolution and the US Constitution; and how thousands of Scottish immigrants left their homes to create the American frontier, the Australian outback, and the British Empire in India and Hong Kong'.

We Scots are fond of the compendium of congratulatory quotes from thinkers of the past. As the Victorian historian James Anthony Froude, biographer of Thomas Carlyle, remarked: 'No people so few in number have scored so deep a mark in the world's history as the Scots have done.'

While we are patting ourselves on the back, let us not forget that is all history – done and dusted. And while it gives us a 'guid conceit' of ourselves and background on which to build, it is no justification for complacency. Scots are comfortable with their history, but find the future difficult.

By all means, we should celebrate our past – and the long-overdue example of the statue of Adam Smith which now stands outside St Giles Cathedral (appropriately unveiled on 4 July 2008, by Professor Vernon L. Smith, winner of the Nobel Prize for economics) is an example of how we should continue to do so. But we should also be open-eyed and honest about our present and more realistic about our future.

As an example, some continue to perpetuate the myth that Scotland is a world leader in education – even though it is more accurate to set that claim in the past tense. Aspects of higher education are still world-class, but it is undeniable that the parish schools and the Scottish Education Act of 1696 created what has been claimed as the first national system of education 'since the days of Sparta', creating the 'lad o' pairts' who could rise in the world on merit and intelligence and not by accident of birth. Scotland was then the nation with the highest percentage of pupils and students in Europe, leading directly to the Age of Enlightenment. However, today's levels of illiteracy and lack of educational achievement in our general population no longer allow us to make such a grandiose claim.

If the case for change is so obvious, why has it not happened? What will rouse Scotland from its comfortable culture of complacency and wake up to the complications and challenges ahead?

There are institutional factors which will either aid or prevent the mental make-over and the various sectors and organisations which dominate Scottish life will have to act as drivers of change in each. It would help if we had a settled political situation, a more inclusive leadership, a national vision of Scotland's role in the new world order and more clearly defined relations, not least with the United Kingdom.

It is all very well to talk about government's leadership role and rely on administrative solutions but there must also be a national consensus. The Irish economic miracle was driven by consensus and willingness for a backward nation to change. They did not want an economic miracle for the sake of it but because as a nation they did not like where they were. They wanted the 'New Irish Dream' and, with massive help from Europe, put in place the economic, political and social machinery to make it come true. In the process, the Irish also underwent a breathtaking psychological change and became the 'Expectocracy' described in David McWilliams' entertaining and unnervingly-accurate *The Pope's Children – Ireland's New Elite*.

Is the Scottish psyche capable of such a transformation? Or is the nation's character too dour, pessimistic and resistant to change to show the necessary confidence, verve and imagination which seems to have come naturally to the Irish? The answer lies within ourselves because, never mind the English or anyone else, we Scots are our own worst enemies.

CASE NOTE: Ours is – in the words of the TV comedy series *Chewin' The Fat* – a 'gonnie no dae that?' culture. It is time for Scotland to start saying: 'We ARE gonnie dae that!'

CHAPTER THREE

'As ithers see us' or The Shrek Effect

*I have been trying all my life to like Scotchmen, and am obliged
to desist from the experiment in despair.*

CHARLES LAMB

ALTHOUGH SCOTS PAY lip service to the national bard Robert Burns, his advice
to 'see oorsel's as ithers see us' is largely disregarded. Around the globe,
whether from 'lack of imagination' or prejudice, advertising executives use the
same lazy shorthand equation: Scot = mean = cantankerous = figure of fun.

Identity matters in an image-conscious world and it would be judged
politically incorrect to subject any other ethnic group to ridicule, yet
Charles Lamb was far from the last influential writer to display a disdainful
anti-Scottish prejudice. P. J. O'Rourke, the American 'humourist', used a
catalogue of clichés to describe the Scots: 'Racial characteristics: sour, stingy,
depressing beggars who parade around in schoolgirls' skirts with nothing
on underneath. Their fumbled attempt at speaking the English language has
been a source of amusement for five centuries and their idiot music has been
dreaded by those not blessed with deafness for at least as long.'

There is a world of difference between a harmless joke and the acceptance of constant stereotyping which blights our national reputation and
impairs the effort to present ourselves as 'smart, successful Scotland'. It is
time to start seeing ourselves as we want to be seen and as we want to be
in the 21st century.

In March 2008, an apology on behalf of the Scottish nation was
demanded from Europe's largest motoring group Automobil Club
Deutscher Allgemeiner (ADAC) after it advertised cheap petrol with a
'puerile' Scottish stereotype. The image in a circular sent to its 15.8 million
members was of a kilted Scot pushing his car because he was too mean to
pay dearer pump prices.

The protest caused some surprise in Germany, since price reductions on
products as diverse as mobile phones and condoms are commonly labeled
with the tag of 'Schottenpreis', meaning 'Scotsman's price'. It has been a
long-standing marketing practice in various European countries to advertise
sales with the commonly recognised assumption that Scots are penny-pinchers
who do not like to open their wallets.

Neither ADAC nor its advertising company had thought any offence would be caused by the cartoon of the grimacing kiltie pushing his Mini uphill, with a funnel in his petrol duct as a sign he could not bear to waste a drop of fuel. The caption was 'Who wants to push? It doesn't have to be this way ...'

One of the ADAC members who received the circular was Glasgow-born Scot David Mackay, based in Germany, who said: 'I thought it was vaguely amusing at first, but then I got annoyed to think that they were taking the mickey out of Scots. It is insulting.'

The Scottish National Party's Westminster leader Angus Robertson MP called for the advert to be withdrawn. 'These adverts are puerile and offensive to Scots and should be withdrawn' he said. 'Why a leading German institution such as the motoring club ADAC would run such a pathetic campaign is beyond me.' The German consul general in Scotland, Ingo Radcke, agreed: 'My general advice would be not to use national stereotypes in adverts. I would urge caution.'

The response from a Scottish Government spokesman was wearily disappointed that the Germans are still portraying Scots with such an overworked stereotype but, perhaps from a desire not to dignify the insult, there seemed to be no inclination to make the protest official: 'I suspect this says less about the real views of Germans and more about the lack of imagination of some advertising executives. Germans love Scotland, our people, culture, music, and scenery, and the many who travel here will not recognise this silly old stereotype. When Scotland's international reputation is strong and growing, it's disappointing that this nonsense is still peddled.'

Indeed. But should Scots not be doing something to counter this negative propaganda?

In Canada, with its strong direct links with Scotland, the type-casting is taken for granted. Canadian Tyres chose the frugal Scot Sandy McTire as their mascot and a recent campaign for Keith's beer in Canada featured a strident Scotsman with sideburns going completely berserk in a bar because the drinkers are not handling the bottles with respect. Typical of the comments from customers on the brewery's website were: 'Your beer is fine, your commercial with the screaming Scotsman re the beer with its neck broken is the worst! I mute the TV every time and a lot of people I know do also. One friend of mine has quit buying Keith's because that commercial is so obnoxious ...

'Since your TV commercial (shown during curling games), I've ceased purchase of your product ... One of the worst and most obnoxious ads I have ever seen ... The Scotsman has got to go, those commercials are an embarrassment to us all ...'

Among these typically touchy Scottish reactions, there were more good-humoured responses: 'I am not anywhere near being insulted by those commercials. I think they are absolutely hilarious, and I also come from a Scottish background. Maybe that is why I find those commercials so entertaining, he is not obnoxious, he makes me think of those great family get-togethers I remember as a young child ... I am Scottish and the Scot on the commercials reminds me of some of my Scottish friends and relatives ...'

The justification for the commercial was that the brewery in Halifax, Nova Scotia, was founded by a 25-year-old Scottish immigrant Alexander Keith and the trademark bears the Saltire Cross and labels show the head of a Scottish stag. A sympathetic Dan Brown of CBC News drew attention to similar advertisements including 'the impossibly small spokesman for Kellogg's to the tight-fisted uncle in the Money Mart spots' and asserted: 'The Scots are the most over-represented minority in TV advertising.

'It's hard not to notice these characters for one simple reason: they yell a lot. In fact, they behave exactly as non-Scottish people expect the Scottish to behave: they're quick to anger and slow to spend money. They're stereotypes, in other words.'

Andrew Clark, an expert on Canadian comedy and lecturer at Humber College, Toronto, pointed out that making fun of things Scottish is a tradition in North American comedy that extends decades into the past although there would be an outcry if, say, a Jewish character were portrayed in a commercial as cheap: 'I think it's a fair question: why are they picking on the Scots? I think the answer is: because they can, and people don't get too offended.

'The idea of a miniature person promoting a Kellogg's mini-bar isn't necessarily a bad one. Why that miniature person speaks with a bad fake Scottish accent, I don't know. I don't see the relevance.

'It seems to be the ethnicity that it's OK to make fun of. I think people look at Scots and they don't consider the Scots an oppressed minority, although the Scots do – they feel alienated inside Great Britain. But to Canadians I think it's just a funny guy with a funny accent.'

And who have we to thank for the image of a niggardly nation of meanies? More than any other figure in history, a Scot – Sir Harry Lauder. His early 20th century musical hall persona perpetuated the most damaging Scottish myth – tight-fistedness ('The Grand Canyon was created when a Scotsman lost a coin while digging a ditch.' 'Who invented copper wire? Two Aberdonians fighting over a penny.' Or, if you want to make it really mean, a ha'penny. And: 'If folk think I'm mean, they'll no expect much.') Perhaps Winston Churchill was being a touch ironic when he described Lauder as 'Scotland's greatest ever ambassador'!

A more modern entertainer who has contributed to the Scots caricature is the Canadian comic actor Mike Myers, who provided the voice of the main character in the Oscar-winning world-wide film success *Shrek*. Myers both of whose parents came from Liverpool and is of English, Scottish and Irish ancestry, was dissatisfied when he first recorded the lines without an accent and asked to re-record the part of the anti-social swamp-living ogre. At the cost of millions of dollars, he re-voiced the character as a Scot who says things like 'Yer gawn the right way furra smack'.

Myers had also employed this character voicing for the character Stuart MacKenzie in his film *So I Married an Axe Murderer* and 'Fat Bastard' in the Austin Powers films 'thirty stones of sweating, foul-mouthed Glaswegian', obese, foul-tempered and flatulent and, as if that were not enough, with 'vulgar manners, unusual eating habits, and a taste for babies and anything that looks like a baby, e.g dwarves'!

Myers claims he chose the Scottish brogue his mother had used when she told him bedtime stories because he has had a long standing affection for the accent from the time he spent on the Edinburgh Festival fringe Fringe in the mid 1980s: 'I just love the Scots accent because it can go from very soft to really angry so quickly.'

In his farewell column for the *Daily Record,* Tom Brown commented: 'When anyone wants to portray a character who is rough, tough and gruff, they assume our accent. That's why Mike Myers should be Scotland's Public Enemy No. 1. The Canadian comic could have voiced Shrek, this summer's monster cartoon hit, in his own accent. But it wasn't nasty enough.

'Shrek is gross with terrible manners and appalling personal habits. So far, so Scottish, eh?

The clever thing is that Shrek's accent is Lowland Scottish. It's impossible to take anyone seriously, far less be frightened, in the away-with-the-fairies Highlands and Islands lilt. Shrek obviously comes from Pumpherston, Cumbernauld or some breeding-ground of ogres.

'Above all, he is unromantic. The film starts as a fairytale until Shrek, sitting on the lavatory, rips a page from the book to use as bum-paper. No doubt, some Scotswomen will recognise him.'

In films and TV, 'Scottish' is all-too-often shorthand for 'nasty'. Even Rikki Fulton and Chic Murray, much-loved comedians in their homeland, played villains in thriller movies because of their ability to convey a flinty severity. And why does Sean Connery never change the world's most famous Scottish accent, no matter if he is playing an Irish policeman, a US colonel or a Russian submariner? Because he plays heroes with a hard streak and that streak is supplied by Big Tam's Scottishness. (The much-imitated Connery accent, by the way, is all his own; it is a filtered Edinburgh voice, with a mid-Atlantic moderation of the broad delivery of the Fountainbridge tenements where he grew up in the shadow of a brewery.)

What is unwarranted is that those who subscribe to these clichés fail to acknowledge the cultured nation behind the accent. As the well-educated doctor in Tony Hancock's classic *The Blood Donor* says: 'We're not all Rob Roys, you know.' Well, we're not all Shreks, either.

The Scottish Government's *Scotland Now* website ('Connecting you to modern Scotland') gamely describes the Myers travesty as 'one of the funniest – and best – Scottish accents ever committed to celluloid by a non-Scot'. It also goes into a sickly swoon when extolling the accents of native-born Scots: 'Are there many women over 40 who don't go weak at the knees at the sound of Sir Sean Connery's silky purr? Or many women under 40 who don't have the same reaction when they hear Ewan McGregor's honey-dipped tones?' (We hope this was written by a woman on the *Scotland Now* staff and not some patronising male chauvinist, living down to another Scottish stereotype ...)

In the real world, as *Scotland Now* points out, there are more positive reasons for making the most of a Scottish accent. In a recent survey by the Aziz Corporation, which provides training courses for business leaders, 55 per cent of business executives said they believed a Scots accent was desirable because it conveyed 'above average honesty in the personality of its owner', particularly in advertising and telemarketing. some English regional accents scored as low as 22 per cent. Two-thirds believed if they met someone with a Scottish accent, they would generally assume that person was successful. Chairman Khalid Aziz said: 'If you want to get ahead in business, it is better to sound as if you are from Scotland than from any English region.' An advertising executive interviewed for the survey put it more succinctly: 'The Scottish accent sells.'

CASE NOTE: It could be regarded as a healthy sign that we are prepared to laugh at ourselves – but should we be making it easy for others to laugh at us, not *with* us?

CHAPTER FOUR

'We arra peepul!'

'A glower says mair than a smile.'
Scottish saying quoted in 'A Wee Book of Calvin'

AT AN INTERNATIONAL football match (in the days when the Scottish football team were allowed to play against England on English soil), one of the authors was trapped on the terracing amid a particularly rowdy section of the Tartan Army. A police squad was preparing to plunge into the crowd and extract the worst trouble-makers, when one of them bawled: 'Who are we?' To a man the thousands around him responded: 'We arra peepul!' In the face of that united front, the police tactfully retreated ...

But who are 'the peepul' and why is this unity only shown in such circumstances? The common toast in Scotland is: 'Here's tae us – wha's like us?' 'Wha' indeed? What are we really like?

The problem about changing the Scottish character is firstly to know what that character is. Over the years, particularly since devolution focused attention on questions of nationhood and identity, many attempts have been made to define the Scottish psyche but no-one has succeeded in pinning it down.

Pin-pointing the Scottish identity is an impossibility. Many people think they know what it is and have used their version to engender 'the politics of identity'; but they failed because they have tried to define what is really a confused mixture of myth, mood, caricature, history, delusion, stereotype, self-promotion, sentimentality and schizophrenia.

Perhaps an Englishman, Melvyn Bragg came closest to the answer in his 2008 TV series *Travels in Written Britain*, in which he presented an admiring and affectionate portrait of Scottish life and letters down to the present day, but confessed: 'Scotland is a nation that can only be defined by its contradictions and differences. Scotland is, and always has been, a country profoundly divided ... dualism is at the heart of Scotland.'

A 14th century chronicler defined the division between Lowlanders and Highlanders, later known as 'House Scots' and 'Wild Scots'. 'The people of the coast are of domestic and civilised habits, patient and urbane, decent in their attire, affable and peaceful' he said. 'The Highlanders and people of the Islands, on the other hand, are a savage and untamed nation, rude and independent, given to rapine, easy-living, of a docile and warm disposition, comely in person but unsightly in dress, hostile to the English people and, owing to the diversity of speech, even to their own nation and exceedingly cruel.'

J. M. Barrie from Kirriemuir had one of his characters observe: 'You Scots are such a mixture of the practical and the emotional that you escape out of an Englishman's hand like a trout.' Only Scots could have written those classics of the ambivalent nature, Robert Louis Stevenson's *The Strange Case of Dr Jekyll and Mr Hyde* (said to have been inspired by the story of Deacon Brodie, whose double life combined being a respectable tradesman and town councillor with a dissolute low-life of crime) and James Hogg's *Confessions of a Justified Sinner*. Perhaps significantly, it was a Scottish psychiatrist, Glasgow-born and educated R. D. Laing, who wrote *The Divided Self*.

Lord Byron picked up on the Scottish split personality in Robert Burns: 'What an antithetical mind! — tenderness, roughness — delicacy, coarseness — sentiment, sensuality — soaring and grovelling, dirt and deity — all mixed up in that one compound of inspired clay!' Byron was simultaneously attracted and repelled by the two types of 'love' poems penned by Burns.

The same national bard who penned some of the most tender and romantic verses in the English language in *Ae Fond Kiss* and *My Love is Like a Red, Red Rose* also wrote some of the crudest, bawdiest and most insulting to women. His coarse parodies of some of his love-songs and his collection of *The Merry Muses of Caledonia*, were regarded as so pornographic they were suppressed for 170 years. While he may have written *The Rights of Woman* criticising the time when 'rough, rude man had naughty ways', *The Merry Muses* (and his bragging letters to cronies about his conquests) are truly offensive in the leering, sexist attitude they betray. No doubt there are women who say that aspect of the macho Scotsman persists to this day …

Other examples of dualism in the Scottish character are not hard to find. The persistent sectarianism which still bedevils our nation uses religion as an excuse but modern Scotland is basically an irreligious nation in that church attendances have plummeted and, while a majority may profess themselves to be 'Christian', the hard evidence is that they are more atheist than anything else.

We have a broad sense of humour and are able to laugh at ourselves, as is evidenced by richly comic creations like the Rev. I. M. Jolly and Rab. C. Nesbitt; but the point is that we have to be the ones making the jokes – there is a national touchiness about outsiders who lampoon the Scots. There is a fine line between character and caricature and, unless we change and present a more positive image of ourselves, we Scots are in danger of becoming the living embodiment of these comic caricatures.

To the world, we exhibit a brimming self-confidence overspilling into arrogance; internally, we are riven with self-doubt and qualms that we may not be as superior as we claim. It was a relief when the (then Labour) Scottish Government scrapped the cringe-making slogan describing Scotland as 'The best small country in the world', which actually summed up Scottish dualism by simultaneously making an overblown boast about the nation's standing in the world while accepting diminutive status. The phrase, particularly when it was so freely used during the G8 Summit at Gleneagles in the presence of world leaders and major nations, was an embarrassment. It certainly did not represent the national self-image because, throughout the centuries, Scotland has never thought small and in modern times it was a strange marketing tactic to present ourselves as a diminutive minor league player.

Scotland's reputation is for hard-headedness and thrift also contrasts sharply with a misty-eyed idealism and a strongly sentimental streak. As G. K. Chesterton pointed out: 'Of all the great nations of Christendom, the Scotch are by far the most romantic. I know it is always said that the Scotch are practical, prosaic, and puritan; that they have an eye to business. But the Scotch are not one-eyed practical men, though their best friends must admit that they are occasionally business-like. They are, quite fundamentally, romantic and sentimental.'

The far-travelled Robert Louis Stevenson pointed out that the idealised view of Scotland and fellow-countrymen is strongest when they meet up abroad: 'When I am at home, I feel a man from Glasgow to be something like a rival, a man from Barra to be more than half a foreigner. Yet let us meet in some far country, and, whether we hail from the braes of Manor or the braes of Mar, some ready-made affection joins us on the instant ...

...I do not even know if I desire to live there; but let me hear, in some far land, a kindred voice sing out, 'Oh, why left I my hame?' and it seems at once as if no beauty under the kind heavens, and no society of the wise and good, can repay me for my absence from my country. And though I think I would rather die elsewhere, yet in my heart of hearts I long to be buried among good Scots clods.'

This Scottish romanticism stems from our infatuation with the past, particularly a fixation with wrongs, real and imagined, over the centuries. It is one thing to take pride in our culture and achievements; however, it also feeds the grudge mentality that is so pervasive in Scottish society and is the well-spring of Scottish nationalism.

Stevenson from his vantage point on the other side of the world, on the west coast of America and the South Seas, was conscious of the indelible influence of history on the Scots character: For that is the mark of the Scots of all classes: that he stands in an attitude towards the past unthinkable to Englishmen, and remembers and cherishes the memory of his forebears, good or bad; and there burns alive in him a sense of identity with the dead even to the 20th generation.'

When Strathclyde University sociologist Isobel Lindsay, who was Convener of the Scottish Constitutional Convention, carried out a small-scale survey in Scotland and Birmingham on national identity, she found perceptions were dramatically different on either side of the border. Scots overwhelmingly regard themselves as 'friendly/warm/kind-hearted' and a third declare themselves as 'patriotic/proud', while only one in 10 admit to low self-esteem and the same proportion see ourselves as 'aggressive/paranoid'. The view from England is decidedly that Scots are concerned with national symbols such as kilts and tartan and are 'patriotic/nationalistic'; while other distinguishing characteristics are accent (32 per cent), mean/careful with money (30 per cent), aggressive/tough/hard (24 per cent), friendly (23 per cent) and heavy drinkers (21 per cent). Only 12 per cent of English interviewees thought Scots are anti-English and a mere 11 per cent regarded us as having a sense of humour.

Scots, on the other hand, were far less charitable about the English, with more than two thirds regarding our southern neighbours as 'arrogant/snobbish' or 'Lager louts/hooligans' (30 per cent).

Some of the individual comments she gathered were revelatory. A fire-fighter in Birmingham said: 'The Scots like to drink. They're friendly individually but can be hostile in larger groups. National pride. Good friends, bad enemies. Excellent soldiers. Hard workers. Passionate. The English are stand-offish. Obstinate. Xenophobic. They don't panic. Large regional variations between North and South.' An Ayrshire student was unsparing about both nations: 'Scots are friendly, unhealthy, overweight, down to earth, funny, unconfident, under-achievers. English are inconsiderate, arrogant, thin, fit, no sense of humour, football hooligans, full of themselves but have no reason to be.'

There have been attempts over the years to get Scots to admit that we may have the odd fault or two and one anonymous observer went further: 'I suppose we are what we are because of the climate, or Calvinism, or some racial inheritance, or even Dr Gregory's mixture. We're damned thrawn, loyal to the point of lunacy, lousy lovers, clumsy, suicidally arrogant, socially graceless.'

There are other, more serious, faults which are a serious handicap in a modern nation and which others have learned to overcome. Commentators have regularly referred to a prevalent feeling of 'grievance', 'sense of victim-hood' and the 'culture of complaint', which have been skillfully exploited by the Scottish National Party – and disastrously mishandled by the Labour Party.

Prof. John Kay, visiting professor at the London School of Economics and a member of the Scottish government's Council of Economic Advisers wrote tellingly in his column in the *Financial Times*: 'A Scottish childhood is an education in the ready acquisition and dogged pursuit of grievance – a trait that has proved so damaging to Gordon Brown, the prime minister. Impotent resentment has for long been the dominant theme of Scottish politics. For Labour, Scotland's economic and social problems have been the fault of international capitalism. For Scottish nationalists the blame lies squarely with the English. Both claims are absurd.'

He added: 'Scotland's economic problems, like its opportunities, are of its own making.

A Scottish government cannot protect the country from the vagaries of the global economy and should not try. The need is to develop and exploit the competitive advantages of Scottish businesses on an international scale.'

'Begrudgery' is not confined to Scotland and has been often been identified as the 'Irish disease', whose main symptom is 'a predilection to begrudge other people their success and wealth'. Phrases such as 'It's far from that he was reared', i.e. 'He may be a successful/wealthy/powerful now, but I knew him when he was just a guttersnipe/corner boy/snot-nosed pup' have been quoted. Bono, the rock band leader who has also been highly successful as business-man, activist and campaigner, summed it up, presumably from his personal experience: 'An American will look up at somebody living in a big house on a hill and say 'Someday, I'm going to be like him'. An Irishman will look up at the big house and say 'Someday I'm going to get that fecker!"

Samuel Johnson observed that the Irish were a very fair people insofar as they never spoke well of one another. He could have said the same about Scots – and probably did.

Prominent Scots, instead of being celebrated, find themselves victims of the national tendency to find fault with their success, otherwise known as the 'ah kent his feyther' syndrome. A classic case in point is Sir Sean Connery who was at first lauded for his global success as a screen actor, but was soon attacked for living in exile and then spurned by the Scottish 'Establishment' for his espousal of the nationalist cause. Connery's generous, and largely unsung, charity work in his native country and his constant advocacy of Scotland overseas are disregarded; his nationalism is written off, instead of receiving credit for at least caring about his nation's future.

Comedian and actor Billy Connolly is another whose world-wide popularity will not be allowed to go to his head – because, he says, his fellow Scots continually put him in his place. 'We have a saying in Scotland, 'I ken his faither', which is a put-down' he explained. 'The TV show *Nationwide* once did a programme on me in Glasgow. At one point I was in the street where I grew up and a girl was asking me for my autograph. A little crowd gathered and two little old ladies were watching. One of them looked over at me and said, 'And his father was such a nice man'.

'Some of being famous is great. You know, to begin with, you get a following and they love you then they start seeing you in the street and pointing you out and that's nice. Then shortly after that you get this other degree of fame through television and films and you're known to everybody.

'Sometimes I don't like it because some people feel they're entitled to say that they don't like you. They say you are rubbish and they say it to your face: 'I don't like your stuff' and I think, 'Who asked you?' They don't seem to care if they are deeply insulting you.'

Even real-life heroes are not allowed to spend too long on the pedestal of public acclaim before being dragged down. John Smeaton, the baggage handler who became an international celebrity and was awarded the Queen's Medal for Gallantry after helping police tackle a man in a blazing jeep which had been driven into Glasgow airport terminal on 30 June 2007, found himself being criticised because the limelight had been turned on him.

His comment about his feelings as he helped to tackle the terrorist – 'This is Glasgow, you know – we'll set about you.' – caught the international imagination. Yet 'Smeato' had continually stressed: 'What I did wasn't just myself. A lot of people did that. But it went round the world in a flash on the Internet. I didn't expect the attention. I didn't ask for it and I don't see myself as anything special.' While insisting he never sought to exaggerate his contribution, he added philosophically: 'It is a strange world when some people try and blow out your candle to make their own grow brighter.'

In another field, Jim Traynor, *Daily Record* sports writer and radio presenter, voiced his exasperation with Scottish 'begrudgery': 'Scotland is overrun by people who live to revel in the demise and misery of others. Everywhere you look, there's someone delighting in the trauma of another, and, of course, a media pack, huddled like fishwives, nodding to one another and saying, 'told you so'.

'It is pathetic the way we can't wait to see people fall on their backsides. Even better if it's flat on their faces.'

He was commenting on the collapse of Gretna Football Club which in five meteoric years rose from obscurity to the Scottish Premier League, where they struggled, ended up unable to play fixtures, crashed out of the senior league and only the dedication of a small group of loyal supporters keeps the club alive in a minor league. It was a brave but doomed attempt by a small-town club and one benefactor-businessman to fulfill every football fan's dream and Traynor found the lack of compassion for Gretna was shameful but not surprising: 'The emergence of this tiny club has never been welcomed by the establishment and particularly those horrible two-bob clubs that have been hanging around the game for donkeys' years accepting handouts without giving anything in return.'

'Every silver lining has a cloud ...'

Schadenfreude, pleasure in others' misfortunes, may be a German word but it is an all-too-common Scottish vice, closely akin to the Great Scottish Gloom and the national negativity which believes in the lament of the lugubrious Private Fraser in *Dad's Army*: 'We're a' doomed!'

The late Rikki Fulton's portrayal of the lugubrious Rev. I. M. Jolly was a richly comic creation but it had its roots in his sharp observation of Presbyterian pessimism and the Scottish propensity for dourness with which this book began. As the Rev Jolly confided: 'I think I'm suffering from depression. It doesn't show with me – I always look like this.'

The Scot's ability to revel in despondency led Bill Duncan, the Head of English at Carnoustie High School, to compile his satirical and defiantly non-PC *Wee Book of Calvin*, a collection of aphorisms and essays described by *The Bookseller* as 'a self-help book full of sorrow... quintessentially Scottish'. It begins with the characteristics of a north-east Scottish childhood: 'Guilt. Sin. Misery. Fear. Self-Loathing.' – and lists such depressing maxims as: 'The bonniest flooer wilts the quickest' ... 'Millions of women bring forth in pain/ Millions of bairns that are nae worth haein' ...'Ye can tell the criminal fae the face in the crib' ... 'Soap and waater waash dirt awa' but a sin stains black forever' ... 'A hangover is yer payment fur havin a guid time' ... As they say elsewhere in Scotland: 'Ye have to laugh or ye'd greet' ...

In recent times, the image of the dour Scot has been misused as an easy jibe against Scotland, its politicians and even its sportspeople. The serious 'Scottish banker' persona of the late John Smith was seen as an asset when he was Shadow Chancellor, Leader of the Labour Party and potential Prime Minister; yet the same qualities are seen as deficiencies in his successor and fellow-Scot Gordon Brown, whose strong points – intellectual, workaholic, serious, sober and 'not Flash, just Gordon' – are seen as defects.

His supporters have pointed out that this not only a personal attack on the Prime Minister, but obvious anti-Scottish prejudice ('too many Scots running our country …'). And the philosopher A. C. Grayling, although disappointed with the policies on civil liberties and performance, declared: 'Gordon Brown is a fundamentally thoughtful man, and it is absurd that part of the reason why he should be so pilloried is for lacking the oily slickness of his predecessor.'

He can take comfort from the fact that, if being dour is a fault, then most Scots are deficient. Brown says: 'It is character that people look for in the end, not personality.'

Similarly, the Scottish tennis star Andy Murray has been subjected to inane criticism for failing to smile when he is concentrating on winning important matches. As a 21-year-old who became the last British player in the fourth-round of Wimbledon and coping with the pressures of new-found celebrity, the *Daily Mail* reported what had become a common criticism: 'There is clearly no problem with Andy Murray's tennis prowess. Now all he needs to learn is how to smile. A major proportion of the viewing public appears to concur with Tim Henman's assessment of the 21-year-old Scot as 'a miserable git'.'

And one English fan among the Wimbledon crowd went further, describing Murray as 'Gordon Brown's love child'. He's a dour Scotsman who comes across very badly.

Scots who like to take offence at such things will have noted that once he became one of the world's top tennis players and the UK No.1, 'Oor Andy' became 'Britain's Andy Murray' … And, make no mistake, offence will be taken; as the too-true jibe says: 'How do you spot a well-balanced Scot? He has a chip on both his shoulders …'

Glasgow MP and UK government minister Tom Harris was pilloried for making a light-hearted comment about a nation that is happiest when it is moaning: 'Why is everyone so bloody miserable?' He was only trying to be a ray of sunshine in the gloom of the 2008 financial down-turn, but he should have known better.

Harris's mistake was to remind people on his blog that things were not really that bad: 'Despite the recent credit squeeze, our citizens have never been so wealthy. High-def TVs fly off the shelves at Tesco quicker than they can be imported. Whatever the latest technological innovation, most people can treat themselves to it. Eating out, a rare treat when I was a child in the '70s, is as commonplace as going shopping. And when we do go shopping, whether for groceries or for clothes, we spend money in quantities that would have made our parents gasp.'

However, he was naïve to hope he could spark a thoughtful dialogue about what he believes to be a deep social, spiritual and cultural malaise. Harris was right to point out that the more we have, the more we fear we have to lose. When we've never had it so good, we refuse to be satisfied and the next question is: 'Why can't things be better?' The hope must be that there are Scots who are prepared to point out our national failings and teach us to laugh at ourselves.

CASE NOTE: The chip-on-both-shoulders mentality and begrudgery, the denigration of the success of others, are unattractive traits. Worse, we only succeed in depressing ourselves. Now that 'The best small country in the world' has been jettisoned as our national slogan, we should adopt another from the school of Scottish folk wisdom: 'Self pity never biled a haddock ...'

CHAPTER FIVE

Auld Enemy – or New Friend?

Some people hate the English, I don't. They're just wankers.
We, on the other hand, are colonized by wankers. We can't
even find a decent culture to be colonized by. We are ruled by
effete arseholes. It's a shite state of affairs to be in, Tommy!

IRVINE WELSH *Trainspotting*

An Englishman, roused by a Scot's scorn of his race, protested
that he was born an Englishman and hoped to die an
Englishman. 'Man,' scoffed the Scot, 'hiv ye nae ambeetion?'

Us & Them ...

WHAT DO PARAGUAY, Sweden, Trinidad and Tobago, Ecuador and Portugal
have in common? The fact that in the summer of 2006 thousands of allegedly
patriotic Scots – otherwise rational, fair-minded and devoid of enmity –
became honorary citizens of these countries.

Sadly, it had nothing to do with the international idealism for which
Scots used to be known because this 'citizens of the world' status had a
baser reason: these countries were all 'Anybody but Eng-er-land' in the
World Cup football finals. Scotland having (yet again) failed to qualify,
there was a national debate about which team Scots should back and even
the BRITISH Broadcasting Corporation had a site asking: What team should
Scotland support?

For most Scots, there was no debate. The unequivocal and unthinking
answer was: Any team playing against the English. In an attempt to assuage
Scottish disgruntlement at failing to qualify while England did, one commentator wrote: 'Never mind. We'll soon cheer up when England is knocked
out of the World Cup.'

A father from Yorkshire whose daughter was born and raised in
Scotland recalls an incident at his daughter's school in Lanarkshire: 'During
the 2002 World Cup my daughter was in a Religious and Moral Education
lesson where the teacher knew there were a small number of English pupils
present. Instead of an uplifting discussion on the benefits of tolerance or
some other moral or ethical issue, he set up a TV in the classroom so that

everyone could watch the live TV broadcast of England playing Argentina in Japan and – you've guessed it – cheer for the Argies.

'That has stayed with our family. Somehow this is harder to deal with than the usual sort of 'English bastards' type of abuse. I seem to recall that as a youngster myself I always supported the Scotland soccer team – except when they were playing England. Innocent days!'

Not to support our fellow-members of the not-so-United Kingdom when they are taking on the world, in a tournament for which we were not good enough to make the grade, may seem churlish and mean-spirited (and, of course, it is). It is also a symptom of one of Scotland's most demeaning faults, because it typifies the Scots' use of the English as a psychological crutch and excuse for our own failings. As Pope Pius II said in the 15th century (and it still remains true today): 'Nothing pleases the Scots more than abuse of the English.'

This mentality, ancient and modern, is a manifestation of Renton's rant in *Trainspotting*, combining Scottish self-loathing and begrudgery with an ingrained hatred of the English – or, rather, our idea of 'Englishness'. Nothing personal, you understand; we just loathe everything you stand for ...

Politicians who stray onto the football field usually find themselves sucked into a morass. Gordon Brown, as potential Prime Minister of the UK seeking to stress his 'Britishness', offended some of his more rabid fellow-Scots by saying he would support the English team and compounded the offence when he added Paul Gascoigne's goal against Scotland in Euro '96 was his favourite football moment.

By contrast, the then First Minister Jack McConnell was accused of pandering to an 'unpleasant side of Scottish nationalism' that devolution had failed to cure, by declaring before the tournament began that he would be supporting Trinidad & Tobago and any 'underdogs' or 'teams with flair' – but not England.

Although it IS only a game, for Scots it is also an excuse to revive ancient hatreds and long-harboured grievances. Eleven men in white shirts kicking a ball, and any of their supporters caught on the wrong side of Hadrian's Wall, become the scapegoats for Culloden, the Act of Union, sundry invasions over the centuries, Cromwell's cruelty and the theft of our oil.

Any excuse will do to take umbrage against the English – even the choice of theme tune for the BBC's World Cup programmes. Some neurotic Scots saw it as deliberate provocation by the ENGLISH Broadcasting Corporation to use Handel's See *The Conquering Hero Comes*, written to celebrate the English butchery at Culloden in 1746.

Clearly, this anti-English prejudice has its comic side, especially when the more extreme among the Braveheart brigade are prepared to rewrite history to assert Scottish superiority. There is a story about a Scots bus driver's commentary to his passengers: 'Over there, the Scottish PULVERIZED the English …Here, we MASSACRED the English. …On this battlefield, we WHIPPED the English …' When a tourist with an English accent protested 'Didn't the English win any battles around here?', the response was 'No' when I'm driving the bus!' Ridiculous, of course, but it makes the point.

Perhaps surprisingly, the Scottish Nationalist First Minister Alex Salmond scorned those Scots who adopt this 'anybody but the English' attitude. In a recent interview, he said: 'When you become national leader you're under a different set of rules. Anything I say can be interpreted as the view of the country. People should back their own country. No-one is obligated to support anyone else, but I don't think you should get your kicks by some proxy. It's pathetic. I have never indulged in it.'

There was a similar change of tune by Kenny MacAskill, the SNP MSP and long-serving foot-soldier in the Tartan Army, who, when England lost to Sweden, exulted: 'The Great Satan has been slain!' In another example of how power brings responsibility now that he is a minister in the Scottish Government, he says: 'If England win the World Cup, I won't begrudge them it. Scotland has to move from people standing in pubs cheering on England's opposition. Scotland has to lighten up about England.'

All of this may seem trivial to those with a more grown-up attitude to questions of patriotism and national identity but there are more serious consequences which cannot be ignored and which, to be fair, are deplored by all shades of sensible Scottish opinion, including the most committed nationalists.

Among the more extreme anti-English incidents reported in recent times were unprovoked attacks on a seven-year-old boy in Edinburgh and a disabled, 41-year-old man in Aberdeen who were punched and racially abused because they were wearing England football shirts.

The boy, whose family came from New Zealand but had moved to Edinburgh, was punched on the head as he rode his scooter through a park in Edinburgh with his family. The assailant called him an 'English w*****'. When confronted by the boy's father, the man pointed to the football shirt he was wearing and said: 'This is Scotland, not f***ing England' and then attacked him as well.

A £1,000 reward was offered for information leading to the conviction of the attacker and, in an attempt to retrieve the situation, First Minister McConnell took the unusual step of making a statement in the Scottish

Parliament, describing the two attacks as 'entirely unacceptable' and declaring that English people, who will make up 10 per cent of Scotland's population by 2015, were always welcome in the country.

As recently as January 2009, a young woman was the victim of a brutal attack in Aberdeen city centre because of her English accent. Lucy Newman, 22, was punched in the face by a man and suffered two black eyes, one of which was swollen shut, a cracked cheekbone and damaged nerves in her eyes. She had moved with her family from Cheltenham, Gloucestershire, 18 years before and her father said: 'Lucy's been in Scotland since she was four but sometimes she's still got an English twang. She was talking and singing with her pal. The guy heard her accent, made a comment about her being English and just smacked her in the face.'

The ingrained nature of anti-English racism in some communities was revealed by the case of a family who had lived in Brechin for seven years but announced in April 2009 that they were returning south because of racism. Mr James Allen, originally from Manchester, was a firefighter in the Royal Navy for 23 years and said he had never came across racism until settling in their adopted home town in Angus.

After a trial at Forfar Sheriff Court, Mr Allen was found not guilty of charges of assaulting two local youths after his defence argued that the incident followed a campaign of racial abuse against the Allen family. After the trial, he said: 'We adore our home, we have lots of friends in Brechin and the police have been absolutely tremendous but we can't take this any more.

'They are still after me— the kids have won. I feel sorry for whoever becomes their next target.'

The problem escalated from youngsters knocking on the door and running away to the door being kicked in and people in masks entering their home.

'It started as a group of about 20 kids and it is now their younger brothers who are involved,' Mr Allen said. 'When we go out to the shops or walk the dog we face a torrent of racist abuse. I can see no solution until parents start admitting that their children are not always going to the youth club. They are out terrorising people. They should take responsibility.'

Police said that out of a dozen crimes against Mr Allen and his family which had been reported to them, nine had been forwarded to the procurator fiscal. Angus Provost Ruth Leslie Melville, in whose ward the family lives, said she was disappointed Mr Allen had to leave Brechin: 'However, the situation appears to have got out of hand and is beyond intervention.'

This damaging darker side to racial bigotry is most visible on the Internet, which has bred a sub-species of 'CyberNats', bloggers and bigots. It is nothing new for the present authors and others who support the Union to be described in public as 'traitors' and 'Quislings' for rejecting Scottish separatism.

English People in Scotland: An Invisible Minority, a study by Stirling University's Department of Applied Social Science in 2008, posed the question of what kind of belonging an inclusive, differentiated, plural society can offer where peoples share a common language and code of conduct and yet continue to identify in culturally distinctive ways. It was a follow-up to previous research papers entitled *'It's as if you're some alien....' Exploring anti-English attitudes in Scotland* and *'We hate the English except for you, cos you're our pal': Identification of the English in Scotland.*

The work confirms the existence of anti-English prejudice and, while the discrimination is low-level, it is persistent. It creates a danger of 'alienating and marginalising' the largest minority living in Scotland, seven per cent of the population, who are regarded as 'white settlers' and given the feeling, even after decades of residence, that they do not belong. Other quotes from English residents in Scotland included 'I don't think we were made particularly welcome' and "English bastards' – it's like one word.'

Joint author and department head Dr Douglas Robertson says: 'This is a major issue in Scotland, yet very little research has been done. English people who have settled in Scotland increasingly identify with their adopted country, but small differences in the way they are treated can make them feel like permanent outsiders, making it impossible to integrate even if they want to. There is no overt racism as with some other minorities, but hearing an English accent raises a moral panic among some Scots.

'Reinforcing the myths and stereotypes of the English as colonial invaders, an English accent – and especially a middle-class southern one – was shown to set off powerful anxieties about national weakness, political dominations, economic colonisation and cultural insecurity on the part of Scots.'

Like the poet Hugh MacDiarmid who said in *Who's Who* his hobby was 'Anglophobia', even the mildest of Nationalists feel obliged to belittle British nationality. The previous SNP party leader John Swinney in an unconvincing Mel Gibson-as-William Wallace impersonation urged in a conference speech: 'Tell the Brits to get off'. Another SNP front-bencher insulted the Union Jack as the banner of British imperialist occupation, unconcerned that his words were an affront to the generations of Scots who proudly followed that flag into battle for the freedoms we now enjoy.

This is an attitude problem which, through long-dead issues and the need to find a scapegoat for our own failings, has been absorbed into the Scottish psyche and has been all too easily reinforced by English counter-attitudes and other layers of contemporary concerns, special interests and tensions. Three centuries after the Union, it is plainly preposterous to regard England as 'the enemy' as the more extreme nationalists do; to heap wholesale blame on the English for Scotland's ills, as most nationalists do and it is a pathetic admission of our own inferiority complex to be perpetually looking over our shoulders at the looming shadow of England.

The Wars of Independence, the loss of a Scottish monarchy in the 1603 Union of the Crowns, the loss of a separate Parliament in 1707 (after the humiliation of the Darien scheme which created the lasting image of a proud nation becoming subsidiary and having to go cap in hand to London) and the repression of the Covenanters and the Jacobite rebellions all fed into the national sense of grievance. Yet how far back down the centuries do we go to feed this resentment? Should we hate Scandinavians for the Norse invasions of the ninth century?

As befits Scotland's First Minister, Alex Salmond (perhaps in a softening-up process for the proposed referendum in 2010 on full Scottish independence) now exudes goodwill and neighbourliness towards the English. Salmond expressed the wish to be 'the best of pals, the closest of buddies' with the English. However, when he voiced this at the SNP manifesto launch in 2007, his audience of nationalist activists and MSPs burst out laughing at the improbability.

There is a suspicion that his tongue is in his cheek when he argues that independence for Scotland would have benefits for the English: they would get their own 'democracy' and he foresees us as 'independent countries united by a monarchy that symbolises the social union between the two.'

In an interview with Iain Dale for *Total Politics* in August 2008, he said he had 'huge sympathy' with the resurgence of English nationalism:.' By choice, SNP MPs have abstained from every vote on English legislation that does not have an immediate Scottish consequence. If you're asking me should people in England be able to run their own health service or education system, my answer is 'yes'. They should be able to do it without the bossy interference of Scots Labour MPs.

'We had this in reverse through the 1980s. Because I believe in independence for Scotland, I also believe in independence for England. I know there are a lot of doom-mongers who say that England couldn't stand on its own two feet. I deprecate that sort of talk. I have great confidence in England's ability to be self-governing!'

Backing up this argument, Salmond commented 'Who needs a moaning lodger?' This image of Scots as transient tenants in the British guest-house betrays Salmond's and the SNP's attitude that the Union is only temporary (after 700 years?!) and Scots have never wanted it, begrudge being in it and would be better off out of it – a blinkered prejudice that is not shared by two-thirds of Scots.

In any case the Scots and English are more than mere neighbours. Perhaps the image should be that of a couple who have started as a marriage of convenience, lived together for many years (perhaps in twin beds?) but have now to find a new way of living in harmony with each other ...

Them & Us ...

God help England if she had no Scots to think for her!
GEORGE BERNARD SHAW *The Applecart*

Jeremy Clarkson, presenter of the 'Top Gear' TV show, seems to successfully cultivates the image of a boorish bigot, for a very good reason: he makes big money out of being obnoxious.

So why should we pay any attention to anything he says? For one reason only: he represents a mirror image of knee-jerk nationalism south of the border and the growth of an increasingly vocal anti-Scottishness. He typifies the 'Little Englander' mentality which combines latent English nationalism with a reaction to Scottish self-government and a resentment of the dominance of Scots in the UK government.

When Clarkson described Prime Minister Gordon Brown as a 'one-eyed, Scottish idiot', he intended to be provocative. Clearly, he did not have the sense or decency to know how offensive he was being. The fact that he later 'apologised' does not mitigate his offence because the 'apology' was half-hearted and had to be forced out of him. Anyone in the public eye who does not know instinctively that using a disability as an insult is unacceptable or that sneering at a nationality is dangerous ignorance, is beyond excuse.

On those occasions when many English people think about Scotland at all, they instinctively agree with Edward Longshanks, so brilliantly portrayed in the film *Braveheart,* when he drawled disdainfully: 'The trouble with Scotland is that there are too many Scots in it...' They also add: 'too many Scots in government over us'. And, insultingly, 'too many Scots picking OUR pockets' – when they really mean the UK Treasury, to which Scottish taxpayers contribute.

A prominent Westminster figure (who has to watch his tongue because his job is dependent on an English boss) told us: 'The English are definitely becoming more English and Scottish dominance is something people talk about a lot down here. They see all the Scots in the Cabinet and they resent what

Jeremy Paxman called 'The Scottish Raj'.' (This comment was described by MPs as 'insulting, irresponsible, divisive and snobbish'. Cabinet Minister Dr John Reid, with typical Scottish forthrightness, described the presenter as 'doolally'.)

The automatic response from Scots is: Why on earth should the English hate the Scots after all they have done TO us – and all we have done FOR them? It is akin to Churchill's verdict on the French: 'They can't forgive us because they owe us too much.'

'They' unthinkingly say 'England' when they are talking about 'Britain'. Even during World War Two, when Scots as well as Welsh and Irish were giving their lives and suffering the same privations, there was a backs-to-the-wall song: 'There will always be an England'. North of the border, it was resentfully rendered as: 'There will always be an England – as long as there are Scots to do their fighting.' Nowadays, it is 'as long as there are Scots to run it. …'

Nor is there much sign of respect, and indeed gratitude, for the many inventions and discoveries we have given them and the world – from the steam engine to penicillin and cloning, through the Scottish Enlightenment which led American historian Arthur Hermann to title his book *How the Scots Invented the Modern World – The True Story of How Western Europe's Poorest Nation Created Our World and Everything in It.*

There should be credit given to the many Scottish politicians, thinkers and statesmen who have governed Britain with distinction. With the clear exception of Sir Alec Douglas-Home, there are good reasons why there were eight Scottish Prime Ministers in the last century. That the Anglo-centric attitude has permeated the most influential quarters was shown by the indiscreet remark of Prime Minister Tony Blair's chief of staff Jonathan Powell that 'You could never get a Scot as Prime Minister'. Gordon Brown has, of course, proved him wrong and thee is no reason why some Scot should do so again in the future.

In the sharply-observant political TV series *The Thick of It* (written by a Scot, Armando Iannucci) a character toadying to the evil Scottish spin doctor explains: 'I'm not a Scot, so I've got to do something to get on.' The disproportionate number of Scots in the Labour-led governments since 1997 may get up English noses, but we would argue they are in the British government and other high places, not out of favouritism or bias but on merit.

The BBC's supposedly neutral *Politics Show* ran a poll asking 'Is it right for a Scottish MP to be Prime Minister now Scotland has its own Parliament?' and a majority answered 'No'.

Of course, it was a loaded question thought up by the ENGLISH Broadcasting Corporation to reflect the 'Little Englander' mentality. It panders to those who cannot come to terms with the undeniable fact that a smaller country has exercised such disproportionate influence and still does, snaffling so many of the top jobs and great offices of State. We simply have to ask the corollary question 'Should the Prime Minister of the United Kingdom only be English from now on?' in order to see it is gross prejudice that ignores the place of Scotland, Wales and Northern Ireland in the UK.

On the same programme, the English (of course) presenter Jon Sopel asked questions about Scots getting too much money 'from the UK taxpayer'. As any Scot who pays tax will tell you, the Inland Revenue return makes it clear that Scots and the other British nations are UK taxpayers. We get our fair share to meet our needs, and we do not moan too much that Londoners get a whoppingly disproportionate amount of *our* money to sort their self-created problems; the recurrent indignation at the national burden of the cost of the 2012 Olympics in London is still confined to a minority.

Columnists in allegedly UK 'national' newspapers indulge their English readership with anti-Scottish jibes. Richard Littlejohn in the *Daily Mail*, referring to Gordon Brown and John Reid, demanded: 'Why should England put up with either of the Tartan Terrors?' Another ultra-English commentator, Simon Heffer in the *Daily Telegraph* huffed that the Scots in Cabinet are 'an over-represented and increasingly unaccountable minority whose job it is to raise taxes from the English to spend on the Scots'.

Like them or loathe them, they articulate a narrow-mindedness which may be unthinking among the wider English population but in politics and media is deliberately calculated to aggravate anti-Scottish (and therefore anti-government and anti-Labour) feelings. The dangers for the UK in this cynical stirring are overlooked in the interest of short-term electoral advantage in England.

An all too easy target is the perceived advantage for Scotland in public spending per head of population which takes no account of the complicated calculation involved, of comparative need and spread of population, nor of the ongoing debate about the tax powers of the Holyrood parliament and the acceptance of the need to revise or replace the 'Barnett formula'. Instead, Scots are characterized as 'subsidy junkies' sponging off the long-suffering and indulgent 'English' taxpayers.

When the economic crisis was at its deepest and UK recession was declared official in January 2009, Heffer was moved to hysteria: 'The sooner the bunch of Scots who govern us are booted into history the better. I don't say that the English would be any better, but at least we would be paying for our own mistakes rather than someone else's.

'Never has the case for English independence from the Scots been so overwhelming. Sadly, I suspect that in the present state of penury England will be saddled with them for another 302 years of high-end welfarism at least.'

At least it shows that Scotland does not have a monopoly of nationalist ranters but, depressingly, Heffer and Littlejohn and their ilk speak for a growing number of their fellow-Anglos. Even more depressing is that these deliberately provocative tirades trigger letters and website responses from the more rabid anti-Scots, the flagrant racism of which caused one correspondent to point out they would probably lead to prosecution if they were applied to blacks or Jews.

The result is a predictable polarisation on both sides of the border and, according to the Institute for Public Policy Research North, a major contributor to this has been the way newspapers and broadcasters have operated in the post-devolution era. In his paper, *Nation Speaking Unto Nation* (which is after all the BBC's motto) as part of the IPPR's 'Future of the Union' project, journalist Douglas Fraser (former political editor of *The Herald* and now BBC Scotland's economics editor) concentrated on a largely baleful media influence and concluded: 'The early years of devolution have shown division to be more apparent than unity and ignorance of each other to be a bigger factor than increased interest.'

The institute's senior research fellow, Guy Lodge, commented: 'During a time when there is so much debate about the future relationship between England and Scotland, what is clear is that since devolution the English and Scots are drifting further apart and growing more ignorant of each other.'

Fraser identified a 'metropolitan myopia' in the London-centric media: 'More than in any similar large country, the national conversation is mediated by people who do not get out of its capital city enough. Is it possible that London, in establishing itself as the most cosmopolitan and outward-looking of world cities, suffers simultaneously from a metropolitan myopia about its own hinterland – English as well as Scottish?

'Those in England who learn about their country from their morning papers will have very little knowledge, and even less understanding, of the fundamental changes in Scotland. The UK is badly served by a media which fails to reflect the regional and national diversity of the country.

'It is easy to dismiss these issues as more whingeing from the Jocks, but there are important issues here about how Britain understands itself as a nation.'

That the Scottish cringe still persists was demonstrated by the all-too-predictable reaction to remarks by the historian and professional controver-sialist Dr David Starkey on BBC TV's *Question Time* on St George's Day, 23 April 2009. To laughter from the audience, who knew what he was about, Starkey answered a question on whether it should be an English public holiday with: 'If we decide to go down this route of having and English nation day means we become a feeble little country, just like the Scots and the Welsh and the Irish.

'Once upon a time England was a great country. Remember we're dis-tinguished by the fact that we don't have national dress. We don't make a great fuss about Shakespeare like the Scots do about that deeply boring provincial poet Burns. We don't have national music like the awful bagpipes.

'What the Scots and Welsh are, are typical small nations with a romantic 19th style nationalism. Do you just want to be a little country rather than the great one we once were?'

Failing to appreciate that the mischievous Starkey was being deliberately provocative, thin-skinned Scots responded with a typical knee-jerk 'Wha does yon Starkey think he is?' reaction; unthinking Scottish MPs and MSPs hurled themselves into Starkey's trap and fumed that his remarks were offensive and insulting. The BBC, which carried the item on UK and Scottish news bulletins, received hundreds of protests and, amid a media storm in which the *Scotsman* rumbled that Starkey 'sparks fury of a nation' while contradicting itself by saying in an editorial 'Let's not rise to Starkey's bait'. It was a classic Scottish boob – instead of ignoring Starkey, they had gifted another victory to the English ...

... *Staying Together*

We cannot, of course, answer for English extremists and would not dream of answering for the more bigoted of our fellow-Scots. However, there is a general attitude problem in Scotland that needs to be addressed: until we stop looking at ourselves through the eyes of another nation, we will never properly grow up.

As the actress Elaine C. Smith pointed out, this can have a crippling effect on national confidence: 'There's a thing about Scotland – we were always stuck in permanent adolescence, constantly blaming the parents for what has gone wrong. It was so easy – 'Och, blame everything on the English', which is an argument I've never had any truck with.'

Why have only the negative aspects of Scotland's relationship with England throughout history been so deeply absorbed into the Scottish psyche? Why do so many Scots fail to realise it is ridiculous to regard England as the dark shadow looming over us and our affairs? And why does a proud nation playing its full part in the United Kingdom see itself as a cap-in-hand inferior partner?

This perversion of patriotism which is rightly derided as 'the Scottish cringe' has been reinforced as a result of the rise of the Scottish National Party, which required the establishment of a grievance culture, a strategy of blaming 'London' for Scotland's ills and, now that they are in government at Holyrood, consistently complain that they are deprived of finance and powers to do what is best for Scotland.

The anti-English, and therefore anti-UK, mentality is succeeding by default because no effective case is being made for the Union and the ties with England, Wales and Northern Ireland. The Unionist parties in Scotland and at Westminster (in particular Scottish MPs and Lords) are failing to take every opportunity to point out the advantages for Scots of membership of the Union and the value of Scotland's contribution.

It seems the nation of the Enlightenment, where the impulse was to question everything in search for the truth, has unthinkingly adopted a miasma of ideas, innuendos and prejudices about England that are now part of the folklore of Scotland. This has seeped so deep into the souls of some Scots that the belief in continuing 'English oppression' is held as fact, when it is no more than irrational, unhelpful and unhealthy pettiness.

It should be obvious that with such a mental handicap Scotland cannot face the future, either as a progressive country within a reformed Union or as a separate nation. It will require a concerted effort to debunk much of the mythology, a debunking that must begin with the acknowledgement that England is the major – but by no means overpowering – player within the United Kingdom and that between are nations we have serious relationships that should not be the subject of the politics of denigration, envy and bickering.

With the Union undefended, either because of inactive complacency or active separatism, it is no surprise that the English are disenchanted. An even greater danger is that in the wake of the global economic crisis, as social unrest spreads, these differences and divisions will increase. Hard-pressed English taxpayers could become more susceptible to the complaints that Scotland is somehow doing better at their expense.

The devolved powers of the Scottish Parliament have brought such benefits as free personal care, tuition fees and the ban on smoking before it was introduced south of the border. Yet while Scotland has its own Parliament with the ability to legislate on most of its own affairs, the English are subject to government by Scottish ministers and by MPs who can vote on vital English concerns while they have no power over the same issues in their own Scottish constituencies.

The risk that must be faced by the Unionist parties, not least the Labour Party in government, is that anti-Scottishness is fermenting in England while anti-Englishness is being fermented by nationalists in Scotland. Scots are left with no clear perspective of the Union and the Union, by default, is being undermined (as we explore in our chapter on the Union).

The public are not receiving a healthy analysis from either politicians or the mass media. The antipathy, pretended or otherwise, towards our partner-nation in the UK may be fine as comedy or knockabout politics, but when it enters the political, constitutional, economic and social arenas it undermines Scotland's advance into the future.

We Scots need to recalibrate where we stand with the English and we should be big enough to admit that they are not responsible for all our problems. Breaking free from that is not breaking free from the Union but it means shedding our own ingrained faults and rejecting the prejudices of the past.

In return, the English should also have a more mature attitude to us and do something about their own problems. Reform of the Union would give England a better view of itself and alter the perception that 50 million people, one of the biggest populations in Europe, are being short-changed by the present Westminster settlement.

The government of England is done in London, not Manchester nor Birmingham nor Newcastle nor Liverpool nor Bristol. Why do the English accept that? Among themselves, they are no more homogeneous than the Scots with the English. Scouse, Geordie, Tykes, Brummie or West Country have their different cultures, attitudes and needs and if these were reflected in regional assemblies there would less cause for grievance about Scotland's measure of self-government.

Learning to be new friends on equal terms would teach Scots and English to see ourselves in a different light. It is ironic that the successful pressure for a greater say in our own affairs came from the fringes of the UK; the Celtic nations in the Union are driving devolution while the English are on the sidelines. They do not have their own English Parliament but Scotland, Wales and Northern Ireland do; they do not have separate legislation, we have. England is the biggest country in Europe with no devolved power. Perhaps it is a time for us to be less hostile to the English and more sorry for them ...

It may be galling for the English to have a minority government in Scotland (a country with a tenth of their population) administrating, annoying, cheer-leading and needling London on the issues of the day. It is for England to move on and stop being an extension of London and the south-east. Scots have thrown off the metropolitan elite: Why don't the English?

Scots need have no problem asserting their own identity within the Union but in doing so they have to throw off the shackles of history, especially recent history. Under the Thatcher' government, there was a perception that Scotland was being used as laboratory for experiments with Tory policy and the author William McIllvanney said: 'We have had bad governments in the past. We have had governments whose awareness of Scotland's problems seemed on a par with their knowledge of the other side of the moon. We have never until now had a government so determined to unpick the very fabric of Scottish life.'

It is unthinkable that any other government would be callous or careless enough to repeat that mistake (although there would be no harm in remaining alert to the possibility, in the event of future changes of UK government).

However, the most powerful reason to end cross-border prejudice is not political, but purely personal. Many Scot-Brits have over-riding individual reasons to want to live together in diversity: their families and personal friendships. Through migration and inter-marriage, Scots have 'English' kinfolk. One of the authors (TB) has a United Nations of grandchildren and says: 'The blood that flows in their young veins is a mixture of Scottish, English, Irish, Indian and Chinese. I am glad to say they have a certain pride in their Scottish ancestry – but the nationality that binds us all together is being British.'

Racism, whether by colour or narrow nationalism, is offensive to such families. Scots and English alike should celebrate what we have in common, not what divides us.

Of course, we Scots should be good neighbours and, in the words of First Minister Salmond, England's 'biggest pal'. But it would help if the English could learn to be just a bit more lovable.

CASE NOTE: We should not constantly look over our shoulder to England, nor use them for comparison, nor as the excuse for our failures. And, instead of carping about Scotland, the English should wake up and start taking their own politics of devolution seriously.

CHAPTER SIX

'Beastly, Filthy Foreigners'

All through the story the immigrants came,
The Gael and the Pict, the Angle and Dane
From Pakistan, England and from the Ukraine
We're all Scotland's story and we're all worth the same.
                    Scotland's Story, THE PROCLAIMERS

A large alien race in our midst, people of different ideals and
faith and blood.
        Church of Scotland General Assembly debate in 1923
                            on Irish immigration

Decent working men are not going to be turned adrift to make
room for beastly, filthy foreigners without knowing the reason
why.

                            KEIR HARDIE

A 'SOMEWHAT DESPERATE' LADY from the Glasgow area made a generous offer on an Internet dating website early in 2009: 'I have a thing for European men! I simply love the foreign accent! So if you are Spanish, German, Portuguese, Danish, Swedish, Dutch, Polish, Czech, French, Italian or whatever and are finding it a pain in the ass to find a decent lover who will treat you like a prince and you have all the wonderful charms and qualities to give to a girl who is looking for love, why don't you contact me?'

Whether she had a queue of Continental gents at her door or whether she is still looking for love, we do not know. But one thing is certain: not all Scots share her open-hearted attitude to incomers, whatever their origin.

Scots like to think of themselves as welcoming and hospitable; they are justifiably proud that Scotland's national bard wrote the definitive declaration of the brotherhood of man. Yet historically and still today, the attitude to immigrant communities has too often been the opposite – and a hostility to immigrants has in the past been displayed, to their discredit, by some unexpected sources.

It is a human failing to be concerned about any influx of 'foreigners', particularly economic migrants who are seeking jobs, homes and a better way of life. As Professor Christopher Smout, the respected historian who has written extensively on demographic history, said in a TV interview in February 2009 on the publication of an academic study of national attitudes: 'There is always going to be some hostility where there is immigration, whether you come from Kent or Tashkent. People are always going to dislike immigrants because they are different, because they are competing for housing, jobs, health care and homes. Some hostility is always going to take place in any country.'

This may explain but, of course, cannot excuse intolerance and certainly not the more extreme reactions, ranging from discrimination and abuse to violence. Irrespective of attempts to create cross-community harmony (and in some official quarters to gloss over the problem by talking about the 'modern Scotland, a rich and diverse society'), racial tensions are a fact of life in that modern Scotland.

It remains to be seen whether the 'British jobs for British workers' mentality will become as pronounced north of the border as it has in England, but the state of race relations in Scotland has to be continuously and carefully monitored. A more sensible and sensitive debate is needed on what has been described by one national newspaper as 'the changing face of Scotland', with a recognition that the nation actually needs MORE immigration.

Recent individual incidents of racism are symptomatic of something deeper; they echo the unpleasant earlier history of bigotry hostility towards newcomers who sought sanctuary in Scotland. To understand today's dangers it is worth learning the lessons of history.

One of the most notorious examples was actually perpetuated by the national church which used a supposed threat to 'nationality' to disguise religious bigotry. It led to an infamous debate in the General Assembly of the Church of Scotland in language so deeply racist that it still shocks.

Irish immigration had contributed significantly to the mainland population and was first measured in the 1841 census as 125,000 in Scotland of Irish birth, rising 20 years later to 204,000, seven per cent of the population. The potato famine in the 1840s led to a major inflow, reported to be at the rate of 1,000 a week in Glasgow alone in 1848.

Eighty years later, Irish immigration was still a contentious issue (in fact, in the light of the secular divide that still persist in the West of Scotland, the question could be asked whether it has ever really gone away) and was debated by the 1923 General Assembly.

Following overtures from the Presbytery of Glasgow and the Synod of Glasgow and Ayr, an Assembly committee report claimed that the Irish population in Scotland had doubled in the previous 40 years and that in the previous 20 years the increase of the Irish population was six-and-a-half-times as great as that of the Scottish population.

The committee's convener, Rev William Main of Edinburgh, said this was not because of any greater fertility of the Irish race: 'It was not a matter of the birth-rate at all; but for the most part, if not entirely, it was due to the emigration from Ireland and as the Irish settled in an area, the Scots departed from it. The two races could not fuse.

'The political influence of the immigration was already seen in the West. It was very largely due to this fact that they had in the Commons at the present time men who were supposed to represent constituencies in Glasgow and the west but did not represent them really. (Applause)

'They had been elected Members of Parliament by the fact that they had this enormous Irish Roman Catholic population in these areas. Hence, the type of men sent from these areas to Parliament, bringing disgrace and scandal into the House of Commons. (Applause)'

Mr Main 'was not afraid of proselytism by the Roman Catholic priests, but increased Roman Catholic populations brought with them a certain power, and in educational, municipal and Parliamentary elections they held the balance.' There was even louder applause from the ministers and elders when he said the facts and figures warranted the Assembly calling on the government 'to institute an inquiry into the condition of matters which, to say the least of it, was a menace to the Scottish nationality'.

Seconding this call, Rev Duncan Cameron of Kilsyth said there was 'a danger that the Scottish nationality would be imperilled and Scottish civilisation subverted'. In what would nowadays be seen as inflammatory racist language, Mr Cameron fumed: 'It was time that the people of Scotland realised the situation. The complexion and the spirit of our Scottish civilisation were being altered by a large alien race in our midst, people of different ideals and faith and blood.

'The time might come when political parties would not touch this question, when men in positions of public authority and power would be afraid to speak, to see this land passing into strange hands.'

By contrast, the rational and far-sighted comments of Rev Dr John White of Glasgow, a future Moderator of the Kirk, are still valid today: 'The problem was how to regulate the incoming of these new forces from Ireland, Italy and Jewry so as to be a strength and not a menace – how to fuse those heterogeneous elements into one essential whole so that they should be Scottish and not foreign.' However, for accuracy, it should be added that the Rev White advocated 'regulation of immigration, as every other nation did'.

One speaker, Rev G. W. Mackay of Killin, deprecated the references to

Labour members in Glasgow and suggested it was exceedingly dangerous to use the word 'alien': 'Were the majority of the English an alien race? Was the great mass of Protestants in Ulster an alien race?' (Shouts of 'No').

The anti-Irish Catholic prejudice was also demonstrated outside the Assembly by at least one academic who should have known better as Professor Andrew Gibb, Regius Professor of Private Law at Glasgow University, declaimed: 'In the heart of a dwindling though virile and intelligent race there is growing up another people, immeasurably inferior in every way, but cohesive and solid, refusing obstinately, at the behest of obscurantist magic-men, to mingle with the people whose land they are usurping; unaware, or if aware, disloyal to all the finest ideals and ambitions of the Scottish race.'

For a lawyer and professor to use such scare-mongering language as 'usurping' and 'disloyal' and insulting descriptions of the new population as 'immeasurably inferior in every way' and priests as 'magic-men', demonstrates the pernicious nature of the prejudice in every level of society.

One of the most surprising racist campaigns in Scotland was conducted by, of all people, Keir Hardie, founding father of the Labour Party. While mounting a working-class crusade against the 'white slavery' of capitalism, he was not above conducting what has been described by his biographer as 'a virulent xenophobic campaign' against immigrant miners from the Baltic countries.

The root cause of opposition to the employment of Lithuanians and others loosely (and wrongly) described as 'Russian Poles' was the threat to the jobs of local miners and the fear that they would undermine their wages. While it is true the mine-owners and steel-masters of Ayrshire and Lanarkshire did make use of immigrants to show native Scots that they had another source of cheap labour and other commentators described them as a new breed of 'serfs', Hardie's articles and speeches nonetheless stooped to the lowest level of racism.

He alleged they brought the Black Death and immorality to Scotland and declared: 'Decent working men are not going to be turned adrift to make room for beastly, filthy foreigners without knowing the reason why.' In one speech, Hardie asserted: 'These men, I am informed, are growing fat on four shillings a week. Their chief item of diet is said to be train oil. These Russian Poles are not allowed to go down the mines to work as they might blow out the lamps and drink their oil.'

In *The Miner*, which he edited, he gave a nakedly inflammatory warning: 'Much indignation is being expressed and the upshot will be bloodshed unless a stop is put to the disgraceful proceedings.'

John Millar, historian of the Lithuanian community in Scotland, points out: 'To call them Poles or Russians was an insult, considering their centuries-long struggle against being absorbed by both.'

Scots-born Mr Millar, whose given name was Jonas Stepsis and whose father and uncle fled Lithuania to escape Czarist persecution for being 'book-carriers' who smuggled their native Lithuanian literature, says the attitude of the Scots to the incomers is all the more remarkable when one considers the history and similarity of both nations: 'Both were small nations, over-run and occupied by their more powerful neighbour. Both had their national dress, language and culture proscribed. Both countries produced a hard core of nationalism, seeking authority ... both peoples emigrated, and for similar reasons, economic necessity, religious and political persecution.'

As a result of his researches into the treatment of his countrymen, he states matter-of-factly: 'Contrary to the myth of Scottish hospitality, the history of immigration into Scotland is a history of bigotry, prejudice, intolerance, discrimination, fear, hostility, verbal abuse and even hatred.

'The 'incomer' was regarded with suspicion and hospitality was generally conspicuous by its absence. The least hint of an accent or difficulty with the English language, the possession of a 'strange' or 'unScottish' surname was met with resentment by the Scots in general and frequently made the butt of their humour.

'As a boy and young adult, I was subjected to the prejudice and bigotry, the name-calling, sneers, taunts and general ill-treatment dealt out to 'foreigners' which seemed prevalent in the West of Scotland at that time. In reply to the suggestion that such treatment would not or could not exist in these modern enlightened days, I quote the following incident which occurred in 1992.

'To further the scope of my research, I placed an appeal in local and national newspapers for former residents. In my absence, a man called at my home and when my son-in-law explained the reason for my appeal the derogatory reply was: 'Oh, he's wan o' they Poles then.'"

The Scottish antipathy towards immigrant workers, particularly in the coalmining areas, was not confined to the Lithuanians. Jimmy Reid, the working-class hero turned writer, has told how Mick McGahey, President of the Scottish NUM planned to produce a book about the life of Bob Smiley, one of the founders of the miners' union in Scotland and a pioneer of the wider Scottish Labour movement: 'After a few months I asked Mick how his project was going. He told me: 'Jimmy we can't publish it. Bob's speeches at the time were viciously anti-Irish.'

'Like the racist language currently used by the National Front against Pakistanis today, Smiley had clearly feared that starving Irish workers could undercut the wages that his Union had struggled to achieve for their members over many years of struggle. That was obviously the strategic objective of the mine owners. I wanted Mick to publish. It was the truth from which lessons could be learned. But Mick saw this revelation as bringing shame to the Union he loved. It wasn't published.'

Secretary of State for Scotland Jim Murphy acknowledged the danger of a revival of this latent tendency when he warned at the Scottish Labour Party conference in March 2009 against a rise in 'recessionary racism'. He said all the mainstream Parties shared this worry of a reaction against immigrant workers as a result of the economic crisis and he had joined trade unions and Scotland's faith leaders, Including Cardinal Keith O'Brien and the Right Reverend David Lunan, the Moderator of the Church of Scotland, in opposition to recessionary racism.

He said: 'This is the first recession in a genuinely global labour market. European workers, including Britons have freedom of movement and the UN now estimates that today there are 176 million people living outside the country of their birth. All of this creates additional pressure points that were not so prominent in previous recessions.

'While understanding people's fears and insecurities, no-one should pander to credit crunch racism ... This crisis wasn't caused by Polish plumbers or Bangladeshi shop workers. It was precipitated by international bankers, some of them very close to home. We should continue to make clear that it is irresponsible bankers on million pound bonuses not the industrious migrant worker on the minimum wage to blame for this financial calamity.'

Recent events support the view that racial tensions are never far from the surface in Scotland and can erupt into ugly and violent episodes on both sides of the ethnic divide. The failure is in fostering a national realisation that Scotland is – and always has been – a multi-racial, multi-cultural society whose character must keep evolving. That the nation needs immigrants, that many who are regarded as 'incomers' are actually second, third and fourth-generation Scots living in well-established communities yet whom the host population still does not accept them as fully-integrated; that minority communities are not fairly represented in our national institutions; and that the result is a younger generation of children of ethnic minority families who, although born and raised in Scotland, reject a Scottish identity.

Self-interest dictates that a country with a low birth rate and an ageing population, has to attract more immigrants, if only for economic reasons. Professor Robert Wright of Strathclyde University put the choice squarely:

'I spoke at a conference recently and a person stood up and said immigration will change the character of Scotland. I said it certainly will but you have a choice: you either have the same character of Scotland and a lower standard of living, or a changed character and a higher standard of living.'

It is often said that Scotland's greatest export is its people and trends indicate that by 2030 the population will fall below five million. The country needs a 20–25,000 net migration surplus year on year, with the condition that these immigrants take up residence in Scotland. A shortfall would mean reduced output, lower economic growth and insufficient tax revenue to maintain services and support the 'economically inactive' ageing population.

A recent surge in immigration, mainly from east European countries, is drying up in the aftermath of the global economic downturn as newcomers find job prospects and earning levels, particularly for those with higher skill levels, are not much better than in their home countries.

Suggested solutions have included 'tilting'; the United Kingdom's points-based immigration system to allow more flexibility with added points under a work permit system which would encourage prospective migrants to choose Scotland as their destination. The Fresh Talent: Working in Scotland immigration scheme was meant to encourage foreign students at Scottish educational institutions to stay in Scotland upon completion of their studies, but now applies to general UK foreign graduates, reducing the specific advantage for Scotland.

The contribution by these communities is plain and there is evidence that they will enrich Scottish life even more in the longer term – as was shown in the 2008 school exam results, when children from Chinese, Asian-Indian and mixed-race backgrounds recorded the best results. A tariff system comparing the results of fourth-year pupils showed children from a Chinese background had an average score of 220, those from Asian-Indian families 207, mixed-race children 191, Asian-Bangladeshi 182, Asian Pakistani 174, while children whose families were described as 'white' had a tariff score of 173.

The risk inherent in not fully assimilating young Scots with a different ethnic background was shown when Scottish Executive researchers carried out a census of school pupils' sense of national identity. The findings showed a clear sense of alienation among many of these young Scots and a disturbing hint of radicalisation in the wake of the wars in Iran and Afghanistan and perceived Islamophobia.

The census in September 2008 showed that a quarter of children of ethnic minority families rejected any sense of British identity, compared with only one in ten in 2002. The only group with any sense of 'being Scottish' was white indigenous youngsters, where the figure rose from 74 per cent to 79 per cent. A third of pupils with Indian heritage defined their nationality as non-UK, while the rate had doubled among Pakistanis and trebled among children with a Caribbean background. The bad news for the creation of a well-integrated and cohesive Scottish society was that Muslim young people were reacting to being 'labelled negatively' and chose to describe themselves as coming from the country of their families' origin, rather than the country of their birth, education and residence.

Extremists will take advantage of any indication of latent racism, as has been shown by the increased activity of the British National Party in Scotland which has included putting up candidates for local and parliamentary elections and, for the first time in the May 2009 European election, 'a full slate of candidates that all live and work in Scotland, a sure sign of the advances we have made in recent years'.

The BNP have concentrated on multicultural communities in the central belt, particularly Glasgow which they describe as being 'on the receiving end of a never ending build-up of economic migrants, asylum seekers, failed asylum seekers, illegal immigrants etc. and has become the immigrant dumping-ground of Scotland' They caricature the city's south side Govanhill area as 'Govanhell', with scare stories of open drug dealing in the streets, social ills and criminality which are unrecognisable to the long-term local residents whose votes they seek.

With the BNP hoping to rekindle the resentments displayed by previous generations of Scots, others in the public eye also have to be careful in their statements and their actions. Problems have been caused by concentrating UK asylum seekers in council houses in Glasgow because houses were available – houses and neighbourhoods of such poor quality that Scots would not want to live there.

Similarly, immigrants are filling the more menial jobs at the lower end of the employment market that Scots have hitherto not been prepared to do. Many European workers are over-qualified for the jobs they do in Scotland, university graduates working in bars and restaurants and workers with much-needed skills taking jobs in the fields.

The population decline of Angus since 1995 has been reversed in recent years entirely as a result of immigration. A Scottish Economic Research study in Tayside showed that in the summer of 2005 there were up to 4500 migrants working in the region, 22 per cent of them in Angus. The majority of the jobs undertaken by these migrant workers were in rural areas, primarily in elementary or low-skilled occupations in the agricultural, tourism-hospitality and food processing sectors. Employers said there was a shortage of workers and of certain skills locally, and they felt that migrant workers were more flexible and productive.

The economic crisis with the widespread loss of jobs and rising unemployment is changing that; the phrase 'British jobs for British workers' may be inflammatory but in such a climate it strikes a chord and is easily converted into 'Scottish jobs for Scottish workers'.

Social problems caused by this influx led to ill-judged comments by the chairman of a community council, who commented after a notorious murder case that the arrival of hundreds of eastern European immigrants in Angus had brought with it 'an unwelcome culture of violence'. (Lithuanian Jolanta Bledaite was murdered in Brechin by two of her countrymen, who dismembered her body.)

In a sweeping general comment on immigration, the community council chairman said: 'We are how having a number of Scottish and UK convictions for murders, with bodies dismembered or otherwise disposed of in an attempt to defeat the identification of victims.' More sensibly, he added that for closer integration of the local community with its growing population of foreign nationals: 'We should be looking at how their presence is going to impact on Brechin and the whole of Angus and how we are going to address their needs in the future.

'We have to welcome these incoming populations. They are playing an important role in filling what would otherwise be big black holes in the local economy.'

The message at a seminar held in Edinburgh in June 2007 by the Equality and Human Rights Commission was that Scotland needs to stop fooling itself into thinking it is a tolerant and welcoming nation. With Scotland increasingly dependent on migrant workers, work needs to be done to transform attitudes towards them.

The EHRC said half of those surveyed for the most recent Social Attitudes Survey believed that Scotland would begin to lose its identity if more Muslims moved to the country, while 30 per cent felt that ethnic minorities and people from Eastern Europe take jobs away from Scots. Morag Alexander, Scottish commissioner for the EHRC, said these figures betrayed Scotland's perception of itself as a tolerant society and warned Scotland that unless we learn to tolerate foreigners, by 2030 she may not be economically or socially fit for purpose.

She added: 'It's too easy for us as a nation to talk a good game about our decency, but the truth is often less noble. We like to think we are free of racism and other inequalities because we prefer that to the truth. In order to live up to our own self image, we have to make the sentiment of our songs real and openly say 'this Scotland is not good enough' and then work to make it better.'

The cool reception for incomers – including isolated pockets of ill-feeling against 'white settlers' from England – is especially ironic when we consider the welcome the Scottish diaspora has received around the world. There are 100 million people around the globe who feel that being Scots is part of their identity; no other country has a comparable number of exile organisations – Burns clubs, Caledonian societies and St Andrew societies – as Scotland.

Yet their attachment to 'home' is clearly more sentimental than real. The nation is failing to keep those young Scots who want to leave and to attract the diaspora in the way that Ireland managed to do in recent decades. They take pride in their nationality, but not in the country nor in the Scottish society.

Ulrich Hansen, a Dane living in Glasgow, summed it up succinctly in a newspaper article on Scotland's Homecoming Year: 'It has often struck me how the locals are slightly puzzled that I have chosen to live here. When you list the reasons they are always flattered but never convinced.

'It seems when young Scots are dreaming, they dream of Melbourne, not Milngavie. It seems people are keen on being Scots, but less so on Scotland.'

Scots are capable of being more insular and intolerant than we like to admit, giving the lie to the popular and self-congratulatory mythology that Scotland is a welcoming and open-hearted country.

CASE NOTE: Scots like to say 'we're a' Jock Tamson's bairns' as a statement of the nation's sense of fairness and equality – when the truth is that we love the world, but only as long as it does not want to come and live here.

CHAPTER SEVEN

'A Cup o' Kindness'?

There's nae harm in taking a drappie.

WILL FYFFE

Surfeits slay mare than swords.

OLD SCOTS SAYING

IN A PEACEFUL VALLEY in Devon, where 'since time immemorial, deer have been drawn to graze in the sheltered meadows which line the River Dart and quench their thirst in the cooling waters', lies a Benedictine abbey – a place of 'beauty, silence and tranquility where God might easily be found'. The monks in their black robes, between their prayers and spiritual duties, produce an elixir which they allow grateful customers to buy as 'a tonic wine'. The brothers named it after their religious house, Buckfast, meaning a place where deer feel safe.

And there the idyll ends. In Scotland, the Benedictine beverage is regarded in official circles as a blight and a social evil, with something approaching a cult status among problem drinkers. It is known colloquially as 'commotion lotion', 'vino d'Jakie', a bottle of 'who-the-****-are-youse-lookin'-at?' and 'wreck-the-hoose juice'.

It is particularly condemned as the preferred tipple of under-age drinkers and a trigger mechanism for crime and anti-social behaviour in parts of Scotland, especially Lanarkshire – where an area covering Airdrie, Coatbridge and Cumbernauld is known as the 'Buckfast Triangle' – and Ayrshire, where broken green glass on pavements and streets and empty 'Buckie' bottles in parks and play areas are territorial markers. It even achieved a kind of fame when Rab C. Nesbit, in one episode of BBC-TV's series about the uncouth Glasgow drunk, made a pilgrimage to Buckfast as his spiritual home (in the sense of alcoholic spirits!).

Apparently it has become so acceptable in Lanarkshire that a restaurant in the county has begun serving a 'Buckfast cheesecake'. This delectable dessert is part of a 'typical Scottish menu', which also includes whisky and haggis fritters – this may reflect the tastes of the local clientele but there is such a thing as carrying authenticity too far ...

At around £6 a bottle, there are cheaper wines but Buckfast has a particular appeal for the younger drinker. Originally sold from the abbey on a small scale, as a medicine with the slogan 'Three small glasses a day, for good health and lively blood', it is promoted and distributed nationally and internationally by a commercial company, with sales believed to be in excess of £30 million, as 'a smoother, more mature medicated wine'. The basic red wine from France is sweetened with vanillin flavouring and the additives include caffeine; this sweetness, along with its accessible price and 15 per cent strength (marginally higher in the UK than the same product in the Republic of Ireland) gives Buckfast the same potent appeal for younger drinkers as alcopops and strong cider.

Research into alcohol and violence in young male offenders, carried out in 2007 in the Polmont Young Offenders Institution, found four out of 10 young offenders drank Buckfast before committing their crimes. A startling 81.3 per cent had drunk alcohol before offending and agreed that drink had contributed to their offending: nearly double the figure ten years earlier.

The acceptance in certain sections of society of drinking among young people and Buckfast's particular effects was demonstrated by one mother in Irvine, Ayrshire, who said: 'I would describe my son as a mellow drunk. I've seen him drinking alcopops, cider, beer or vodka and he'd get a bit silly, then fall asleep. There was never any trouble. But drinking Buckfast was a different kettle of fish. He would binge drink on it and become aggressive and destructive.

'My younger son had his first experience – and hopefully his last – of Buckfast on Friday and he was exactly the same. It's the first time I've every seen him aggressive and I'd love to see it banned.'

Helen Liddell, who was MP for constituencies in 'The Buckfast Triangle' and Secretary of State for Scotland, called for a ban on sales of the wine; her campaign resulted in a 'safer streets' policy with a ban on drinking in public places. Cathy Jamieson, MSP for Carrick, Cumnock and Doon Valley in Ayrshire, and former Justice Minister, suggested a voluntary suspension of sales by local retailers (only to met in her constituency by 'teenagers chanting 'Don't Ban Buckie' and a 'substantial rise' in local sales was reported). Andy Kerr MSP for East Kilbride in Lanarkshire, then the Health Minister, described it as 'an irresponsible drink in its own right' and held inconclusive talks with the distributors about lessening the impact in the West of Scotland. And Jack McConnell, when he was First Minister of Scotland, criticised its particular attraction for young people and said it had become a 'a badge of pride amongst those who are involved in antisocial behaviour.'

Rarely has a single product been scapegoated in such a specific way for what is actually a much more general problem and targeting Buckfast is attacking the symptom, not the disease, since most – but not all – of these problem areas are localities with high unemployment, particularly among the youth, large housing areas and social deprivation. Buckfast is only one of a number drinks which are misused in the national heavy-drinking culture and accounts for only 0.5 per cent of all alcohol sales in Scotland, rising to one per cent in parts of the West of Scotland. The monks and the distribution company, J. Chandler & Co, partners have always strenuously denied their product is especially harmful, pointing out it is responsibly and legally enjoyed by the great majority of purchasers. They have suggested the real cause for serious misuse is that these areas have been socially and economically deprived for decades. Politicians are shifting blame instead of dealing with the real problems which lead to anti-social behaviour.

In 2005, in reply to Justice Minister Jamieson, a spokesman for Chandler & Co. said: 'She may blame our product, but our sales at £28m are tiny compared to alcopops which are about £300 million. To answer critics who blame Buckfast for anti-social behaviour, I would say 'Is it the individual, is it the bottle or is it the alcohol?' If a particular type of car was taken off the road, would it stop accidents happening?'

Drink problem – or people problem?

So there you have it in a bottle or a glass: Scotland's problem with drink is not just 'Buckie' but ALL drink. Official figures showed that Scots drank 50 million litres of pure alcohol in 2007 (equivalent to 42 bottles of vodka per person, a figure met with the black humour of 'So who's drinking my share?') and the unfunny statistic that alcohol misuse is costing our public services £2.25 billion year (a figure that includes the cost of alcohol services, absenteeism from work, drug-related crime and in-patient treatment in hospital – and much more in terms of human misery). On average, almost 1,000 Scottish men and 448 women die from alcohol-related illness each year, while in 2007, there were 455 drug deaths.

Scotland's booze crisis has dramatically worsened at a time when other countries are improving and the drinks industry analysts Neilsen's state Scotland has the eighth-highest alcohol consumption level in the world. The 50 million litres of alcohol in 2007 was considerably more per person than England and Wales.

Alcohol consumption in Scotland has more than doubled since 1950, with the rate of increase particularly noticeable since the early 1990s. Drug and alcohol-related deaths in Scotland are now among the highest in Europe and show no signs of abating, having doubled since 1995, and Scotland has one of the fastest growing chronic liver disease and cirrhosis death rates in the world. The report said: 'This is at a time when indicators of drug and alcohol-related harm are reducing in other countries in Europe.'

Sales data for 2007 indicated that Scots drank the equivalent of almost 23 units of alcohol per week, compared to just over 19 units in England and Wales – and, since this is an average, some people are clearly drinking much more than others and far more than recommended levels.

Like the rest of the UK, Scotland is still predominantly a nation of beer drinkers but beer's share of the UK alcohol market has been in steady decline over the last 30 years, from over 60 per cent in 1976 to 43 per cent in 2006. Wine and, more recently, cider have grown in popularity, with a market share of nearly 30 per cent in 2006, compared with just over 10 per cent in the mid-1970s.

The clear difference between Scottish drinkers and the rest of Britain is the higher consumption of spirits – 29 per cent of all alcohol sold in Scotland in 2007 but was less than a fifth of the alcohol drunk in England and Wales. And 'binge drinking', consumption of large amounts in single sessions, accounts for a higher proportion of drinking occasions than in the rest of Europe.

One in 20 of Scottish adults are dependent on alcohol to some degree and across Scotland, about 1,500 people are drinking themselves to death every year. In May 2008 the estimated overall cost of £2.25 billion a year was more than double the previous estimate (which was no more than an official guesstimate) and showed the size of the drinks bill that is being paid by the NHS, social services, police and courts, business and industry. The figure was spread over the NHS (£405 million); social work services (£170 million); criminal justice and the fire service (£385 million); wider economic costs (£820 million) and human/social costs (£470 million) – with the warning that even that might be a significant underestimate.

Lower productivity at work and days off from hangovers could be costing Scottish business £400 million; the use of hospital beds to treat drinkers could be costing the NHS more than £150 million; accident and emergency services another £32.3 million; police response to alcohol misuse £288 million, with alcohol assumed to be behind 40 per cent of violent crimes; and premature deaths caused by alcohol abuse an estimated £328 million.

The study by the University of Glasgow and the Medical Research Council in February 2009 showed the men's death rate from alcohol at 38 deaths per 100,000, and the women's rate at 16 per 100,000. When these deaths are mapped it exposes the 'shocking effects of the increasingly entrenched drinking culture on Scottish women' in certain areas. The female death rate reached a high of 59 in Glasgow Ibrox, an economically deprived area on the city's south side.

Dr Richard Mitchell, of the university's public health department, who compiled the map along with Dr Carol Emslie of the university's Medical Research Council public health sciences unit, said the death rates in some areas were 'astronomical' and indicative of a growing national trend.

'Scotland is facing a huge public health problem, which will require strong and radical action by the Scottish Government,' he said. 'The results suggest to us that men and women are both vulnerable to the social, economic and cultural pressures which can make people drink too much.'

In March 2009, it was reported that Barrowfield, an area in Glasgow's east end with serious social and economic problems, is 'the alcohol-abuse capital of Scotland' with one person dying prematurely from drink every month – almost 60 residents dying from alcohol-related illnesses such as cirrhosis of the liver, over five years. Fifteen of the 20 worst affected areas were in Glasgow; the city centre had the second highest rate with 38 drink-related deaths, followed by the same city's Govan and Linthouse South districts (37), Greenock town centre 35 and Calton, Gallowgate and Bridgeton 34. These statistics are quadruple the deaths in better-off areas and the least afflicted postcodes were in prosperous neighbourhoods in Dyce in Aberdeenshire, Markinch in Fife and Strathaven North in Lanarkshire, where alcohol abuse did not figure at all as a cause of death.

A report by the World Health Organisation found Scotland has the second highest murder rate in western Europe and earlier research showed that half of murders in Scotland are committed by people under the influence of drink or drugs.

'Lessons for Mental Health Care in Scotland', a report commissioned from Manchester University by the Scottish Government, studied all homicides and suicides in Britain over a six-year period, showed Scotland's high rates of drug and alcohol misuse mean people north of the border are twice as likely to kill or commit suicide than those in England and Wales.

Suicide rates in Scotland equated to 18.7 per 100,000 compared to 10.2 per 100,000 for England and Wales. Murder rates were 2.12 per 100,000 people in Scotland, compared to 1.23 per 100,000 in England and Wales. In the case of Scottish suicides, well over half of patients had a history of alcohol abuse; for murders, two out of every three killers had a drink problem.

Louis Appleby, Professor of psychiatry and director of National Confidential Inquiry, commented: 'Alcohol and drug misuse runs through these findings... suggesting that alcohol and drugs lie behind Scotland's high rates of suicide and homicide and the frequency with which they occur as antecedents in our report are striking.'

Scotland has the eighth highest level of alcohol consumption in the world, equivalent to 21 pints of pure alcohol a year for everyone over the age of 16. It is estimated that up to 50 per cent of men and 30 per cent of women are drinking more than the weekly guideline of 14 units for women and 21 units for men. It is no surprise, therefore, that Scotland also has one of the highest rates of drink-related liver disease and cirrhosis in the world. Nation-wide, an average of 860 people per 100,000 are admitted to hospital because of illnesses linked to alcohol; the number of patients discharged from hospital with alcoholic liver disease more than doubled from 1,731 in 1996 to 3,541 in 2006.

And Scottish drinkers are getting younger: between 1990 and 2004, there was a 50 per cent increase in reported drinking by 13-year-olds and a 33 per cent rise by 15-year-olds. An audit of emergency departments found that nearly 650 children were treated for alcohol-related problems, including an eight-year-old.

Perhaps the most telling fact of all is that expatriate Scots who live in England and Wales are twice as likely to die from alcohol-related conditions than their neighbours, a clear indication of the effects of the Scottish drinking culture.

In the face of such appalling statistics, the question becomes: Does Scotland have a drink problem, or is it a people problem – a SCOTTISH people problem?

'The most drunken nation on the face of the earth'

Another name for the 'drinking culture' could be 'national addiction' or, more accurately, 'national excuse'. Despite all the shameful statistics already quoted, many Scots take pride in their consumption of alcohol and regard binge drinking as a sign of prowess.

Attitudes range from the 'likeable drunk' as portrayed by Scottish comedians to the 'big man' ethos, where the ability to remain standing – and fighting drunk – after a bender is a sign of machismo. Getting 'stocious', having 'a good swally' or a 'richt guid bevvy', being 'well-ersed', 'stoatin' fu'' or 'fu' as a puggie' ... are laughed off as 'having a good time' ...

One anonymous contributor to a newspaper debate, clearly spoke from heartfelt experience: 'The pathetic almost hero-worshipping tones of 'you should have seen him/her last night, man, right out of it they were, but it was a right laugh!' make me sick to my stomach.

'Aye a right laugh, right enough. Tell that to the lassie who gets so drunk, she doesn't know which bloke she ended up with or, indeed, how many; tell that to the families deprived of money for essentials so that father/mother can come in from a 'good night out' falling about all over the place; tell that to the hospital staff who have to deal with the results of this 'good night out', tell that to the relatives of someone killed by the drunk driver, who was really just an good bloke who enjoyed 'a good laugh'; tell that to the families and relatives of those who lose loved ones through liver disease and other premature deaths caused by alcohol abuse.

'Oh aye, Scotland, let's continue to humour these folk and let's laugh ourselves to death! But 'we're not doing any harm', 'only enjoying a wee swally' they cry – I've seen too many of my peers die through the long-term effects of this drug to find it 'good for a laugh' any longer. Get honest, get real and get some respect for yourselves and your families!

'Yet propose putting a few pence on the price of this dangerous drug and you get the usual crap about the wee pensioner who won't be able to afford his favourite tipple now and how ridiculous it is that we can't get ripped out of our faces on the cheap. Give me a break!'

Attempts have been made to explain, if not excuse, this attitude as a historic hangover but, this cannot justify its survival into the 21st century. As Shona Robison, the SNP government's Minister for Public Health, said: 'Scotland has a long and complex relationship with alcohol. Certainly the drinking of alcohol is well-established in our culture. One of our major exports – which might even be called a national emblem – is an alcoholic drink, whisky.

'But when people ask why Scots drink the way we do – meaning to excess – I think they imagine that we've always been a nation of heavy drinkers. Some like to put our drinking habits down to romantic notions about our national psyche. They say we Scots are a melancholy bunch who drink heavily to inure us to our sometimes harsh climate. That sounds like the drink talking if you ask me.

'I suppose we need to ask ourselves if we want to be a nation that can't control our drinking. Are we proud of that?'

Jack Law, chief executive of Alcohol Focus Scotland, agrees: 'We've always been famous for our great hospitality – alcohol is deeply ingrained in our culture. No social occasion is complete without plenty of booze on offer. We use alcohol not just to celebrate and commiserate, but drinks companies have successfully persuaded us that it should be part of every leisure occasion, night in or out. It's become just another product on supermarket shelves, we've forgotten it's a drug with the potential to cause a great deal of harm.'

Historians and sociologists suggest today's drink culture has its roots in the grinding poverty of past eras, the male-dominated industrial society and the resulting repression by moralists and temperance crusaders. Professor Tom Devine, commenting on the SNP government's attempt to change attitudes, wrote: 'Drinking was built into the very fabric of society – everything from completion of a job to the sealing of a bargain required alcohol to be consumed and plenty of it. Countless numbers of Victorian Scots endured a hard life of unrelenting poverty and grim, overcrowded housing conditions. The bottle offered a temporary escape from these miseries and the male-dominated world of Scottish heavy industry also encouraged a macho culture of heavy drinking as a public test of virility.'

Certainly the Robert Burns dictum that 'Freedom and drink gang thegither' reflects the belief (still seen today in the indignant reaction to the new drinks policy) that booze consumption is a right not to be challenged and attempts to curb drinking must be resisted.

The Burns Nicht celebrants who put away copious amounts of drink may think they are following the Bard's example, but he was not really a toper. A fellow-Ayrshireman, Professor Donald Stewart of Edinburgh University, who frequently met Burns recalled: 'He told me, indeed, himself that the weakness of his stomach was such as to deprive him of any merit in his temperance.' Burns's reputation as a drinker grew from his last years in Dumfries, where it was noted: 'His dissipation became more deeply habitual. Foolish young men such as writers' apprentices, young surgeons, merchants' clerks and his brother excisemen pressed him to drink with them that they might enjoy his wicked wit.' One way or another, drink is accepted as a contributory factor to his early death at the age of 37. The persistent legend has it that, already ill, coming home after having over-indulged in the Globe Tavern he fell asleep in the snow and never recovered from the effects of exposure. In fact, the eminent 20th century medical man Sir James Crichton-Browne reviewed the reported symptoms of Burns' last illness: weakness, rapid and irregular pulse (auricular fibrillation), fever, thirst and delirium. Sir James diagnosed: 'Burns died of endocarditis, a disease of the substance and lining of the heart, with the origination of which alcohol had nothing to do, though it is possible that an injudicious use of alcohol may have hastened its progress.

'It was rheumatism that was the undoing of Burns. It attacked him in early years, damaged his heart, embittered his life and cut short his career.' But, of course, none of that will stop Scots from having a heavy night on haggis and whisky, in the deluded belief that they are emulating 'rantin', rovin' Robin'.

For at least two centuries, attempts have been made to shame, cajole or force Scots into reducing their national consumption of alcohol. In the mid-19th century, a time when – despite massive over-provision of legally licensed premises – illicit stills, shebeens and clandestine drinking dens flourished even in city tenements, one newspaper editorial scathingly described Scotland as 'pretty near at least, the most drunken nation on the face of the earth'.

Temperance leagues, total abstinence societies whose members agreed 'to abstain from all kinds of intoxicating liquors, except for medicinal and sacramental purposes', the Band of Hope for children, were formed in a common crusade against the evils of drink. The Scottish Prohibition Society for the Suppression of the Sale of Intoxicating Liquor by Legal Enactment fought for decades before achieving a kind of success in the Temperance (Scotland) Act 1913 under which voters in a district in Scotland could vote on whether their district was 'wet' or 'dry', a provision which lasted until 1976 by which time Kirkintilloch was the only 'dry' in the country.

One side effect was that publicans who feared losing their licences if their locality went 'dry' did nothing to improve their premises and working-class Scots became accustomed to drinking in seedy surroundings. Journalist Hugh McIlvanney, recalled: 'Pubs so bare that anyone who wants to drink in sophisticated surroundings takes his glass into the lavatory.' There was also a functionality about pubs close to mines and steelworks, where workers coming off shifts needed to wash the coal dust out of their throats or slake thirsts created by roaring furnaces and working with molten metal. One community-owned public house in Fife, the Goth, had a trough with running water around the bar so that the miners could spit out the filth in their chests.

The image of the hard-drinking worker must have been in the thoughts of working-class hero Jimmy Reid when he started the 1971 sit-in at the Upper Clyde Shipyard with the stern warning to his members: 'There shall be no bevvying.'

According to one Glasgow historian, the temperance movement brought 'blessings to many households once desolated by strong drink, purifying social customs, and shedding a beneficent influence throughout the land'. Not enough, however, because drink is still a pervasive and self-injurious part of Scotland's culture and character.

'A couple o' drinks on a Sa'urday nicht ...'

Government guidelines say the recommended intake for a man is no more than 3–4 units a day, equivalent to two pints of strong lager, and 2–3 units a day, less than two standard glasses of wine, for a woman. Binge drinking has been defined as drinking double the daily recommended unit guidelines.

Scotland's problem is the number of drinkers who are ignorant of that advice and are offended by the suggestion that they are binge drinkers – even while in the middle of a binge.

A 24-year-old in a Glasgow city centre bar told one researcher as she ordered a large (250 ml) measure of wine equal to more than three units: 'At home I've got huge fishbowl wine glasses that hold half a bottle at a time, and I would easily have one of them. So I don't think of this as being a particularly big glass.' Further justifying her 'night on the town' with girl-friends drinking the same amount, she added: 'I can easily go Monday to Friday without having a drink at all. But then I will have a lot to drink at the weekend – I guess I am more of a weekend binge drinker.' Although they had over seven units each, none of them regarded it as big drinking session or a binge and a 30-year-old member of the group said: 'If I go out on a big Saturday night out, I'll probably have a bottle of wine and then at least couple of shots of vodka or something on top of that. I would only ever really count what I was drinking if I had to drive later on or early in the morning. The only time I ever really think I have drunk too much is when I have a killer hangover the next day.'

It was no surprise when Glasgow University researchers found Scots-women were at a greater risk of dying from drink-related diseases than men in England with the average Scottish women's death rate from chronic liver disease and cirrhosis is almost 16 per 100,000 population, compared with 15 among English men.

The SNP Justice Secretary Kenny MacAskill commented early in his term of office: 'It's impossible to walk down the street at night without seeing people who've simply had too much to drink. When nearly half of those accused of murder were drunk when they committed their offence, when one Scot dies every six hours from alcohol abuse, when alcohol is costing our economy tens of millions of pounds, it's time to say 'enough is enough'.'

In Edinburgh, a move was made to curb 'stag' and 'hen' nights which had made the city centre, especially the Grassmarket and Rose Street, the venue for nights of pre-nuptial debauchery. In Aberdeen, a taxi-driver said: 'Union Street is like the Wild West on Saturday night – but it's the females who are the worst trouble. If I see two women who've had a few drinks and two guys, I pick up the guys.'

The comedian Will Fyffe sang 'when I get a couple o' drinks on a Saturday, Glasgow belongs to me!' and his lyric painted a couthy, comradely picture of 'only a common old working chap' and 'a couple o' cronies' having 'six deoch-an-dorises' (probably about ten units or well over the binge level.

However, the real picture of a Saturday night in 'dear old Glasgow town', which is replicated in towns and cities across Scotland, is somewhat different – as personal experience shows:

- Glasgow describes itself as a 'modern, multi-cultural, metropolitan city', 'a major European cultural capital' with 'a vibrant nightlife' and promises visitors 'an eventful experience'. It depends what the city fathers mean by 'eventful'. What I got was a night of in-your-face drunkenness, stomach-turning ugliness, depressing scenes of debauchery and a feeling of menace in the air. On Friday and Saturday nights the bustling, business-like Glasgow morphs into a cross between Gomorrah and the bottom of the Las Vegas Strip (i.e. the raunchier, rowdier and more repulsive end).

It was only between 6.30 and 7 pm, yet groups of young people were reeling across the pavement, shouting raucously in the foulest language. They were only just starting out on their night on the town but already there was no self-control, no sense of decency.

Because of the all-time low in supermarket drinks prices, with Tennents Special at £7 for 20 cans, 35p a can, and super-lager at £8 for 10, 40p each, booze is cheaper than soft drinks. We have up-dated Hogarth's hideous *Gin Lane,* with strong ale in place of Mother's Ruin and preparation for a night out means tanking up with a carry-out at home or on trains and buses, guzzling all the way.

Most disturbing of all was the feeling of menace in the air. In a city centre full of lurching troupes of both sexes, their inhibitions and their tempers loosened by drink and who-knows-what-else, you get the feeling that the slightest accidental bump or wrong look could trigger nastiness.

Compare that with the Continental Saturday evening, where families and old people saunter around their town centres – especially in Italy, with its time-honoured ritual of the 'passagiatta,' the stroll to see and be seen and strike a 'bella figura,' a good image – and if they have a drink, it is sociable and in moderation.

Call me neurotic in my old age, but there is something edgy and threatening about naturally-aggressive Scots hellbent on having their version of 'a good time'. I have spoken to a number of more mature types, who have expressed surprise that we went into town because they no longer dare. Surely that fear of going wherever they want on a Saturday night is an infringement of their civil rights.

And, of course, the only police in evidence whizzed by in a closed van; we saw none on foot, checking outrageous behaviour or cautioning the foul-mouthed bawlers – something that used to be called 'breach of the peace'. No doubt the law was keeping an eye on the scenes via the ubiquitous CCTV cameras, but that is no substitute for their physical presence among the crowds.

Glaswegians will complain this is unfair to their fun-loving town and Saturday night in other cities is just as lively. True, but it is more obvious in Glasgow, thanks to that hostile 'I'm here to have a good time and what are you going to do about it?' attitude.

How did Saturday night become binge night for Scots? When did it become compulsory to get rat-faced? And is it something in our genes that makes us not merry but quarrelsome and confrontational after a couple of drinks? Why do 40 per cent of men and 33 per cent of women binge-drink at least double the recommended level on their heaviest day, usually Saturday?

Six years ago, the Scottish Executive puffed that it had 'called time on binge drinking' and millions were spent on a useless advertising campaign and local action teams to no effect. We have simply surrendered our streets to the drunken and disorderly.

Scots themselves are well aware that the nation has a booze problem but they are either deluded enough or complacent enough not to bother doing anything about their own drinking. The Scottish Social Attitudes survey published by the government in 2005 showed general agreement with the statements: *'Drinking is a major part of the Scottish way of life.'* and *'Adults in other parts of Europe tend to drink alcohol more sensibly than adults in Scotland.'* Almost half 46 per cent of respondents thought alcohol caused more harm than other drugs to Scotland as a whole.

The survey commented: 'Taken together, the findings suggest that while there may be different 'drinking cultures' within Scotland in terms of the patterns of drinking, types of alcohol consumed or the contexts in which alcohol is drunk by different groups, there is relatively strong agreement across all groups that drinking is both a problem for Scotland as a whole and a central part of the country's culture.'

But that was followed up with the self-justifying statement of every drinker that alcohol is a social lubricant: *'It's easier to enjoy a social event if you've had a drink.'* Answers to the statements *'Getting drunk is a perfectly acceptable thing to do at weekends'* and *'There's nothing wrong with people my age getting drunk regularly'* showed condemnation of heavy drinking – but only in others.

Both statements were framed to gauge attitudes to 'binge drinking', and there were fairly high levels of disapproval surrounding getting drunk regularly or at weekends. Yet people were somewhat more likely to agree that getting drunk at the weekends is acceptable than they were to agree that there is nothing wrong with people their age getting drunk regularly. The researchers said: 'This suggests that binge drinking at weekends attracts less stigma overall than getting drunk regularly.'

The extent to which the younger generation are copying their heavy-drinking elders is an increasing cause for concern but information about the problem is scant. So scant that the *Daily Record* mounted its own investigation by submitting freedom of information requests to every health board for a breakdown of their alcohol-related admissions of 10 to 13-year-olds in 2003–7.

They found that hundreds of children, including under-10s, are treated for drink-related conditions in Scots hospitals every year. While health chiefs refused to reveal exactly how many under-10s ended up in hospital, saying the numbers are small enough to lead to individuals being identified, the figures for over-10s are so high they have no such concerns.

In the four year period, 154 boys and girls aged between 10 and 13 were treated in the Glasgow board area and one boy in the age range was treated in a psychiatric unit for mental illness caused by drink. In the Borders, 39 children aged 10 to 13 were discharged from hospital following treatment for binge drinking between 2004 and 2008 and in Lothian, 15 children aged under 13 were treated for 'mental and behavioural disorders due to alcohol use' in 2004.

However, the figures rose sharply for older teenagers; in Glasgow, 939 14 to 17-year-olds were treated in hospital in the period and a further seven in the age range with mental health problems caused by drink were treated in psychiatric wards.

To be fair, this is not an issue unique to Glasgow; the city still has its problems and lack of resources has not helped – but similar scenes can be witnessed in any large town or city in Scotland.

Any idea that drunken behaviour is primarily a West of Scotland problem was dispelled by the CCTV *Cities* programme shown on Channel Five in November 2008, which was given unprecedented access to the 185 cameras that monitor Edinburgh. The capital city's staid reputation was tarnished by as-it-happened scenes of binge-drinking and violence centred on the two-and-a-half square miles in the city centre where there are 540 licensed premises, including 33 nightclubs open until three am of which are full at weekends with capacities up to a thousand.

The cameras pinpointed reeling revelers and drunken brawls which spilled into the street outside licensed premises, as well as shocking images of weapon-carrying thugs in a Wild West-style affray centred on a pub. A lesser offender was the young man caught on camera urinating on a police car while his pals filmed him on their mobile phones; caught after a chase, he showed no remorse: 'I was offered 10 quid to do it. I thought it was a pretty generous offer so I decided to spray my inner fluids all over this police car. I've had a very good night, especially urinating on a police car.'

A constable commented: 'The females are just as bad, if not worse. They get stuck in, hair pulling, scratching, everything. All rules go out the window.' In one incident, a foul-mouthed woman was arrested when her male partner was put into a police car following a disturbance. She screamed at police: 'Well come on then. Detain me — f*****g detain me. Put your handcuffs on me then' then spat at the TV crew shouting: 'F*****g come on then. Think you're f*****g smart videoing me ya f*****g chancer. I'll f*****g kick yer c*** in.'

When she began to sober up at the police station, she sobbed: I'm really sorry. I am. I'm really sorry to everyone.' The arresting officer was not impressed: 'She was more concerned about breaking a false nail and making sure her hair was tidy. That's life.'

That's life, indeed, when Scotland has 'a couple o' drinks on a Sa'urday nicht'. Hic ...

CASE NOTE: Scots take a perverse pride in their drinking culture, many regarding it as a form of national 'prowess', but the statistics show that it is deeply damaging in financial and social terms and, in personal terms, downright stupid.

CHAPTER EIGHT

No Mean Country

We are the Scots – and this is what we do …
RIOTING FOOTBALL FAN IN MANCHESTER

Violence is a cancer in this part of the world.
GLASGOW A & E CONSULTANT

THE NIGHT OF 14 MAY 2008 – a night of mayhem, violence, vandalism and sheer thuggery in the centre of a great city – was a reminder of the ugly streak of violence beneath the surface of the Scottish character. Drink and poor organization were blamed but, after the excuses and accusations, the question remained: Why was it the Scots?

When Scottish supporters, in Manchester for the UEFA Cup final, went on the rampage in the city, it had nothing to do with 'the beautiful game'. It was said at first they had shamed Glasgow Rangers FC, later that they had disgraced Scottish football after a couple of decades of comparatively good behaviour by supporters – but as the appalling scenes were shown internationally on TV (and have had hundreds of thousands of hits on YouTube) it was clear that they had reinforced the wider national reputation for aggression – something the Scottish community lives with, week in and week out.

Those who try to explain, if not justify, the fans' behaviour point out that only a minority of the 100,000-plus supporters who travelled south for the event were involved; and an official report afterwards found that the 37,000 Rangers fans inside the City of Manchester stadium were well behaved and 'a credit to the club'. They claim that the riot was triggered by the failure of a giant TV screen in Piccadilly Gardens, where tens of thousands of ticketless others had gathered to watch in the open air.

One aggrieved supporter complained: 'This is absolutely ridiculous – there's Rangers fans throwing bottles and cans at each other because the game's not on. We've been sat here since 12 o'clock waiting on the game coming on. The coverage started at seven o'clock and then five minutes later the game's off. It's an absolute shambles, shame on Manchester, shame on Manchester – it's let the country down.' Another said: 'Some people are really angry. They've spent a lot of money – maybe £4,000 to £5,000 – to come down here for this.'

However, a report by Manchester City Council's chief executive Howard Bernstein found that the violence had begun hours earlier on the morning of the game in the specially-prepared Piccadilly Gardens 'fan zone': 'At 11.30 am there was the first report of anti-social behaviour – missiles being thrown at the stage and the first reported fight between fans. The first act on stage lasted only 20 minutes out of the 45 minutes scheduled because they were pelted with cans and coins.

'From four pm, the operators of the merchandise unit reported increasing problems in Piccadilly Gardens. Fans jumped over the security barrier and climbed on top of the sales unit.

'Large numbers of people were jumping up and down on the roof and urinating on top of the unit. Although the police were called the sheer numbers surrounding them meant there was little they could do.'

Neither drink nor football fever nor disappointment nor technical failure can justify the mob mentality when hundreds of Scots ran riot, smashing shop and bank fronts, damaging bus stops, wrecking cars and clashing with police. As a sports car was trashed, one of the yobs turned to a woman by-stander and exulted: 'We're the Scots – and this is what we do!'

PC John Goodwin, overwhelmed by the mob, beaten to the ground, battered, kicked and stamped on, thought he was about to die: 'It was just total hatred, really. Some of the mob were trying to take my helmet off and I knew if my helmet had come off, that would have been the end of me.' His colleague PC Mick Regan was pursued down the street by a pack of about 20 Rangers fans before being tripped and set upon before he was rescued by a 23-year-old former soldier Tom Bardsley who had bottles and bricks thrown at him for going to the policeman's aid.

Mr Bardsley said he had served in a number of war zones but had witnessed nothing like the scenes in Manchester: 'I would describe it as wolves who had not been fed for days. I knew that if no-one was going to help him, he wasn't going to make it.'

One commentator, the feminist writer and broadcaster Lesley Riddoch, said the 'Battle of Manchester' should be a massive wake-up call for Scotland: 'Does civic Scotland have the will, the courage or even the insight needed to tackle Macho Caledonia? Can we accept that large parts of our society are out of control, and dominated by the threat of male violence and the misuse of power? Scotland was laid bare. Ours is a society only partly based on reason and partly based on uncontrolled male aggression. Emotional excess is excused by polite society, admired by other men and aped by girls.'

Two of her readers agreed about this ultra-macho culture: 'Lets get down to basics, the entire Manchester disgrace was just another repeat performance of what has been deemed acceptable within the Scottish psyche for generations.' And: 'You're not a man unless you can take a drink! Of course a drink means as much as you can swallow in any given time and generally until the money runs out. Then go home demand your tea is put on the table within the five minutes it takes for the stomach to discharge an amount of the liquid that has been consumed; then throw the tea back at the provider as not being what was wanted.'

The Scottish Government, which has set up a Violence Reduction Team based at St. Andrew's House, and its website Action on Violence.com, asserts; 'Violence is an infection that has crept through society to the extent that it is viewed today in much the same way as the common cold – something that is both incurable and inevitable.

'In Scotland, violence is a chronic problem. Although overall levels of crime have fallen in the West of Scotland, levels of violent crime, in particular knife crime, have remained relatively constant for the last 40 years.'

Strathclyde Police established a Violence Reduction Unit in January 2005 to target all forms of violent behaviour, in particular knife crime and weapon carrying among young men in and around Glasgow and its remit was extended nationwide by the Scottish Executive in April 2006 as 'a national centre of expertise on tackling violent crime', working with the government team with the aim of achieving 'long-term societal and attitudinal change, and, by focusing on enforcement, to contain and manage individuals who carry weapons or who are involved in violent behaviour'.

The need for such an approach has been repeatedly demonstrated by a series of shocking statistics which, unfortunately, have become tediously familiar over the years. A national newspaper, the *Daily Record* carried out its own research in 2006 and reported: 'On average, one person has been murdered on our city streets EVERY week for the last THREE years ... Glasgow is well on the way to being the UK's murder capital with 14 murders so far this year alone. Last year, there were 25 murders in Glasgow, a rate of 4.3 murders per 100,000 people, or more than DOUBLE the rate in London. In Glasgow, there have been 98 murders in the last three years to date – an astonishing average of almost THREE every month – with almost three quarters of them committed in the east of the city. Many of the murders across the country took place in a small number of areas associated with high social deprivation.'

In an effort to identify 'hot spots', the paper found 25 murders in Edinburgh in the three years from 2005-2007, with many clustered in Calder and Southhouse. In the same period, police in Dundee logged seven murders and

Aberdeen nine. In the majority of cases, the victims and culprits were young men and knives were often the weapon used. Knives account for more than 50 per cent of murders across Scotland. The murder toll followed a study which showed Scots were twice as likely to commit homicide or kill themselves as people anywhere else in Britain and alcohol and drug consumption were blamed for the markedly higher murder and suicide rate.

The previous year, a UN report labeled Scotland the most violent country in the developed world, with people three times more likely to be assaulted than in America. England and Wales recorded the second highest number of violent assaults while Northern Ireland recorded the fewest.

The study, based on telephone interviews with victims of crime in 21 countries, found that more than 2,000 Scots were attacked every week, almost ten times the official police figures, and included non-sexual crimes of violence and serious assaults.

The international report said violent crime had doubled in Scotland over the previous 20 years and levels, per head of population, were comparable with cities such as Rio de Janeiro, Johannesburg and Tbilisi. The attacks had been fuelled by a 'booze and blades' culture in the west of Scotland, worsened by sectarian violence, with hospitals reporting higher admissions following 'Old Firm' football matches.

David Ritchie, an accident and emergency consultant at Glasgow's Victoria Infirmary, was quoted as saying the figures were a national disgrace. 'I am embarrassed as a Scot that we are seeing this level of violence. Politicians must do something about this problem. This is a serious public health issue. Violence is a cancer in this part of the world'.

The study, by the UN's crime research institute, found that three per cent of Scots had been victims of assault compared with 1.2 per cent in America and just 0.1 per cent in Japan, 0.2 per cent in Italy and 0.8 per cent in Austria. In England and Wales the figure was 2.8 per cent.

Scotland was eighth for total crime, 13th for property crime, 12th for robbery and 14th for sexual assault. New Zealand had the most property crimes and sexual assaults, while Poland had the most robberies. However, research shows that less than a third of violence may be reported to police.

Predictably, there has been reluctance to accept these unfavourable findings in official circles concerned about Scotland's image in the world. The Association of Chief Police Officers in Scotland, questioned the figures, 'It must be near impossible to compare assault figures from one country to the next based on phone calls'.

'We have been doing extensive research into violent crime in Scotland for some years now and this has shown that in the vast majority of cases, victims of violent crime are known to each other. We do accept, however, that, despite your chances of being a victim of assault being low in Scotland, a problem does exist.'

When the *Sunday Times* published details of the UN study naming Scotland as the most violent country in the developed world, they predicted that the first instinct would be to 'recoil and deny'. The newspaper cautioned in a leader that the easy response was to 'go on the defensive, question the evidence, anything but 'face up to the reality'. Despite this the then Justice Minister Cathy Jamieson told BBC Radio Scotland it was 'simply not people's experience' that members of the public in Scotland were routinely attacked (the report actually said that three per cent of Scots had reported being victims of assault, compared with 1.2 per cent of Americans) and she claimed the figures were out of date while the executive had initiatives in place to tackle the problem.

Said a *Sunday Times* riposte: 'The fact that Scotland can be a warm and welcoming country is not the issue, but the testimony of professionals on the frontline speaks volumes for the fact that the ugly face of the country has not disappeared. However, every town and village is affected to a greater or lesser extent. It is important not to overstate the problem — fuelling the fears of the vulnerable — but the culture that is gripping Scotland, with the violent few spoiling the standard of living of the law-abiding majority has to be tackled head on. This important debate must not be silenced by politicians.'

With a change of government, Jamieson's SNP successor as Justice Minister, Kenny MacAskill admitted: 'We're under no illusion that tackling the high levels of violence in Scotland will be easy. There are no overnight solutions to tackle this macho culture.'

The worst 'hot spot' is in Glasgow, which has a history of weapon-carrying gangs which reached its peak in the 'No Mean City' razor-slashing and pitched battles in the 1930s to 1950s – an ethos that is still very much alive. Police say there are still 55 gangs in Glasgow, involving around 700 young men aged 12–23, the majority of whom have a history of offending and violence. Alcohol abuse is common and many carry a weapon on a regular basis.

Launching a £1.6 million project to tackle the problem in the city's East End, MacAskill said: 'For too long now, areas of Glasgow have been blighted by gangs and gang violence. I've heard of boys following their father, brother or uncle into a gang and I've no doubt that the vicious cycle of drink, drugs and deprivation lies at the heart of this. For some young people the gang is like a family, to them it means having people to look out for them and protect them in a way they've perhaps not been used to.'

The following section contains scenes of strong, graphic, bloody violence – readers' discretion is advised. In other words, it is pretty much what you will see on the streets and in the housing schemes of Scotland, as the district news testifies week in and week out.

In a single issue, one North Lanarkshire local newspaper reported within a five-mile radius examples of violence including a man battered senseless by unknown attackers for no apparent reason; a 25-year-old whose 'face fell apart' after being slashed in a horrific knife assault carried out in a revenge attack; a teenager left for dead after being hit with a bottle then repeatedly kicked and stamped; another threatened with a knife and baseball bat. Subsequent weeks continued the casualty list of deliberate maiming, disfigurement and, sometimes, death.

The carrying of offensive weapons, from knives to swords, machetes and meat cleavers, and 'settling of scores' have once again become endemic. In the past, the bare-knuckle battles in turf wars, the 'square go' to sort out real or imagined slights or a random beating to prove 'machismo' were bad enough; in modern Scotland, no self-respecting thug leaves home without a blade – or worse. The new term is 'plunging' an opponent, ie sticking a knife into him.

Weapon-carrying is, of course, nothing new, especially in Glasgow where the vicious catchphrase that accompanied the blade on the skin during the 'No Mean City' era was: 'Has yer mother got a sewing machine? See if she can fix that!'

It was thought that the knife culture had been brought under control following the reign of the legendary Lord Carmont in the 1950s. A grim-faced and fearsome figure on the High Court bench, he passed into folklore with knife and razor-carrying gangs. In one sequence of sittings he passed sentences of up to 10 years on eight offenders, totalling 52 years and gave minimum sentences of five years for merely carrying a concealed weapon. A long spell in Barlinnie became known as 'copping a Carmont'.

These days, gang membership begins with neighbourhood misbehaviour by wannabes as young as 11 and 12 influenced by older youths; it then proceeds to West Side Story-type territorial or ethnic or (let's be frank) religious and football related violence; graduating to drug-dealing and 'protection' networks.

When the hard men in the criminal gangs commit violence, it is often one drug franchise wiping out another – and, you may think, let them get on with it. But take your life in your hands and visit some of the gang-ridden housing schemes, and it is the younger gangs which create most concern. In 2007, a battle royal on Glasgow's East Side between two gangs, The Torran and The Skinheeds, resulted in 15 arrests for weapons possession and two gang members, aged 18 and 19, being jailed for 27 and 31 months. One former member complained: 'It's that bad we can't even go across Wellhouse Road [the gang boundary] for a Chinese takeaway. We'd get stabbed. We're stuck on this scheme, with different gangs all round.'

Ask any young yob why he carries a knife and he will tell you it is for protection, because he knows members of other gangs are similarly armed and it is stab or be stabbed. Knives with flesh-ripping edges have only one obvious use, yet they are openly on sale in certain shops which do a steady trade in Rambo knives, replicas of Japanese swords and other lethal-looking Oriental ironmongery. As one law enforcer said with heavy irony: 'You're not going to be cleaning your teeth or peeling potatoes with a 12-inch blade. And no young hoodie is going to be buying a Samurai sword because he is a connoisseur of fine weapons.

Although well-publicised, police stop-and-search crackdowns under the Safer Scotland campaign, coordinated by the Violence Reduction Unit, have done little to change the culture. Amnesties and so-called 'enforcement phases', including the use of airport-style Ferroguard poles and hand-held metal detectors in town centres, have taken over 1,000 weapons out of circulation nationally every time yet Justice Secretary Kenny MacAskill had to admit: 'There are still far too many people being injured or killed because they have been attacked with a knife, or other dangerous weapon. In many parts of Scotland, carrying a knife is seen as some kind of fashion accessory or something to be proud of. They are no such thing. They are lethal weapons and there are too many of them on our streets.'

Despite the historic reputation, figures for violent crimes and weapon confiscations show this is not simply a Glasgow or West of Scotland problem. Dramatic evidence was provided on CCTV *Cities*, based in Edinburgh, that showed one incident in which a gang marched on a pub, where there had already been a brawl, baying for blood and led by a man wielding a meat cleaver. As a riot broke out, with chairs flying, the thug with the cleaver was clubbed to the ground by an opponent using a traffic cone and the fighting continued even after the police arrived on the scene. In the aftermath, only the man with the cleaver was convicted, receiving only 187 hours community service.

Other cameras caught similar affrays in other parts of the city; one man was filmed swinging the Korean combat weapon 'twin sticks' also known as 'nunchucks' and in a scuffle outside a busy nightclub a man was seen punching another clubber unconscious.

A worrying factor is the number of children being caught carrying knives;

seven primary school children were among 31 under the age of 16 charged by police after being caught carrying knives in Edinburgh in 2008 and it was revealed that knife possession amongst under-16s had rocketed to a five-year high, compared to just twelve recorded incidents in 2004.

Among those charged in 2008 were two eight-year-old children, three nine-year-olds and two 11-year-olds. The age of criminal responsibility in Scotland is eight and children younger than that are not charged.

Nor is the perpetration of violence any longer confined to the male sex. There has been a marked increase in violence committed by women and the country's leading prosecutor, Lord Advocate Eilish Angiolini told the Scottish Parliament (ironically the Equal Opportunities Committee) in April 2008 that women criminals were becoming more violent, especially after binge drinking, with many prepared to take the lead in appalling crimes. Although, compared to male offenders, the number of such aggressively violent women was 'very small', she said, 'Many women are not just the collaborators or going along with a dominant male partner – being an accessory, carrying knives for the boyfriend, assisting in cleaning up after a murder – but are now prime movers' she said. 'We have seen some appalling acts of torture by women against women and murderous tortures. We have seen increasing signs of groups of young girls using violence against predominantly other young girls and carrying weapons.

'Those are what we might have perceived traditionally as male behaviours – violence which seems aligned with the increasing consumption of alcohol by young women binge drinking. And in the drugs world there are a very small number of women who are leading groups and gangs.'

For the majority of women in Scotland, however, the fear is of becoming victims of violence rather than perpetrators. A 2000 Safety on the Streets study showed nine out of ten women worry about being attacked, most young women have real fears of being raped, many had been followed and others reported having their drinks spiked, they were near-unanimous in expressing fear of physical or verbal abuse and they feel they are less safe than they were a decade ago.

Yet, in a sadly Scottish macho reaction, comments seemed to blame the women for making themselves victims: 'Three in four fail to take sufficient care when they have been drinking' ... 'Most are afraid of going on public transport late at night, yet just one per cent carry a personal alarm' ... 'Today's young women are as afraid of being beaten up by other girls as they are of being attacked by men' ...

Domestic violence has previously been hidden and is deep-seated and, in a sense, accepted. Attacks in the home are estimated to be running at 47,000 a year and are said to cost the Scottish economy around £1.5 billion annually. Yet another campaign, this time costing £10 million, has been launched by the Scottish government.

Experts believe the number of reported cases, 35 000, to be the tip of the iceberg. Heather Coady of Women's Aid Scotland said that, in her experience, most victims suffer up to 35 attacks before even bothering to formally report them. The number of children trapped in violent homes could be as high as 100,000 and, as Coady pointed out, the trauma of the violence they experience and witness on a daily basis can remain with them for years.

'It does not matter where you live or how much you earn, domestic abuse cuts across ever social divide,' she said. 'And sometimes, for women whose husbands are outwardly respectable and pillars of society, it can be harder for them to be believed or find an outlet to make a complaint.'

In April 2009, reporting on the traditional seasonal increase in domestic abuse over the 'festive' period, police attached to Violence Reduction Unit described violence in the home as 'Scotland's national shame' – a phrase which has become an official cliché for a number of the country's social evils. Campaign co-ordinator Chief Inspector Cameron Cavin said: 'These figures are shocking and highlight the fact that despite everything, many people still think it is okay to be violent towards a partner. Domestic abuse is Scotland's national shame, a shame which lies at the roots of much of the other violence we see in our society today and it is not acceptable.'

Meanwhile, the abuse goes on – as does the long-suffering acceptance by the victims of the attitudes of macho Scottish males. A waitress serving a pub lunch in Fife recently had bruises on one side of her face, which her make-up could not conceal. Asked what had happened to her, she shrugged: 'It was ma ain fault – I should've had the football on the telly when he came in from the match ...'

CASE NOTE: Violence is endemic in Scottish society. Politicians and law enforcement spokesmen who attempt to minimise its effects are seriously mistaken. It is an epidemic that has to be recognised and dealt with.

CHAPTER NINE

A Question of Confidence

*God gie us a guid conceit o' oorsels is the Scotsman's most
earnest prayer.*

JAMES BRIDIE

*Boswell: 'I do indeed come from Scotland, but I cannot help it.'
Dr Johnson: 'That, sir, I find, is what a very great many of your
countrymen cannot help.'*

A QUESTION FOR OUR FELLOW-SCOTS: How do you REALLY feel? Weedy?
Wimpish? Wet? Wishy-washy? Has your 'get up and go' got up and gone?
Perhaps you are suffering from what has been diagnosed as the Scottish
sickness: a chronic lack of confidence. We just cannot help ourselves because
we are a nation of pessimists. Others say 'can do' but ours is a 'canna dae that'
culture.

Do not despair, for help is at hand. Scotland, believe it or not, has a
government-supported 'Centre For Wellbeing And Confidence' – otherwise
known to sceptics and cynics as the 'Happy-Clappy Institute for Sunny Smiles,
Feeling Good, Always Looking on the Bright Side and Whistling a Happy
Tune'. All together now: 'You've got to acc-ent-uate the positive, e-lim-in-ate
the negative ...' Or, as one resolutely dour commentator put it: 'May we please
soon see the end of government-funded 'Full of Yourself' training, especially in
our schools but also in self-promoting 'Centres of Full-of-Yourselfness'.'

The reactions show a natural surprise that Scots, whose pride in their
nationhood, history and achievements is as rampant as the lion on their
flag, should be regarded as lacking in confidence. After all, world – not just
British or Scottish – history is rich in significant Scottish achievements,
reaching a pinnacle in the Enlightenment and continuing to this day. National
pride, a sense of community and belief that it is the best of countries in
which to live are undiminished.

Surely a people for whom the words 'gallus' and 'smeddum' had to be
created, cannot be that diffident and shy? (For those readers without a dictionary of the Scottish language, 'gallus' means bold to the point of impudence
– some say it comes from 'gallows' as in a rascal who deserves to be hanged –
and 'smeddum' is full of spirit and energy, as used by Burns when he
described two feisty women with 'muckle smeddum and rumblegumption'.)

The scepticism about the need for a Centre for Confidence (based in gallus and go-getting Glasgow, of all places) perhaps also reflects the Scottish dislike and mistrust of a brash over-confidence. Overweening arrogance is a social sin and the worst things that can be said of another are 'he's fu' o' himself', 'his heid's ower big' or 'he disnae hauf fancy his barra'.

Scots rely on an innate sense of their own individual worth, irrespective of their station in life, put pithily as: 'The erse may be oot o' yer breeks, but ye're still as guid as any other bugger.' This, you understand, is not bragging but simply a cruder re-statement of the Burnsian equality of man (and, if forced to admit it, woman):

> What though on hamely fare we dine,
> Wear hodden grey an' a' that,
> Gie fools their silks, and knaves their wine;
> A Man's a Man for a' that.

But, whisper it, could that noble sentiment, along with the somewhat defiant tendency to insist on inborn Scottish superiority (*Here's tae us, wha's like us?*), in fact be whistling in the wind? Was the slogan 'the best small nation in the world' a boast, or an admission that the national ego is not as big, nor as self-assured, as we make out? Is there, in fact, a genuine crisis of confidence in being Scottish?

That a 'Centre For Wellbeing And Confidence' is active in Scotland, with core funding from the government through the departments for mental health, education and social services, may seem surprising but working on this book has shown us the need for more work to be done on promoting a positive culture in everything we do in Scotland. Its founder, Dr Carol Craig, a leading figure in the field of Positive Psychology – predictably dubbed Scotland's 'happiness tsar' by the media – struck a chord in government, industry, academia and commerce, when she declared: 'I'm continually struck by how we Scots lack confidence in every aspect of our lives.'

In a speech which led to the Centre's creation, *Towards a Confident Scotland,* the then First Minister Jack McConnell said he was committed to building confidence in Scotland: 'Lack of confidence can be a barrier to achieving all that we can in life and making the most of our creativity and potential. I believe greater confidence in ourselves will help to unlock a better future for Scotland.' His Education Minister Peter Peacock stressed the importance of creating a future generation of ambitious, confident Scots: 'We know from research there are issues to be addressed about confidence in young people in Scotland. Confidence will help them adopt a 'can-do' approach, encourage them to take all the opportunities that come their way and will ensure there is no limit to their ambition.'

The Centre's mission statement is to transform Scottish culture so that it supports more 'optimism (for self, others and Scotland); self-belief (an important ingredient in 'can-do' attitudes); a 'growth mindset' (essential for people to realise their potential); resilience (required in helping people keep going when life is difficult); positive energy; sense of purpose/meaning; giving (an antidote to a 'me' centred world) and wisdom (important for good decision-making and leadership) and for advancing the confidence agenda.'

The Centre grew from a book, *The Scots' Crisis of Confidence* by Carol Craig in which she wrote that Scots collectively and individually lack confidence, with 'enormous implications' for economic growth, enterprise, physical and mental health, creativity, personal relationships, parenting skill and the political culture. Craig argued that Scotland's relationship with England (i.e. being the junior partner in an incorporating union) might have contributed to 'the confidence gap' but it is really a question of how the Scots themselves see the world. And she showed her understanding of the Scottish nature by predicting that those who challenged this mental state (presumably including herself) would be 'criticised, denounced or ostracised'.

It could be argued that this so-called confidence deficit among Scots is a mixter-maxter of notions of a national inferiority complex, the rise of nationalism and intellectual arrogance. For decades, it has been fashionable among the Scottish chattering class to chastise us for our alleged national negativity and lack of gumption; the writer Alan Bold dismissed us as: 'Scotland, land of the omnipotent 'No'.' And those nationalists who blame 'the English' or 'the British state' for all our ills have, more than any others, been responsible for the unattractive 'Scottish whinge' which understandably grates on the ears of outsiders.

The successful football manager Alex McLeish, formerly of Scotland and Glasgow Rangers and who inspired Birmingham City's return to the English Premier League, contributed a blog to the Centre's website entitled *Releasing Scotland's Potential: The Importance of Self-belief*. In it, he challenged the ingrained 'negative attitude' of Scots: 'Other nations like to pat themselves on the back and we don't do it enough. We tend to have a wee chip on our shoulder but, for a small nation, we've got some great heroes; Chris Hoy at the Olympics for instance. I believe we have to show more confidence in ourselves.

'As a passionate Scot I've often been asked: how do we as a nation, release our potential? All my working life has been involved in an industry that is all about potential. I've seen young players at 13 looking like the next Ronaldo only to be walking away from the game at 17 because they've not fulfilled their potential and have lost self-belief.'

He concluded: 'I believe there is more fight within us than we know, we have more strength than we think and far more potential than we could ever call upon or even dream possible. I look forward to the day when the people of Scotland begin to understand that the only constant in our lives is the opportunity to realise our potential.'

McLeish was right to target young Scots, since a study of school-age children found that they ranked 23rd out of 29 countries in terms of confidence. Confidence levels among school children in Scotland appear to have risen between 1994 and 2002. While there is little direct evidence about confidence, it is clear that some of the major challenges faced by Scotland – rates of suicide, depression, low life-expectancy, relatively low business start-ups – can be linked to pessimism.

'Confidence is an issue of concern to Scottish Ministers' said a Scottish Government discussion paper in 2005 'Lacking confidence, having low self-esteem or being a pessimist are not only problems for mental well-being, they may also mean that people in Scotland fail to achieve all that they are capable of achieving.'

The research on attitudes of schoolchildren by Edinburgh University in 1998, as part of a World Health Organization survey, found that 11, 13 and 15-year-olds in Scotland ranked low in confidence compared to other countries even though trend data for Scotland suggested confidence increased between 1994 and 2002. On the confidence meter, Scotland ranked 23rd out of 29 countries; Greece, Portugal, Greenland, Poland and France were the top five (indicating, at least, that a sunny climate for not a factor), before America. England, Wales and Northern Ireland were 17th, 20th and 21st, with Scotland only narrowly coming ahead of the bottom six – Austria, Estonia, Sweden, Slovakia, Germany and the Czech Republic. There was a surprising gender difference: in Scotland just over a quarter of 11, 13 and 15-year-old boys, but only 15 per cent of girls at the same ages, said they felt confident 'always'.

By contrast, every survey ever taken shows the near-unanimous strength of people's pride in being Scottish, sometimes as high as 97 per cent (for their own good, that miserable three per cent should make sure they remain anonymous).

By similar margins, the 2003 study *Being Young in Scotland* found young people more likely to identify with positive rather than negative statements about Scotland. (Although a significant number had doubts about statements such as 'There are lots of opportunities for people like me to get on in life' and 'I can imagine myself leaving Scotland and living elsewhere' and a majority agreed that 'Scottish culture is too inward-looking'.)

The Scottish Government researchers found that despite some of the optimism, there was a 'poverty of expectation' in Scotland: 'A palpable sense of resignation was evident in some of the interviews conducted – the 'can-nae' as much as the 'canny' Scot'.

Many felt that modesty is valued in Scotland and wider research suggests that a cultural tendency towards modesty has an impact on self-esteem, with such cultures less likely to produce individuals who regard themselves as highly worthy people. With classic Scottish duality, humility and modesty are regarded as universal strengths, guarding against 'unwarranted self-congratulation, pretentiousness and arrogance', but these same character traits also result in 'reduced happiness'. The research suggests: 'Rates of depression and unhappiness are likely to be higher in a culture which encourages modesty.' The choice for Scots seems to be: 'Be humble and glum; or be cocky and feel better.'

Having made the choice to be glum, Scots have allowed their downbeat nature to invade their cultural, even their humour. The Scottish Government's *Confidence in Scotland* discussion paper pointed out: 'Sayings, humour and literature in Scotland help to underpin modesty and to punish non-conformity. Well-known Scottish sayings are often negative 'putdowns' such as: 'What is he like?'; 'Aye, that'll be right'; 'Can we no dae anything right?'. Scottish comedy is often self-deprecating and pokes fun at individuals perceived to be immodest or who "get above their station".'

Lack of confidence is part of the explanation for a lower-than-average level of entrepreneurial activity in Scotland. The Scottish Executive says the rate of new business formation is lower than in most other regions in the UK and the Global Entrepreneurship Monitor (an international survey of entrepreneurship) found that Scotland's 'total entrepreneurial activity' is slightly lower than the UK average (5.5 per cent compared with 6.4 per cent) and is placed in the lower half in a group of 31 nations surveyed. The same research also found that people in Scotland are much less likely than those elsewhere to invest in a business; the informal investment rate in Scotland in 2003 was about 1.4 per cent. This is low by international standards (the average rate was 3.4 per cent in a survey of 31 nations) – but that, of course, could simply be characteristic Scottish canniness where money is concerned.

A significant reason for the relatively low rate seems to be the fear of failure, in sharp contrast to, say, the US where credit is given for trying something new, even if it ends in disappointment and bankruptcy. Scots – although they possess the necessary start-up skills, ability to identify opportunities and admire those self-made multi-millionaires like Kwik-Fit founder Sir Tom Farmer and the retail tycoon Sir Tom Hunter – were found to have a more cautious attitude to risk. A recent survey suggested that there are no marked differences in the proportions of people thinking about going into business between England and Scotland but also found that more Scots were concerned about getting into debt and business failure.

The Scottish Executive study commented: 'If a culture values modesty, then the members of that culture will be less likely to report that they are highly worthy people. Research suggests that people in Scotland see themselves as modest.'

The irony is that outside of Scotland we are regarded as the masters of innovation throughout history. The original thought from the Scottish Enlightenment is globally recognized and a poll of nearly 2000 people in Britain asking them to name the greatest UK inventors was dominated by Scots, with Alexander Graham Bell, Alexander Fleming, John Logie Baird and James Watt topping the list.

When discussing Scottish confidence, or the lack of it, a more recent and recurring theme is that too many Scots have been absorbed into the dependency culture, with an abdication of personal responsibility in favour of the State. Compared with individuals elsewhere in the UK, Scots are more likely to believe that the State should provide for their needs. The 2001 British Household Panel Survey showed Scottish residents are more likely to agree with the statement that 'It is the government's responsibility to provide a job for everyone who wants one'. Expectations that the government should provide the solutions also led to a culture of blame when social and economic problems occur – even though these problems may be local or individual.

This dependency has grown with the steady expansion of Scotland's high public expenditure economy. The proportion of GDP associated with the public sector in Scotland is amongst the highest in Europe and well over a quarter of employed Scots work in the public sector; social welfare spending in Scotland is nine per cent above the UK average. However, it is worth pointing out that this is less than the per capita averages in Wales and Northern Ireland, which were 20 per cent and 16 per cent respectively in 2002–03.

Another blow to the nation's self-confidence has been the loss of self-sufficient traditional heavy industries and the arrival of 'branch office' industries with headquarters elsewhere, a number of which were then withdrawn as global markets collapsed. And it can also be argued that the banking crisis which engulfed the (Halifax) Bank of Scotland and the Royal Bank of Scotland not only destroyed trust in these institutions but also badly shook the national confidence.

A reputation for soundness and financial commonsense built up over three centuries disappeared overnight and, as the Scot Ian Jack lamented in *The Guardian*, the debacle even damaged the standing of the Scottish accent in call-centres and the like as 'the voice of trust': 'Sadly, remembering that neither nationhood nor social class is a barrier to incompetence and greed, the rest of the world may have to adjust the inferences it draws from a Scottish voice.'

Devolution's return of the Scottish Parliament to Edinburgh was supposed to be a national rebirth that would give the country a new self-assurance. However, the hallmark of the devolution project has proved to be over-optimism from the start. The boundlessly confident First Minister Alex Salmond insists that devolution has changed Scotland 'for the better, and forever', giving people 'a new sense of confidence' but others make a more realistic assessment.

After the first seven years of devolution, the *Economist* declared: 'Scotland has regressed into an inward-looking, slightly chip-on-shoulder, slightly Anglophobic country with no clear sense of direction. Instead of gaining a new self-confidence, it has gained self-doubt, while clinging to an old dependency on the state, which still means, at least in part, England.'

That outsiders regard us in this way can be met with two different reactions. In all-too-typically Scottish fashion, we can take offence, raise our hackles and go into a national huff; or we can dig deep and find the confidence to change the attitudes which are holding us back.

CASE NOTE: The questions and choices for Scotland are: Pessimistic or positive? 'Can do' or 'cannae dae'?

PART TWO
DIAGNOSIS

CHAPTER TEN

The Scottish Psyche

By Anne Ellis
Director of Psychology, PeopleMaps

*I do like Scotland. I like the miserable weather. I like the miser-
able people. I like the fatalism, the negativity, the violence that's
always just below the surface.*

The Devil in the Testament of Gideon Mack
by JAMES ROBERTSON

COUNTRIES, LIKE ORGANISATIONS, have a psychological personality and a
people's collective personality provides the country's essential identity. Climate
contributes to the psychology of nations as can be witnessed between
Northern and Southern nations: most Northern cold weather countries
have a more aloof task orientation (possibly to keep warm?) and Southern
ones, naturally, have a warmer feeling or people orientation.

Scotland is a small country that views its own people as pragmatic and
practical. Alongside England, Scots are (and see themselves as) a minority
nation and there is security and safety in numbers for minorities. People are
more comfortable if no-one breaks the mould and stands out. This has led
to a defensive posture which in turn leads to a tendency to decry success.
Even though Scotland is small, it is still easy to recognise differences in the
psyche, say between the East and the West coast, the North and the South,
internal Scots identities huddling together for security.

The Scots are often referred to in literature or portrayed as irascible and
dour and most Scots would probably at least recognise the descriptions.
Obviously, all Scots are not irascible or dour but the temperament of a great
many could perhaps be so summarised without much resistance. This attitude
might be attributed to being a small country with a larger-than-life neighbour,
maybe more so in times past than the present day; perhaps this proximity,
and constant comparisons, was enough to give the Scots a chip on their
shoulder, manifesting in a sort of arrogance flowing from a defence of their
inferiority complex or an inherent self doubt in the national personality.

95

Psychological description

Carl Jung, the Swiss psychologist, defined personality as a combination of preferences and attitudes. Preferences he defined as: Thinking/Task, Feeling/People, Sensing/Intuition; and Attitudes, he defined as: 'Extraversion' or 'Introversion'.

The people of Scotland boast that, although a small country, it has provided a great many of the world's inventions from a country populated by people with great ideas. They can truly boast about their skilled engineers, scientists, doctors and pioneers who have opened up areas in far flung countries and shared their gifts. They are tremendously proud of the national poet Robert Burns who gave them 'A man's a man for a' that' (a statement that also colours their psyche); their boast is that he is known throughout the world, and this from a country of less than five million people.

Irascible behaviour is most likely to come from people who have a preference for Thinking/Task coupled with an extraverted attitude. This behaviour is found in the irascible Scot, an 'in your face' personality: tell it as it is, straight talking, what you see is what you get, take me or leave me, type.

It is interesting that it is usually the irascible Scot who will boast about their country's contribution to the world whilst, in reality, the Scots they admire and are describing, share with them only a preference for Task or Thinking, the Scots they are boasting about in fact have a very different attitude: Introversion, which creates a different type of Scot. Both are task-focused but their attitudes to life are very different. It is possibly the adherence to task that gave rise to the so-called Protestant work ethic with its Calvinistic streak, seriousness and sober behaviour.

Extraversion-Introversion and the Scottish psyche.

Extraversion and the Irascible Scot

The attitude of Extraversion coupled with the preference for Task/Thinking is the attribute of the irascible Scot, prevalent in the west-coast Scot, with a task culture of 'can do'. People with this preference and attitude confront, challenge, think out loud; they are all about options and consequences and their focus is on the bottom line. They seek feedback, provided it is positive!

The caricature of the Scot who sums up this behaviour could be the minister who when preaching said: 'There will be wailing and gnashing of teeth!' When a voice in the congregation asked 'What if we have no teeth?', the irascible minister replied, 'Teeth will be provided!'

The Task/Thinking type with an Extraverted attitude does represent a wide swathe of Scottish behaviour. The psyche of all the pioneers mentioned above, except for Robert Burns, is one where an attitude of Introversion coupled with Task/Thinking prevails. The only thing the irascible Scot and these other Scots have in common is that they both have a preference for Task/Thinking. It might even be more apt to say that they do not have a preference for 'Feeling' as defined by Jung. Extravert and Introvert would both be in full agreement that they could not abide 'touchy-feely behaviour'.

Introversion and the Dour Scot

The attitude of Introversion coupled with a preference for Task/Thinking are attributes of the dour Scot prevalent on the east coast. They share a task culture but it is more likely to be 'can do... it right'. People with this preference and attitude are reflective. They are inquisitive, questioning everything, taking nothing at face value, and act in a cool calm and collected manner. They internalise everything and beat themselves up over every minuscule mistake. It is a bit like a swan swimming: there's a lot going on under the surface but they give little away.

This type is probably best summed up by the 'Canny Scot' descriptor; they insist on seeing things with their own eyes, they don't trust easily, and accuracy and precision are what's most important to them. 'Where's the evidence?' is their question and they need to ensure that the evidence is robust.

An example that sums up this behaviour is the executive who gets his whole desk cleared, organised down to only one piece of paper, sits back in satisfaction and says 'Now I'm ready for my spontaneity session!'

The dour Scot has no need to share thoughts or ideas with anyone. They do not seek external affirmation and rarely if ever volunteer information. Their purpose is to analyse things and do what is necessary to get things right first time. They tend to upset others because they cannot share feelings. In reality they are unaware of their own feelings therefore it would be very difficult for them to share. They are motivated to do something to help a situation and not to wallow in self pity, or have pity for others. They know that wallowing will not provide a solution. The dour Scot is doggedly determined and not in the least interested in courting popularity.

What both these Scots have in common is a preference for Task/Thinking however the attitudes of Extraversion or Introversion make their response to situations different in all aspects, except that the task must be done. The Irascible Scot's attitude is Extraverted and The Dour Scot's is Introverted.

Extraverted and Introverted Politicians

There are probably a great many Scottish politicians who could ably demonstrate the characteristics of either the irascible Extraverted Scot or the dour Introverted Scot. Some examples currently spring to mind: Gordon Brown, Wendy Alexander, Alex Salmond, Michael Martin and Robin Cook, perhaps it is not difficult to work out which is which.

The Dour Scot

Since he is the Prime Minister, let us take Gordon first. Without a doubt, he is a very typical example of a dour Scot. Here is someone who cannot stand artifice or playing to the gallery. A serious minded individual who emulates the pioneers of old with his great mental abilities. He could be a modern-day Adam Smith, a careful thinker.

As with all serious minded people, he cannot stand flightiness or stupidity. He has no time nor interest in courting popularity as he wants to get on with solving the problems of the world. Some might call it arrogance, which would astonish him. He truly believes he is the best man for the job considering his past experience and connections with world figures. If others could take the hand-clasping PR role of the politician from him, he would be happy getting on with finding the solutions that are necessary to solve all the current problems.

He needs time with peace and quiet to perform best and get the results he seeks. People charge him with prevaricating due to indecision, but this could not be further from the truth. Yes, he does prevaricate but this flows from his need to find the very best solution. His challenge is that he knows that, given just a bit more time, he can find an even more perfect solution to a situation, and he cannot sign off on anything until his need for perfection is met. The danger in this is that the 100 per cent perfect solution might come too late to be of any use and other more pragmatic people would go with 80 per cent if it got the job done.

The contrast is stark between Gordon and his predecessor Tony Blair, who valued expediency and was visible everywhere. Since Gordon took over the role someone has obviously had to tell him that he needs to be more visible and needs to reach decisions more quickly. This has led to some knee-jerk reactions, the response to the 10p tax fiasco might be a perfect example.

Gordon is being advised, almost certainly, that he should be seen as more human and he must smile and press the flesh, all of which are anathema to him as it takes him away from problem solving. He does not appear to accept wholeheartedly that he needs to make changes, at least superficially, to meet the demands of our media age.

That the electorate has to be wooed is not something that appeals to him. Gordon probably believed he was doing the serious work of running the country whilst Tony Blair was courting popularity. Now that he has the PM role, he expects people to appreciate that he is a serious politician getting on with the job of running the country; he deems this to be a major advantage for the country, and one that people will recognise.

What he has failed to see is that in today's terms the role of politician, due to media attention, is more a public relations job than any other. The challenge for Gordon Brown is that he has a very Scottish attitude of being doggedly determined and will probably insist on continuing to do the job his way. It is almost impossible for him to become the politician who will shine through media attention. Right or wrong, elections are won these days on personalities and Gordon's just does not cut the mustard in popularity stakes. His being Scottish has been an issue with the UK electorate; this is not due to racism but more to the fact of him being so typically representative of the disgruntled dour Scot unwilling to give any quarter and play the popularity game. 'Thrawn' is a good Scottish word that sums up his attitude.

The Irascible Scot

Wendy Alexander came to the job with all guns blazing in typical irascible Scot mode. She was going to be the one to sort out all the challenges. She set out her stall in no-nonsense fashion and then allowed herself to be goaded by another, craftier irascible Scot, Alex Salmond, into irrational reactions and making claims she could not keep.

This is a typical example of Extraversion and Thinking/Task behaviour: where the person is more comfortable offering apologies later than by first asking permission. The irascible Scot is often described by the statement, 'Their dander was up' and this would be easy to see in Wendy's behaviour.

A personality with a preference for Thinking/Task coupled with Extraversion is rarely a team player. They are more of a one-man (or woman) band having total belief in their own ability without seeking too much evidence to prove the case. The hierarchy is alive and well with the irascible Scot.

The in-built determination of the Scot, coupled with the 'Wha's like us' mentality, will only exacerbate this single minded activity. Rather than hesitate, regroup and think things through the steamroller rolls right on. Thinking as identified by Jung says nothing about the quality of thinking but describes an objective behaviour with little consideration to feeling. When someone with the psychological profile of Wendy Alexander meets obstacles she responds, much like the 4' 1" drunken Scottish football fan. He squares up to his 6' 5" rival beats his chest and says 'Bring it on', an unfortunate turn of phrase that she actually used!

With her personality, Wendy possibly believed she was giving good, strong leadership. Her style is lead-from-the-front, 'Gung ho!' over-that-hill leadership. This just does not go down well with a more educated population as it may have done in times past. People do question and want answers; it is not enough to hide behind 'I know best'.

Wendy's personality is one for action and to be seen to be doing something, anything, just take action. Her craftier rival, Alex Salmond, shares the irascible Scot personality but is longer in the tooth and knows how to provoke the wrong type of (re)action. Let us face it, he has exhibited this sort of behaviour himself many times in the past.

Unfortunately for Wendy, politics is played out in the public eye and, like Gordon, she too needs to learn that public relations plays a huge role in the public's reaction to their politicians.

And the irascible male Scot will still get away with more than his female counterpart. Even though we live in an emancipated age, people still want their women, although fighters, to be feminine with it; something Wendy must work on if she is to successfully stay in politics.

The Scottish nation has made an inordinately high contribution to the good of the world to this point. Yet increasingly they will need to recognise that they are a very small country made even smaller because we now have a visible global economy. In public life, changes will need to be made to meet the demands of political lives lived out in the glare of publicity. Politicians might need to understand and accept that perhaps no-one has all the answers and that internationalism is what is needed as the world shrinks. We can see by watching television that what happens in one corner of the world can have a knock-on effect in other parts very quickly.

The dour or irascible Scot will not change their core personality easily, nor should they. What they do need to do is to modify their behaviour through recognising that everyone is not out to get them. Could they be more open and calmer in their approach to differences and perhaps more neighbourly to 'big brother' over the border?

Personality changes in the Scottish scene

A week is a long time in politics, so the saying goes, and this has repeatedly turned out to be true. Wendy has departed the scene, probably due to her intense focus on one particular aspect and perhaps the result of an impulsive reaction. Against all the odds her main goad and rival has managed to get himself elected as First Minister – another irrascible Scot? Yes – but one with a difference.

The astute irascible Scot

Alex Salmond shares some of Wendy's personality; however, he straddles the mid-point on the Jungian scale of Thinking and Feeling and can use both interchangeably. This enables him to bring forth a charm to which Wendy could never aspire.

In Scottish terms it is often described as 'sleekit', yet it is charm none the less. He is really gifted in telling people what they want to hear, always putting a positive spin even on bad news, and this is something that the electorate expect from their leader. Interestingly, many presidents in the United States have shared this personality style, Kennedy and more recently Bill Clinton and the world knows how charismatic and charming he could be. It could also be worth noting that there are more people in jail with this personality type than any other! It probably is the ideal personality for a politician to have, charming, charismatic and ruthless!

(President Barack Obama is obviously very analytical and intelligent, yet it is his 'feeling' preference that enabled him to attract and inspire so many loyal supporters. He uses all his gifts and, although subjective feeling is his first preference, he is trained and educated to use his objective thinking preference, certainly as a lawyer and also as an academic. His often-humble take on things, ability to remain unruffled, avoidance of the personal insult and sticking to a steady low-key mantra through thick and thin, rarely rising to the bait, also bodes well for subjective feeling preference. The mantra itself helps corroborate the Feeling over Thinking preference: 'Yes *we* can' never 'Yes *I* can': the 'we' is inclusive, something that comes naturally to him because he has a strong feeling preference.)

Alex Salmond uses his personality well. Unlike Wendy, when he gets upset or is fully into his task mode he can still respond to detractors with the quick quip or a joke. He does not immediately go on the defensive. He may be guilty of whatever he is being accused of but he is so personable in deflecting things that doubts are raised. The difference with Wendy was that she may not have been guilty but by immediately going on the defensive she managed to look guilty and this is the main difference in personality terms between them.

Those people on the Thinking/Task personality scale, as the name suggests, focus on the task at all costs. The people with this personality style are so intense in getting on with solving the problems that they have little time for the niceties and treat any social interaction as an interruption. Gordon shares this preference for Thinking/Task although his attitude of introversion makes him very different. Wendy found out to her cost just what a dangerous mistake it could be for a politician not to court the electorate or even the media.

Those people whose Jungian preference for Thinking/Task is coupled or softened with a Jungian preference for Feeling/People, would never adopt Wendy's attitude. Even while still focusing on the task, they recognise their response to people is equally as important and they make the time for them.

Alex Salmond's way of working is to get his results through people and he understands that he will get more using honey than vinegar. Those who have tackled him and come out on the wrong side of the argument may not easily agree that he is charismatic and charming as in any confrontational scenario the gloves will be off and he will come out as the fighting Scot.

He aims to win and there is nothing 'namby pamby' about how he goes about it. He is secure in his knowledge that he instinctively understands what makes people tick and how he can use this to his advantage. It is this that makes him a very different irascible Scot from Gordon or Wendy. She was so focused on doing what was, to her mind, best for 'the people' she forgot to take account of their feelings even to the extent of confiding in them when this was obviously needed.

Alex Salmond's attitude to the outside world is extraversion and his preferences are shared between Thinking and Feeling yet the preference that makes him so very different from Wendy is his preference for Intuition (which he shares with Gordon), against her preference for Sensing. He looks for potential, which is often far off in the future and she got bogged down in the here-and-now. His potential might never get any closer or become the reality, yet he can paint a picture that motivates others and he is truly skilled at convincing and persuading sufficient numbers of the electorate to believe it.

Post-crunch

To the surprise of many, Gordon the dour Scot is still with us, though almost unrecognisable from the Gordon we knew before the world-changing crunch and the attempted coup within his own party! He has not had a personality transplant, but he has come alive and is visible everywhere. He has the world's problems on his shoulders yet a real spring in his step.

What has caused this shift in his personality? It's the very thing that motivates him most, he sees himself as not only the best person for the job but the only person up to the job. He even manages to smile and laugh now that he is revitalised. He has been seen lining up, smiling in photographs and pecking cheeks with glamorous female politicians from all over the world as they come to seek his advice.

He may not be able to solve the situation but he just loves the challenges it gives him. He can stop worrying about domestic minutiae and get on with dealing with real situations, where the figures demand a brain such as his. He is in his element and if it all goes pear-shape he won't like it; however, he will have gone down fighting on serious issues that his predecessor never had to contemplate and in this he will be vindicated.

He is often accused of not listening and it appears this way. He does listen; however the only person whose opinion he really values is his own. He has not really met anyone whom he would regard as having a sounder under-standing of the problems and the solutions than he has.

His personality type has meant that he never has a need to volunteer information and this can still be seen in the way he dishes out the small amounts he thinks we need to know. No-one has access to the full picture as he sees it, nor will they ever access this. For him, it is enough for the electorate to know he is in control and he knows what he is doing.

He is not going to get this message across using charisma although fear is also a great motivator – and right now the electorate are more fearful than they have ever been. Perhaps the Devil you know may be better than risking any sort of change and from this perspective he may just hold onto power for a wee while longer than was originally thought possible.

Corruption and the crunch

No sooner had Gordon recovered his energy and got moving on sorting the world's financial challenges than the home front erupted again. We have already stated that he gets on best with large serious challenges and prefers the world's stage to dealing with the minutiae of domestic policies; however, the latest battering has come about because he did not pay as much attention as he should have to the smaller everyday issues and, unattended, they grew bells and whistles.

The national disgrace of MPs' expenses claims developed partly because there were bigger things to tackle and, as far as he was concerned. Expenses could only ever be a side show – and surely someone else was dealing with this 'minor' issue?

It turned out that the someone who was dealing with it was another irascible Scot, Mr Speaker Michael Martin, who is out of a totally different mould. He is a west coast irascible Scot, with a background steeped in pursuing his entitlement. He was honest as he saw it and worked totally within the rules. That the rules themselves were the challenge did not occur to him.

If Gordon had not had the cares of the world on his shoulders and if he had had the time and a more urgent responsibility for analysing these rules, he would certainly have recognised that there was a major problem.

Unfortunately Gordon does not sweat the small stuff! Someone with street-savvy equal to Michael Martin did recognise the challenge: yet another Scot. The late Robin Cook, who was more in the mould of Gordon (but not quite), did point this out when it was a small speck on the horizon. He was a Scot on the cusp of irascible and dour; someone with high Thinking/Task but who could apply irascible or dour depending on the situation. He was certainly a more worldly-wise politician who fully understood the minutia that would turn off voters, yet still neither Tony Blair the then prime minister nor Gordon listened.

The challenge for Gordon is that he lives totally in his head. He is not in politics for personal gain. He truly does believe that he is the answer and the only answer at this time to sorting out not just Britain's but the world's financial situation. The expenses scandal and, if the truth be told, the appeasement of the electorate, appeared to be just a distraction to him.

That his party and politics in general are in disarray is something he thinks will be sorted when he finds a solution to the financial situation. The fact that he went on YouTube was his a sop to his advisors. He did what they asked, smiled and tried to look 'cool' and since it was totally out of character for him to do this it came over as false. His reason was that if he could get the advisors off his back he could get back to doing what interested him most, dealing with a world crisis. He was smart enough to know that some nod had to be made in the direction of the electorate, hence he went along with what proved to be a totally misguided gesture.

The Future

There are major challenges to be sorted and the chances are the dour Scot Gordon Brown is the best person to sort them; yet it might be all to late for him. History will give him a better press than the British electorate, as is the case with most politicians.

Today's world is immediate and superficial. How a politician comes across in the media seems to be the guide to electability. By now, Gordon has probably sealed his fate in this department since most of the electorate see him as uncaring. That he cares very deeply does not come across.

The fact that he puts finding a solution to the very major challenges of a world crisis before his personal chances of being re-elected should say something about his sincerity but unfortunately it does not. Charming the media and soothing the electorate's ego pays much greater dividends.

That is a lesson that Gordon could take from the other Scot working on the electorate in Scotland, a consummate politician if ever there was one. Alex Salmond could never solve the sorts of challenges that Gordon could, yet he can knock spots off him when playing to the gallery. Salmond knows that a politician needs to tell the electorate what they want to hear and then tell them again and again. To succeed in politics it is not necessary to solve the world's problems or even the electorate's, just stick with the feel-good mantra!

Gordon may eventually be hailed as the person who got us out of the financial doldrums and averted the depression that was predicted. By the time the UK electorate recognise his worth, they are likely have elected a much more pleasant personality who makes them feel good, even though he could never have got us to the place that Gordon did. All people, Scots and others, seem to want instant gratification in this 'must-have-it-now' society. Perhaps it is true that we do end up with the politicians we deserve.

CHAPTER ELEVEN

Explanations or Excuses

Oh, what miracle has made you the way you are?

LERNER AND LOEWE

Scotland – that bastard land!

LORD BYRON

SO WHAT MADE THE CONTRARY Scottish character? Our 'mongrel' pedigree
… the weather … religion … the hardships of our ancestors … real and
imagined grievances … economic and social blight … the school system
with its origins in the Reformation … being a small nation forced to punch
above its weight … a desperate desire to cling to a separate identity and culture
…? All have been touted as reasons for the way we are and the way we are
perceived.

An ill-advised attempt was made by the Scottish Government to re-package
the Scottish identity with the extremely large claim: 'The best small nation
in the world.' Whatever effect the slogan had on outsiders, the catch-phrase
displayed on official literature and at gateway airports made most Scots
squirm with embarrassment or simmer with anger.

Adslogans, the tagline data base used by top agencies worldwide says in its
'Art and Science of the Slogan' that a catchline should reflect the brand's name,
be campaignable and competitive, and impart positive feelings for the brand.
It should NOT be negative, prompt a sarcastic or negative response, make you
say 'so what?' or 'ho-hum'. Which is exactly what the 'best wee' mantra did.

It was bad enough when others look down on us, but we should not
patronise ourselves. 'Small' never enters the minds of REAL Scots and, while
that may technically apply to our population and land mass in comparison to
other countries, it certainly does not apply to our attainments and influence
in the world. As the late author and custodian of Scottish culture Maurice
Smith almost said, Scotland is a state of mind and we have always had a 'guid
conceit o' oorsels'. And Hugh MacDiarmid, rhapsodising about the natural
treasury to be found on a small patch of hillside, demanded indignantly:
'Scotland small? Our infinite, mulitform Scotland *small?*'

Other government slogans made more credible stabs at re-branding the
country: 'Scotland is the Place' for the Fresh Talent initiative to attract students

from overseas, while the aspirational 'Healthier Scotland', 'Natural Scotland', 'One Scotland', 'Safer Scotland' and 'Smarter Scotland' were more hopes than statements.

Attempts to sloganise Scotland have rarely been successful. 'Confident, Competitive and Compassionate Scotland' was all the 'c's' except catchy and it was followed by the equally-alliterative 'Smart Successful Scotland'. There have also been 'Scotland – the Brand', the trying-to-be-trendy 'Cool Caledonia' and the Scottish Tourist Board's somewhat baffling 'Live It. Visit Scotland', which only works alongside images of people wheezing on mountain tops or hurtling down waterfalls.

An unexpected result of the 'best wee country' slogan was that it provoked a serious examination of Scottish identity and 'lazy stereotypes'. The Scottish Left Review devoted an entire issue to the debate explaining: 'Some people thought it sounded like we were thinking "small", others thought it was bordering on arrogant, some thought it lacked anything distinctive. Some of these criticisms may well have had more than an element of truth about them, but what was the better option? If this isn't how we want to present Scotland, what is? What is the Scottish national identity we want others to know us by?'

The Review asked a cross-section of thinkers, writers, sociologists, artists, activists and others to come up with their own alternative slogans. All that exercise proved was that none of those asked should seek a career in advertising; the offerings ranged from the colloquial 'Scotland – Nae Bother!', to the worthy 'Scotland – Fairer, Greener, Happier', the clever 'Scotland – Matured for a 1,000 Years. Enjoy' to the far-too-clever 'Scotland – It's Still Reigning Here'.

The American Arthur Herrman almost gave Scotland a slogan with the title of his book *How The Scots Invented The Modern World*, recognizing Scottish genius and acknowledging the influence of the Scottish Enlightenment. Would *Scotland – Wha's Like Us?* be too boastful? Probably.

Perhaps any attempt to sloganise Scotland should follow the example of the dog food company that advertised itself as 'so good it doesn't need a slogan'...

'A mongrel nation'

'The most mixed-up small nation in the world' would have been more accurate; and such an endearing admission might even have attracted more visitors (although it would not have met the politicians' need for something more assertive and confident).

Genealogically speaking, however, the Scottish nation *is* mixed up and as William McIlvanney memorably declared at a home rule rally: 'Never forget that we are the bastard people of a mongrel nation.'

There has been no such thing as a 'pure Scot' (any more than there is such a thing as 'pure English') since a hotch-potch of nations combined from Roman times and before to coalesce: Picts, Gaels, Vikings, the Strathclyde Britons, Saxons and, later, Normans. The individual characteristics that constitute this mixture can still be seen in Scottish character types, from the hot-blooded and impulsive to the cool and canny, and in the way we look. From before the beginning the 'nation' was more a political than a racial entity and it took a King of Norman blood, Robert the Bruce, to unite the Scots. He did so in all-too-typical fashion: his 'nation' was created out of a myth of descent from a non-existent dynasty of Scottish kings – and, more importantly, out of enmity to England.

Eventually what the 'Hammer of the Scots' could not do in 1314, economics finally achieved in 1707 when the Darien disaster led to the Union of the Parliaments and the incorporation of Scotland into the United Kingdom, ruled from London. The Scottish 'sense of victimhood' was intensified and aggravated by injustices that include the Highland Clearances in the 18th and 19th centuries, the demolition of the industrial base in the 1980s, the Poll Tax in 1989 and the current question of the powers of the restored Scottish Parliament – the grievance mentality remains a way of life for too many Scots.

Dreich, dismal and dreary ...

Scotland's weather exists only in Scots, in standard English it is indescribable. Scots words are used to portray it that have no English equivalent: 'dreich' to describe a dismal and dreary day; 'haar', the cold mist or fog that creeps from the North Sea and into your bones; the 'souch' or 'sough' of a howling wind; 'snell for a bitingly cold wind; 'mizzle, the adaptation of miserable and drizzle'; the 'smirr,' of light drizzly rain that can somehow make you wetter than a prolonged downpour and in either case, you are bound to end up 'drookit'. In Caithness, they have a 'screever', a strong wind; a 'bleeter', a sharp passing shower and a 'thief-lookan sky', a threatening sky that will steal the good day, which is typically Scottish in anticipating that good will turn to bad.

A *Washington Post* travel writer, aware of these quaint Scotticisms, asked her Hebridean taxi-driver what he would call the day's weather and was told bluntly: 'I'd call it bloody awful.'

There are, of course, occasions when the Scottish weather can be beautiful but even then the pale-skinned, easily-overheated Scot has the words for his discomfort: a warm and humid day is 'mauchie' or muggy and on hot, sunny days it is easy to be 'sweltrie' or even 'roastit'.

The official government website acknowledges the character-building importance of the Scottish climate by devoting a whole chapter to it and admitting: 'Scotland's weather has frequently been made a subject of fun, not least by Scots themselves. The perception of Scotland's climate as unwelcoming has even been a badge of pride, with the bracing air being said to make the men of Scotland hardy, and the women rosy-cheeked.'

It claims there really are climatic compensations: 'When one considers that even Scotland's southerly cities of Glasgow and Edinburgh lie further north than Copenhagen and Moscow to the East, and Calgary and Labrador to the west, it is surprising that our climate is as mild as it is. Washed by warm Atlantic currents rising from the Caribbean, we enjoy more clement conditions than inland nations much further from the pole. Many parts of Scotland have over 1,400 hours of sunshine annually, more than Manchester or Birmingham....

'Sometimes fresh and expansive, sometimes dark with omen, the skies of Scotland are the ever-changing backdrop to the spectacular natural scenery that tempts visitors from all corners of the world to Scotland. The rolling clouds that tumble down the glen, the mist that shrouds the mountains on an early morning, to climb through and out above the clouds to a peak bathed in sun: these are as much a part of the matchless landscape as the mountains themselves.'

Ignore the national bard's 'wert thou in the cauld, cauld blast' and 'o tell na me o' wind and rain', the Scottish civil servant with the soul of a poet prefers 'painting the clouds with sunshine'. Scottish weather isn't really as bad as it's made out to be – official.

Robert Louis Stevenson, brought up in 'the gloom and depression' of winters in Edinburgh which has its own local wind-chill factor, was convinced of the effect on the national character and culture: 'The Scotch dialect is singularly rich in terms of reproach against the winter wind. Snell, blae, nirly, and scowthering, are four of these significant vocables; they are all words that carry a shiver with them; and for my part, as I see them aligned before me on the page, I am persuaded that a big wind comes tearing over the Firth from Burntisland and the northern hills; I think I can hear it howl in the chimney, and as I set my face northwards, feel its smarting kisses on my cheek.

'Even in the names of places there is often a desolate, inhospitable sound; and I remember two from the near neighbourhood of Edinburgh, Cauldhame and Blaw-weary, that would promise but starving comfort to their inhabitants. The inclemency of heaven, which has thus endowed the language of Scotland with words, has also largely modified the spirit of its poetry.

'Both poverty and a northern climate teach men the love of the hearth and the sentiment of the family; and the latter, in its own right, inclines a poet to the praise of strong waters. In Scotland, all our singers have a stave or two for blazing fires and stout potations: to get indoors out of the wind and to swallow something hot to the stomach, are benefits so easily appreciated where they dwelt!'

Why did the poets Fergusson and Burns spend so much time drinking in low dives? Stevenson has no doubt: 'The kindly jar, the warm atmosphere of tavern parlours, and the revelry of lawyers' clerks, do not offer by themselves the materials of a rich existence. It was not choice, so much as an external fate, that kept Fergusson in this round of sordid pleasures. A Scot of poetic temperament, and without religious exaltation, drops as if by nature into the public-house. The picture may not be pleasing; but what else is a man to do in this dog's weather?'

Those Edinburgh winters must have seared themselves into Stevenson's consciousness and frail body: 'There is something almost physically disgusting in the bleak ugliness of easterly weather; the wind wearies, the sickly sky depresses them; and they turn back from their walk to avoid the aspect of the unrefulgent sun going down among perturbed and pallid mists. The days are so short that a man does much of his business, and certainly all his pleasure, by the haggard glare of gas lamps.

'The roads are as heavy as a fallow. People go by, so drenched and draggletailed that I have often wondered how they found the heart to undress. And meantime the wind whistles through the town as if it were an open meadow; and if you lie awake all night, you hear it shrieking and raving overhead with a noise of shipwrecks and of falling houses.

'In a word, life is so unsightly that there are times when the heart turns sick in a man's inside; and the look of a tavern, or the thought of the warm, fire-lit study, is like the touch of land to one who has been long struggling with the seas.' Small wonder that Robert Louis Stevenson travelled to Provence, California and ended his days in tropical Samoa.

And even if the weather is at its most glorious, the Scot will find reason for foreboding. Alastair Reid summed it up in his poem in which he meets the woman from the fish shop on such a day and cries 'What a day it is!' In reply:

Her brow grew bleak, her ancestors raged in their graves
As she spoke with their ancient misery:
'We'll pay for it, we'll pay for it, we'll pay for it!''

A *hard* life

The weather, the poor diet (derisively summed up in Dr Johnson's dictionary definition of 'oats: a grain which in England is generally given to the horses but in Scotland supports the people') and the harsh conditions of everyday life all combined to create a hardy people ready to face centuries of adversity.

They were well-suited to the privations of pioneer life on the frontiers of the Empire or soldiering and chroniclers tell of Highland soldiers who marched overland carrying just a bag of oatmeal and a small stone on which to heat it at night: 'For rest, they rolled up tightly in their homespun wool plaids and stretched out on the bare ground. When the temperature dropped near freezing, they would occasionally dip their plaids into a stream to freeze them and sleep inside a coating of ice not unlike a snow cave. One clan chieftain was chaffed by his men as 'soft' when he was seen making a pillow out of snow (sometimes out of a rock).'

In the Old Statistical Account of Scotland, the first-ever statistical 'portrait of Scotland' compiled in the 1790s from reports by over 900 parish ministers, Sir John Sinclair described the Highlander thus: 'He has felt from his early youth all the privations to which he can be exposed in almost any circumstances of war. He has been accustomed to scanty fare, to rude and often wet clothing, to cold and damp houses, to sleep often in the open air or in the most uncomfortable beds, to cross dangerous rivers, to march a number of miles without stopping and with but little nourishment, and to be perpetually exposed to the attacks of a stormy atmosphere. A warrior thus trained suffers no inconvenience from what others would consider to be the greatest possible hardships, and has an evident superiority over the native of a delicious climate, bred to every indulgence of food, dress and habitation and who is unaccustomed to marching and fatigue.'

In more modern times it is often forgotten that the industrial revolution and subsequent years of enormous economic vitality and vigour in which ironworks, coalmines, textile mills, foundries, engineering works and shipyards thrived side-by-side with appalling disease, poverty and squalor in which working people were treated as slaves and the under-class were ignored.

The women of Scotland matched (and out-matched) the men in their hardiness. In addition to the never-ending struggles of bearing and raising children in severe conditions, they shared the most grueling forms of work.

They often went barefoot (wearing shoes only for special occasions such as church) and on a visit to the Highlands in the 18th century, diarist Edward Burt was shocked by women treading their washing in tubs 'when their legs and feet are almost literally as red as blood with the cold.' In the herring season a female labour force lived rough as they walked scores of miles to the east coast fishing harbours where they gutted fish in all weathers. It was reported: 'Each woman cleaned about thirty-five fish a minute and could keep up the pace for hours on end.'

The word 'feisty' had not arrived from America but it perfectly describes the spirited Scotswomen who fought with police and soldiers in the Clearances, the 'Women's Housing Associations' who led the popular movement and opposed sheriff's officers in the Glasgow rent strikes; and the miners' wives who emerged from their secondary role and provided the key community support which kept the 1984 miners' strike going as long as it did.

A direct line to God

Question: Did the Protestant religion, particularly in its austere and dogmatic Calvinist form, shape the Scottish psyche – or did the dourly democratic Scottish character mould Protestantism? Either way, the two are entwined and religion has had, for good AND ill, an ineradicable effect on the nation.

The Reformation established Protestantism as the national established Church of Scotland, 'the true religion' as it is described in the National Covenant of 1638, and the ensuing strife and struggles created an almost Biblical sense of identity. A similarity between Scotland and the Old Testament Israelites has been argued: 'Scotland was a poor and seemingly insignificant nation. But like Israel, God had chosen it to play a leading role in His plans for the establishment of true religion and the betterment of humankind.' To which an appropriate response might be: Holy Moses!

The old faith, Roman Catholicism, was replaced by Presbyterianism and it is no coincidence that this essentially democratic form of church government had a special appeal for Scots. Without the debatably 'God-given' authority of priests and bishops, no-one is regarded as better than anyone else, including the ministers who are appointed by their congregations and responsible to them. Kirk sessions administer parish affairs and, instead of a rising hierarchy of bishops, cardinals and Pope, the church is governed by presbyteries, synods and, ultimately, the General Assembly.

This egalitarian approach to matters spiritual is a reflection of the 'we're a' Jock Tamson's bairns' attitude of Scots, typified by the argumentative trade unionist and workers who rightly see themselves as every bit as worthy as the boss. It also gives every Presbyterian Scot a direct line to God without the intervention or intercession of priests: 'very God and very man, yet one Christ, the only mediator between God and man'.

In the Westminster Confession of Faith, compiled by 'an assembly of divines' and presented to Parliament in 1647, is still the 'subordinate standard of doctrine' of the Church of Scotland (subordinate only to the Bible), 'the Popish sacrifice of the mass' is dismissed as 'most abominably injurious to Christ's one only sacrifice, the alone propitiation for all the sins of the elect'. The Bible is God's way of 'better preserving and propagating of the truth, and for the more sure establishment and comfort of the Church against the corruption of the flesh, and the malice of Satan and of the world'.

Man and woman are 'unprofitable servants' who are burdened 'by the debt of our former sins' and 'defiled and mixed with so much weakness and imperfection that they can not endure the severity of God's judgment'. Public church censures included admonition, suspension from the Sacrament of the Lord's Supper for a season, excommunication from the Church and the public humiliation of standing on the 'cutty stool of repentance' before the entire congregation, as Robert Burns was forced to do as penance for fornication and getting Jean Armour pregnant. These censures were deemed necessary 'for the reclaiming and gaining of offending brethren; for deterring of others from the like offences; for purging out the leaven which might infect the whole lump ...'

The rigid Sabbatarianism which lay across Scotland until the mid-20th century (and is still evident in island communities) was laid down in the stricture that the Lord's Day was 'to be continued to the end of the world, as the Christian Sabbath'.

And in language which still bedevils inter-church and inter-sectarian relations to this day, The Westminster Confession says non-reformed churches are 'subject both to mixture and error and some have so degenerated as to become no churches of Christ, but synagogues of Satan'. In particular: 'There is no other head of the Church but the Lord Jesus Christ: nor can the Pope of Rome in any sense be head thereof; but is that Antichrist, that man of sin and son of perdition ...' While that remains unrevoked as the Kirk's standard of faith, is it any wonder that sectarian extremism exists in Scotland and runs far deeper than the crude displays at 'Old Firm' football matches?

And is it any wonder that generations through the centuries, having absorbed such severe and unbending moralizing, produced a race with somewhat gloomy expectations? This characteristic was gloriously parodied by Rikki Fulton's comic creation, the lugubrious Rev I. M. Jolly, and in the story of the minister who thundered about the eternal fires and damnation which awaited his congregation to such effect that a terrified parishioner cried out: 'Lord! Lord! We didna ken!' To which the minister replied with relish: 'Weel, ye ken noo ..!'

The darker side of this kind of Calvinism is embodied in the doctrine of predestination – that God has foreordained all things and has elected certain souls to eternal salvation or damnation. As church correspondent to the newspaper baron Lord Beaverbrook, one of the present authors was told that his Lordship (son of a church elder from West Lothian who migrated to Canada and became a Presbyterian minister) believed firmly in predestination and that he had already been selected for the wrong place! Which seems a gloomy way to live, but may explain some of the damned (in his view) Lord B's more ruthless actions during his life.

In the 1950s–60s, Beaverbrook ordered his Scottish newspapers to wage a holy war, declaring 'No Bishops in the Kirk' in response to a move to the Kirk and the Scottish Episcopal Church with the blessing of the Church of England. It says something for the deep roots of religion in the Scottish psyche that a crusade (the crusader being Beaverbrook's front-page emblem) run by the *Scottish Daily Express* (then the biggest-selling newspaper in Scotland with over half-a-million sales) could command popular attention and influence the establishment. The 'Bishops Report' was thrown out by the 1959 General Assembly after a heated debate and the *Express* exulted: 'The spirit of Knox is not dead.'

Caricatures and parodies apart, the Kirk should be given full credit for its benign influence on Scottish life. For centuries, the nation's reputation rested on the learning and scholarship which have been a direct result of the Kirk-created education system. Since Presbyterianism was a Bible-based religion without priestly intermediaries ordinary people should be able to read the Scriptures for themselves and a vital part of John Knox's Reformation was the establishment of a school in every parish to teach reading, writing, and catechism. From that, there grew the system of grammar schools in every town, high schools and colleges furthering classical studies and the ancient universities with three-year courses in arts, medicine, law, and divinity.

Far superior to the education systems in England and Europe, Scottish education created what has been called the 'democratic intellect' – personified by the 'lad-o-pairts', that penniless local lad walking to the university town with his supply of oatmeal and herring, whose intelligence alone was enough to raise him above his station in life. Over a century later, Scotland led the Western world in the realms of medicine, economics, history, and jurisprudence when it was possible to stand at the Mercat Cross in Edinburgh and 'shake hands with fifty men of genius in an hour'.

The historical importance of the Kirk was praised by the United Free

Church Moderator, Principal Alexander Martin, in a report on the 1929 Union: 'No-one who knew their Scottish history would deny that the Church had fulfilled many a notable public service in the past. It had been on the floor of the General Assembly rather than in the corrupt estates or Privy Council that the battle of the Scottish people for freedom had been won. The burden of the poor was borne for centuries by the Church unaided and in her system of education she laid during the past ages the foundation of a democracy in which all barriers were down and the way was open and free for all.'

Thomas Carlyle, commenting on the flowering of Scottish genius in the Enlightenment, saw 'Knox and the Reformation acting in the heart's core of every one of these persona and phenomena'.

As the established national church, the Kirk was also the 'people's church' and 'the voice of Scotland' and Rev Professor Archibald Main of Glasgow University wrote: 'After the year 1560 the ordinary man gained what the extraordinary cleric had lost, no more was the layman a humble puppet of the Mother Church – he could voice his views in Kirk Sessions or General Assembly, he had the opportunity of influencing public opinion.'

From the Union of the Parliaments in 1707 until the re-establishment of the devolved Scottish Parliament in 1999, the annual General Assembly of the Church of Scotland – although narrow-based in religion, class and ethnicity – was the nearest thing Scotland had to a Parliament. It acted as the forum for debate, often national indignation, on important social, political, industrial and moral issues.

The Church & Nation Committee, always described in the popular Press as 'powerful', had the remit 'to keep under review all aspects of the development of the nation's life and to recommend ways in which the Church of Scotland can act in the highest interests of the people of Scotland'. Throughout the 20th century, the Committee's reports were always the occasion for showpiece debates on the spectrum of Scottish concerns from poverty, housing and industrial decline to nuclear warfare and the presence of NATO missiles on Scottish soil. Now called the 'Church and Society Council', it continues the tradition of engaging in today's issues – from the treatment of asylum-seekers and ecology to adoption and education.

The Kirk played a leading part in the Home Rule campaigns in the late 1940s, the 1979 referendum failure and again in the Constitutional Convention in the 1990s. Although it has always been assumed that the Kirk, being established and Protestant, would be pro-Unionist, it has always supported a measure of home rule as the will of the people – indeed, as 'the voice of Scotland', it could do no other.

One Scot who embodies the questions of religion and identity is, of course, Prime Minister Gordon Brown. In his rise to power he mainly shied away from public discussion of his basic beliefs, but when campaigning for the Leadership of the Labour Party – and subsequently as PM – he has spoken unambiguously of his 'moral compass' and the values instilled in him as a son of the manse. He also said that the scandal of MPs' expenses at Westminster offended his Presbyterian conscience.

His father, the Reverend John E. Brown, was the embodiment of Christian Socialism and – as well as a powerful pulpit-style of oratory – the young Gordon absorbed those values. He told the 2008 Labour conference: 'I don't romanticise my upbringing. But my parents were more than an influence, they were – and still are – my inspiration. The reason I am in politics. And all I believe and all I try to do comes from the values I learned from them.'

In the Kirk's manse in Kirkcaldy, prayers were said before meals and debate was encouraged, although the father's views were dominant. The minister's sons played their part in the life of the church and, somewhat unfairly, were expected to set an example of good behaviour to other 'teenagers'.

The Brown boys had to earn their pocket money, selling evening papers around the town and programmes at Raith Rovers' ground to gain free access at half-time. Oldest brother John edited a mimeographed youth fellowship magazine, with high-flown and idealistic editorials by his younger brother on world events, the proceeds of which went to Third World charities.

Years later, the Prime Minister spoke with feeling of the impression made on a young boy by the procession of hard-luck cases to the kitchen door: beggars looking for food, mothers of young families with not enough money to last the week, the unemployed, the bereaved and the troubled: 'As a minister's son you see every problem coming to your doorstep. You become aware of a whole range of distress and social problems. I suppose it's not a bad training for politics.'

To mark their father's 80th birthday, his three sons published a collection of his sermons under the title *A Time To Serve*. The book resonates with practical Christianity, in which theology and doctrine are important, but even more important is the treatment of others, especially the less-fortunate. One chapter outlines the Reverend John's concept of 'the plus factor': 'In appearance, the cross is very like the plus sign, suggesting to us that Christianity symbolises something more. Nor is this to be regarded as a false or erroneous idea. Christianity is such a religion. It has a Plus Sign right at its centre. It gives more and it expects more.'

This voice echoes in his son's Manchester declaration: 'I will never forget

– the only reason any of us are here is that we are in politics as servants of the people.'

Poignantly, given Gordon Brown's loss of the sight of one eye in a rugby accident in his teens, the first sermon in the book is titled 'Our need of vision'. Written with a father's obvious feeling, it says: 'Blindness is surely one of life's sorest handicaps. Those who are deprived of sight miss much. For them, vistas of loveliness are shut off and bring no joy and gladness.'

All his life, the Rev John had a passion for the Third World, not merely as a missionary field but as a cause to be championed and he preached against the unfair distribution of wealth in the world. It was no surprise to learn that Gordon Brown's vision of 'the good society' includes programmes for the poorer countries.

Setting out his Prime Ministerial creed, Gordon Brown openly confessed: 'I joined the Labour party out of faith.' And: 'The Labour Party must stand for more than a programme, we must have a soul.'

Times have changed and, with them, the influence of the Presbyterian church in Scotland – or, indeed, of religion itself.

So is Scotland still a Christian country? Perhaps a more accurate answer would be that Scotland has become an increasingly irreligious country – because, although the overwhelming majority claim adherence to one of the Christian denominations, they certainly do not fill the pews in the churches of those denominations. And whether they practice Christian morality is a question for them ...

The question on religion in the 2001 Scottish Census still showed over two-thirds of people identifying themselves as Christian (Church of Scotland, Roman Catholic and 'Other Christian'), while over a quarter (1.4 million) stated flatly that they had no religion.

The true picture is given by steadily declining church attendance and participation in parish and other events. Although 42 per cent, or over two million, of Scotland's population identify themselves as 'Church of Scotland' by religion, the Kirk's communicants recently dropped below the half-million mark for the first time and the number of new members joining each year has dropped by nearly 80 per cent since 1981. Similarly, while some 750, 000 Scots identify themselves as Roman Catholics, the number attending Mass is only 200,000.

In 2001, the Muslim population was 42,600, with 52,000 of other religions and it is expected that these numbers will have grown, not least because Muslims have the youngest age profile with 31 per cent aged under 16 years.

According to Article xxv of the Act of Union: 'Presbyterian Church

Government and Discipline. Shall be the only Government of the Church within the Kingdom of Scotland.' Not only that, but the act binds all British monarchs to 'inviolably maintain and preserve the True Protestant Religion'. As part of the modernisation of Scotland, it seems time to accept that we are now a multi-faith society, even if that means disestablishment and the separation of church from state. To many, that would be more honest – but do enough Scots care about religion to re-examine that relationship?

An even more honest assessment would be that from once being the nation that considered itself 'chosen by God', Scotland has turned to atheism or religious apathy and the harsh verdict of the *Undiscovered Scotland* tourism guide: 'In practice, a visitor to Scotland could leave without really having noticed the religious life of the country.'

With so many influential factors – are they explanations or excuses? It is not surprising that the Scottish character is such a paradox. We are emotional, yet stolidly undemonstrative in personal relationships; Scots do not do 'touchy feely' nor kissing in public, especially mwah-mwah air-kissing – a habit introduced from London but in Scotland something only posh posers do. When a Scot says 'it's no' bad', it may seem grudging, but is actually meant as praise.

Scots are aspirational and still produces as many successful entrepreneur; the 'lad o' pairts' from a lowly beginning who became a multi-millionaire in post-Industrial Revolution times now has his counterparts in Sir Tom Farmer, Sir Tom Hunter, Brian Souter and many others. Yet Scots who have climbed the class ladder continue to cling to their working class credentials, especially those who have risen from poor to middle-income ranking. (The term ' bunnet hustler' denotes the middle-class type who puts on a 'cloth cap' manner and harps on about his under-privileged origins.)

We cannot change our blood-lines and history, nor our climatic conditions, but we can do something about the character flaws which continue to blight our nation and our prospects of success in the 21st century. Before we can change ourselves for the better, we have to understand who we are.

PART THREE
TREATMENT

CHAPTER TWELVE

What Kind of Scotland?

Change we need

BARACK OBAMA Campaign slogan

THE FIRST TWO PARTS of the book have set out Scotland's symptoms, provided a diagnosis and identified the reasons why Scotland, a nation of such potential, is underperforming, why it is that it is failing to shape up to old problems and new challenges and falling short of the world-class nation we must aspire to be.

We now need to look at possible remedies and at how a Scotland with such changing characteristics can deal with change and challenge in this new era. This new agenda is formidable and needs a Scotland able to make real and informed choices about its future. After we have described and discussed the new character we (the authors) envisage for our country we will explore in what ways this new character will lead to a better Scotland.

We need to make the case for change. Change is tough to deal with and can far too easily intimidate and threaten, ensuring that the contented and the complacent win through. The case for change has to be compelling but the consequences of inaction have also to be spelled out. In this new era we have choices to make. We can continue as we are and muddle through or we can accept that we face challenges that require us to have a national personality transformation. Are we into modifications and minor character adjustments or do we want a total make-over?

What kind of Scotland do we want to live in? Do we need a Scotland that is inclusive and significantly more equal? Do we value the quality of 'solidarity' of, say, the Scandinavians or should we emulate the enterprise of the USA or can we combine both in this fiercely competitive and global world?

What are our dreams, hopes and ambitions for ourselves, families, friends and country? Do we want a quality of life that achieves a better balance between materialism and our desire for a less frenzied life-style, peace of mind, tranquillity and a more spiritually uplifting sense of being? As a nation, post-credit crunch, how do we rise above the grudge, greed and grievance mentality into which so many of us lapse?

Don't we want a Scotland where the most intractable problems can be solved and where inequality starts to be seen as the corrosive and destructive force that it is? Don't we want to be more successful in embracing and tackling the big challenges of this new era, including climate change, global warming and energy security?

What does a high standard of living and quality of life mean in 2009? How do we achieve the goals of becoming a modern, innovative, secure, confident and progressive country? How do we measure our progress against our own individual and national potential rather than relying on myths and make-believe and our uniquely unhelpful comparisons with our neighbours to the south?

These are only some of the questions we need to consider as we make the transition as a nation from 20th to 21st century thinking and behaviour. The world we live in is in a remarkable state of change and offers enormous challenges to Scotland. It could provide successes and achievements we do not dare to imagine. But we can only transform ourselves in to this new enlightened age if we build solid foundations and adopt a new outlook.

While taking stock of who we are and where we are, we also need to ask who we want to be. If the answer to that question necessitates change (and the authors believe it does) then how do we change and what will that change look like? This is the challenge, change and choice continuum in which we move from a nation with a curious combination of contradictions, inner conflicts, confusions and complacency to a nation which is full of positives, that is confident, innovative, modern, focussed, positive and ambitious.

At a time when every section of society is facing serious challenges, when dramatic change is everywhere and failure to respond could bring devastating consequences, the stakes are necessarily high. If we are being honest, we sail in uncharted waters. Old signposts are of no help and the dividing line between staying still, sliding back and moving forward can be difficult to see.

We have talent, we have assets, we have a record of achievement in so many areas, but do we have the will to make a real difference in the decades ahead? Do we have the leadership in our society and in our politics and is there a consensus on the need to radically alter our approach?

This book has shown that like all nations Scotland is a product of a complex and rich mix of cultures, history, education, religion, politics, climate, geography, language, industrialisation, beliefs, values, myths, economics, family, law and education. Because of these we are where we are. And when we turn to look forward, the issues we face need more than superficial description, simple analysis and easy solutions.

The 'change we need' impacts on everything we do and we should not forget we are dealing with human beings with all their complications and unpredictability. We also have to recognise the social, economic, constitutional and political structures we have created to organise our society and make sense of a complex world, a world which now extends from our homes and communities through to our nation, the United Kingdom, the European Union and the global community in all of its bewildering and troubled reality. And all of this complexity is linked by extraordinary systems of information technology, global communication and an electronic revolution focussed on the internet. This is a truly connected world.

Today, Scotland is interdependent and international in a world without borders or boundaries. Our environment, our economics, our energy do not fit neatly in the space we call Scotland or the UK. As a consequence, our politics, which are fixed by geography, are finding it hard to cope and respond to problems and issues which local and national governments no longer control. Our debates about independence and sovereignty have a hollow and dated ring to them. They seem to ignore these new and emerging realities and the fact that we are citizens of a completely new era.

In trying to capture a snapshot of Scotland in this complex reality, we have attempted to be honest, rigourous and open in our thinking. Since we have decided that Scotland IS a suitable case for treatment, this section of the book recommends remedies based on optimism and the basic truth that we *can* have a better future for our country. It is up to us, since no-one else has the same interest in our future!

New thinking can take us forward; facing the future and making a difference is within our grasp. In this context, leadership and building personal and collective responsibility become crucial. How does the new Scotland – based on our work on its condition, diagnosis and treatment – measure up to change? And what are the drivers of change that can provide this more inspiring future? We will attempt to bring these tangled issues into a straightforward narrative comprising four broad themes:

Scotland, A Nation In Transition: change, choice and challenge; a new era recasting the national character; a nation in transition; Inspiring futures, the drivers of change.

Scotland, The Opportunity And Challenge Agenda: Bridging the gaps, poverty, aspiration and confidence; a new agenda for a new era, global, European, UK and Scotland; an ideas' world, innovation, thinking, a new enlightenment.

Scotland, Aspiration And Achievement: The new politics, devolution and the union; the new economy, beyond the crunch; the new society, old problems, new solutions; the new diaspora, Scotland's strength abroad.

Scotland, How Do We Reshape The Nation: Redefining the national purpose with a new sense of Scotland; mood, morale, motivation and momentum; media and the message.

This provides the best way of taking us from *Scotland: A Suitable Case For Treatment* to a Scotland that has, at least inside the pages of this book, been successfully treated. This would be a Scotland fit for the purpose of a modern era, a confident, positive and competitive player in the global order, reshaping our role in the United Kingdom and Europe, providing new solutions to old problems and changing for ever our national mood.

The key elements that we discuss in more detail later are:

- The national psyche and the forces that shape it.
- The new economic order; recession and the financial and banking crisis are taking their toll but have we reached a tipping-point where we can see beyond debt, unemployment, mortgage collapse, collapsing pensions and see new opportunities, new ways of doing things?
- Politics and our political system in the wake of the Westminster expenses crisis and the opportunity to build a new politics. Our democracy: is it fit for purpose and what purpose is that?
- The future of the Union and Scotland's role in it: nationality, identity and diversity, independence and the alternatives
- Recognition of the new global order and the importance of Europe
- Old problems, new opportunities: social, health, inequality – how they combine to determine and either enhance or damage life-chances.
- The economy: indicators; the new energy-climate industries; productivity, competitiveness, growth, poor workforce participation rates, unemployment, innovation and small business development; economic inequality; beyond the banking and financial crisis; technology, communications and learning.
- National character; dependency, responsibility, respect, tolerance; risk and recklessness, negativity; success and achievement; enterprise, individuals, the family and other structures.
- Closing the gaps: inequality, aspiration, contentment, confidence
- New era, new challenges: progress in different political spaces – global, the European Union, United Kingdom, Scotland.

- Influencing the national mood: opinion formers and the media. Press, broadcasting, electronic communications. The Internet, new era – new media?
- Leading the way – leadership, innovation, vision, consensus and collective responsibility, partisan politics; confidence, comparative advantage and achievement; tipping point politics.

TREATMENT: Scotland has the potential – talent, assets, resources, backed by a credible history of achievement – to be a world-class nation. What is in doubt is our ability to acknowledge, comprehend and manage change in a world of increasing complexity, competitiveness and challenge. We face a range of social, economic, demographic and political issues which require imagination, innovative ideas and a real sense of national purpose.

CHAPTER THIRTEEN

'Cannae be Bothered' Scotland

IN *THE CULTURE OF CONTENTMENT*, J. K. Galbraith asserts that as affluence advances the political class, other organisations and collective bodies have weaken. Their collective resolve to tackle difficult issues and intractable problems, despite still being part of the political rhetoric, has been diminished.

His book provides a fascinating insight into two aspects of the Scottish dilemma: our failure to tackle inequality and the inability of the political process and politicians to escape from the middle-ground of politics and distribute scarce public funds to any other group than 'the politically deserving'.

Galbraith's analysis explains why massive inequalities in Scotland do not represent a priority issue. As he points out, these are not just issues for the poor and disadvantaged, the discontented minority (one million people in Scotland), but an issue for the contented majority and national well-being.

This raises the question of whether democratic societies have either the political will or the incentive to take serious action to tackle inequality. At present nearly 20 per cent of Scotland's population lives on or below the official levels of financial poverty – which, of course, masks a myriad of other inequalities keeping people excluded and unable to escape the life-style and generational and geographical aspects of exclusion in 20th century Scotland.

Politics becomes, in Galbraith's argument, a matter of satisfying the culture of contentment, the affluent majority who have the most clout in elections, lobbying and advocacy. For Galbraith, this means that citizens are viewed as consumers while collective, common and civic needs and responsibilities are sidelined. Political parties are seen as seeking to outbid each other in safeguarding the affluence of the contented and so the centre-ground of politics becomes congested.

This argument is complicated in Scotland by the success of the Scottish National Party, who are centrists in the accepted political sense of the word but have added new layers of concerns to the debate north of the border. Seeking to transform the sovereignty and authority of Westminster, impose an imprint of nationality and reinforce the issue of identity, the SNP has provided a new focus for political and social cohesion. The SNP reinforces the importance of the 'culture of contentment' theory by relegating the interests of the poor and other significant minorities and promoting instead new aspirations of nationhood regardless of social and economic issues and problems.

This divorce of social and economic conditions from pride, patriotism, nationality and identity is similar to the United States. The poorest, most deprived, least educated and least affluent sections of society embrace moral issues, family values, religion and the defence and security of the US and vote consistently for the Republican Party who are unlikely, indeed unwilling, to provide economic and social policies to help those in greatest need.

In Scotland, we are in danger of combining a culture of contentment with a cult of nationality, neither of which is interested in inequality and exclusion. Yet inequality remains the most important and intractable of Scotland's social and economic problems, a signature issue for government failure, lack of investment and national resolve. Galbraith confirms the more subtle pressures at work on this issue. Without a major change in approach, then, inequality will continue to cast a shadow over a modern Scotland.

On this particular issue, the years ahead look difficult. Post-2011 government spending from Westminster will be reduced and the battle over priorities will adversely affect poverty and social and economic minorities. Uncertainty over the Constitutional question will undoubtedly divert political attention away from serious policy change. Reinforcing this is the fact that the SNP Government has not given poverty and inequality much of a priority in its first two years.

Any serious efforts to be world-class will be undermined if we simply waste the talent and potential of 20 per cent of our people: if comparable situations don't exist in Scandinavian countries, why should this unacceptable state of affairs exist in Scotland?

Poverty continues to cast a long shadow over our claims to be modern. The frustration of the contented is likely to increase as they press governments for help as mainstream services are affected by the austerity coming in the aftermath of the crisis in public finances. As the margins of existence become tighter for the contented, there is a real danger that the political will to help the disadvantaged will decline.

We need to shift focus on the inequality question. While we have rightly been investing in the social aspects of poverty and inequality, we have been less concerned with the economic issues. Learning and education, improving social mobility, building confidence and aspiration and economic opportunity are key to a new deal for hundreds of thousands of Scots. The achievement gap must be closed.

The narrative must be about economic inclusion and this requires a much greater intellectual and political effort to confront entrenched attitudes as well as demanding new modes of thought and behaviour. As a policy national inclusion will value a million people as an economic asset that could contribute to our economic output.

At the same time, we could reduce the financial burden of supporting the generational workless, promote a culture of reduced state dependency and greater individual responsibility. The idea of two nations living in the same country is not sustainable. Against these social and economic demands, the importance of a more productive and competitive economy becomes more pressing. Again without that fundamental shift, we are likely to content ourselves by opposing cuts and maintaining the size of the public sector, rather than seizing the opportunity of addressing the economic weaknesses that are endemic in our economic and industrial policies.

Part of this debate will be whether we need more economic powers for Scotland or whether we should leave it to Westminster. Accepting that globalisation and Europeanisation are now the key determinants of UK economic policies, there is still scope for debate on whether Scotland's economic needs are being adequately met from London. So far, the devolution debate has failed to focus on the simple issue, that by devolving more economic power to Scotland, Wales, Northern Ireland and the English regions we stimulate independence of thought, motivate areas out of their dependency on London and devolve more responsibility to for dealing with the economy. Surely a new approach would provide Scotland with the impetus and dynamic to tap the potential of Scots in a more direct and immediate way.

Is there a Tipping Point?

In his book *The Tipping Point*. Malcolm Gladwell puts forward his take on what creates change in a modern society. The theory of Tipping Points is a very simple idea which requires us to reframe the way we think about the world. Gladwell believes Tipping Points are a reaffirmation of the potential for change and the power of intelligent action. His central thesis is that the world around us may seem like an immovable and implacable place but it is not. We are powerfully influenced by our surroundings, our immediate context and the personalities of those around us. He argues that with the slightest push in just the right place, it can be tipped.

What, then, is the thinking behind his view of how change can be created? For Gladwin it is the best way to understand the emergence of fashion trends, the ebb and flow of changes that mark everyday life and to think of them as 'epidemics', ideas, products and messages and behaviour that spread like 'viruses'. The epidemics such as this share an underlying pattern: they are all clear examples of contagious behaviour; their distinguishing characteristic is that little changes have big effects; and the changes happen very quickly.

In looking at change in Scotland, of particular interest is the notion that the tipping point is the moment of critical mass when the unexpected becomes the expected and where radical change is more than a possibility, it is a certainty.

Continuing the analogy with epidemics, Gladwin outlines some detailed thinking which is very relevant to our debate in Scotland. The three rules of epidemics or agents of change are Law of the Few, the Stickiness Factor and the Power of Context. The Law of the Few relates to bringing people together, accumulating knowledge and having skills. Stickiness is all about the product, the packaging and the sell. The Power of Context is important as activity is sensitive to the conditions and circumstances of the time and places in which they occur.

Within Scotland, change can happen but it needs the conditions to be created. Change can emanate from the top or evolve from the bottom of nations, institutions and communities. Change needs to be relevant and intelligible. Change needs to inspire and enthuse. Change needs leadership and outcomes. Change needs a message and a positive medium. Change needs new thinking and new behaviour. Change needs confidence and courage.

The expenses crisis at Westminster could be described as a shock to the system and a tipping point but, while we have all the factors that might occasion a radical shift, we still need all of the concepts outlined by Gladwin if radical reforms of our constitution, politics and governance are to be anything more than an angry public and press outburst about MPs' expenses.

Our potential tipping points for change in Scotland are:

- The prospect of further constitutional change – federalism and independence
- The economy – the banking and financial crisis and recession
- Major problems in critical parts of our society
- People becoming disillusioned with materialism and the grudge and grievance society we have – a search for a deeper meaning to life
- Climate change, global warming and the carbon footprint
- The breakdown of trust and confidence in our politics, governance and democracy
- Cuts in public expenditure and concerns about dependency
- Poverty and the politics of inequality
- A new politics involving a realignment of parties and more consensual politics
- Inspiration from other countries and more attractive models of solidarity and enterprise – the Scandinavian experience?

These issues – potential tipping points for change – may individually or in some combination generate the momentum for change. There is clearly enough evidence in Scotland to convince us that change is both inevitable and desirable.

Bridging the aspiration and achievement gaps should be a logical focal point for a nation that wants more success, more prosperity and an end to our enduring problems, including poverty. Consensus on ideas, rather than confrontation around ideology, also makes sense. We do have the ability to make choices but do we have the courage? Political, business and social leadership is absolutely critical.

A nation of contradictions; thinking one thing and doing the other

What we say, what we think and what we do are often contradictory. This could be explained as just part of politics being the art of the possible, as we give way to realities in the face of problems that seem impossible to solve. It could be the politics of contentment, where enough of us are comfortable and feel there is little point in making a bigger effort. It may also be a lack of leadership, vision, courage and confidence. We may deny the existence of a problem in the hope that something will come up to make it better. We could be failing to appreciate the significance of issues and problems and the real damage they are causing to our society. More likely, is a combination of factors.

These questions lie at the heart of our political, cultural and ethical dilemma in Scotland. Do we have a split personality and face multiple ways at the same time? Do we fail to appreciate that being world-class is about focus and a clear direction and having the collective will to do the unpopular, the difficult, the challenging and the long-term instead of the comfortable?

Sadly, it's this short-term approach is now characteristic of our political culture. We have reached a critical point and seem unable to see how abnormal and unacceptable this behaviour would be in other countries. We are normalising the abnormal and fitting it to our way of life. Issues and problems nudge along incrementally, as a consequence we fail to see how thing are worsening or to see in objective terms how bad things are; as a society we let things slip and do not appreciate their significance.

We abdicate our responsibility and leave it to others – the police, social workers, teachers and doctors – to deal with problems that individuals, families and communities should also be dealing with. A nation is in denial when the abnormal is accepted as the normal. We seek crisis responses from professionals to deal with the symptoms but rarely tackle the underlying causes.

- Why do we have a reputation for a strong work ethic following on from our early Calvinism but allow so many people to be idle and workless? Do we have a problem not so much of welfare-into-work but welfare *instead* of work?
- Why, when three-quarters of crime, criminals and victims are found in one quarter of our local government wards, are we still doing little to tackle the root causes of crime and criminality in these communities?
- Why, when our prisons are filled with people with drug and alcohol problems and mental and physical illness, do we have so few treatment facilities and concern for their health issues?
- Why, when our prison re-offending rates are so high, are we putting so many people in prison when faced with evidence that for a large number of people prison does not work and places us out-of-step with every other western European country, except England?
- Why is it that, when our nation is awash with drugs and we are a world embarrassment in terms of alcohol consumption and when drink is driving domestic violence, crime, 'yob' behaviour and taking such a toll on our health, do we seem outraged to be asked to make some concessions on our drinking habits for the good of Scotland ?
- Why is it that, faced with an escalation of knife-carrying and knife-using, we allow vicious knives and weapons which can only be used to harm to be sold on our high streets with no licensing, identity or age-check being carried out? And in this area of policy, who needs an air rifle in this day and age? What is it to be used for? Why should Westminster not allow us to ban them?
- Why, in a country that claims to be correct and Christian, do we have some of the highest incidences of teenage pregnancy, domestic violence, knife crime, violent crime, antisocial behaviour, alcoholism, male suicides and teenage violence in Western Europe?
- Why, in a country that lauds 'the lad o' pairts', 'the democratic intellect' and our much-vaunted education system, is nearly one in seven of our population functionally illiterate?
- Why, in a country that prides itself on its socialism, collectivism and the history of heroic struggles in steel, shipbuilding and coal and the heroes of red Clydeside, do we have in 2008 one of the widest inequality gaps in Western Europe and some of the highest levels of deprivation and exclusion?

- Why is it that in terms of a world class economy we have such low growth rates, low rates of productivity, an overall lack of competitiveness and a low rate of business formation and, despite having record low levels of unemployment and high levels of employment. we have large numbers of people who can work who won't work and make no contribution to our economic effort?
- Why, as we face a crisis of rapidly increasing numbers of children with obesity and morbid obesity, are we closing down opportunities at school for exercise, fitness and health?

These are only snapshot examples of our inherent contradictions which speak volumes of a nation that is self-contradictory and unsure of itself. Clearing up inconsistencies and pursuing sustainable and honest politics requires us to have a sure sense of national purpose and well thought-out policies. We need to confront the consequences of confusion and contradiction.

Even accepting the range of excuses – legacy thinking, learned behaviour and innate conservatism – it is hard to escape the conclusion that in failing to address these contradictions at the heart of our social order, we are leaving some of Scotland's most intractable and enduring problems to worsen over time.

A better life for Scotland will not be reached without the will to change how we think and behave and in viewing the bigger picture we need to acknowledge certain realities:

the nation state is too big for the smaller things and too small for the big things. That is why the United Kingdom will continue to cede more powers and authority to the European Union and will devolve or share more powers with Scotland. The political and constitutional debate will continue creating uncertainty but with the prospect of a more sensible and settled structure in the longer term.

Globalisation holds out the possibility of more uncertainty but also enormous opportunities as national borders and boundaries give way to more interdependence and interconnectedness. This new global order requires Scotland to be adaptable, innovative and entrepreneurial.

We need a richer and much more intellectually challenging public debate to achieve sustainable politics and a more expansive vision for Scotland in the first quarter of the 21st century. To bridge the aspirational and achievement gaps necessary for success we need a 'new Enlightenment'.

Scotland has to free itself from the negative consequences of history and start to promote national self-interest and self-belief. Converting to a positive case for change will challenge the political classes to the limit. Insecurity and the desire to feed a habit (don't break the mould and don't over-reach) are typical of a national attitude which values dependency over personal independence, solidarity over enterprise, public over private, caution over risk, and a Scotland that has difficulty with success.

In other Western European countries, which had change forced upon them by the forces of history, modernity and success have been more enthusiastically embraced and celebrated. Conditions which may have been appropriate for different period in our history now lack relevance and resonance in a fast-changing world.

There are real choices to be made. There is no doubt that the positive aspects of collectivism are important in any progressive society but we have reached a point where the dominance of the state, public provision, dependency, the power of government and a blurring of rights and responsibilities are holding us back.

Scandinavia provides different models where powerful and well funded public provision lives successfully with a much more innovative and enterprising culture. The US model is one of minimum welfare or solidarity with a real emphasis on enterprise, individualism and entrepreneurship. The UK model, of which we remain part, provides an example where solidarity and enterprise co-exist in an uneasy relationship.

Scotland has a chance to pursue a new model which combines the positive elements of collective provision but with a new approach to enterprise and the entrepreneurial economy. By looking at the process in this way, we are breaking new ground in our consideration of change in the context of understanding the condition of Scotland in 2009 and the challenges we now face.

The priority areas for change are:

- We have to be focussed on change and innovation, our thinking needs to be wider and deeper and we need to be comfortable with ideas and create an inquiring and challenging society.
- The constitutional challenge and the extent to which our current set-up serves our needs and is fit for purpose or whether we need to have a new settlement which sees Scotland with far more autonomy but still within a new and modern Union. Does our relationship with the Union and England demand independence? Put simply, what is the best political configuration for Scotland to progress, create a higher standard of living for all and win world-class status?
- We need to locate enterprise and entrepreneurship at the heart of Scotland's thinking. It needs to permeate our national psyche and, like the Scandinavians, it must be more comfortably linked with solidarity.
- Dependency is becoming a corrosive and constraining aspect of our

national life which impacts on our thinking and makes us less able to deal with the new economic order. It distorts the debate about rights and responsibilities; it weakens individuals, families and communities and makes us less resilient. This is about more than 'the public sector' or 'big government' or 'high taxation or 'public spending', although these play their part. It is a way of thinking which is deeply embedded in our subconscious, diminishes the spirit of our nation and puts us out-of-step with other successful countries.

- Bridging the aspiration gap and, in turn, the achievement gap.
- We have to start taking our demographics seriously, especially the reduction in those of working age and the predicted rise in the number of older citizens. These have significant implications for shifts in voting power, the undermining of economic growth and significant increases in social, pension and health costs.
- Learning is the key to success in the knowledge society, both for a civilised approach to life and a successful economy. It is also the principal route out of poverty.
- A million Scots on or below the poverty line are symptomatic of lack of social mobility, social and economic exclusion, poverty, deprivation and the social aspiration gap. This deserves new thinking and new initiatives.
- Economic performance requires improvements in competitiveness, productivity, growth, small business formation and removing the culture of worklessness in parts of Scotland.

TREATMENT: We need a richer and much more intellectually challenging public debate to achieve sustainable politics and a more expansive vision for Scotland in the first quarter of the 21st century.

Our new world view is about the power of ideas and, within the context of change, altering attitudes to overcome powerful cultural and character obstacles in our path.

Scotland has to break free from that debilitating cycle of being complacent-comfortable-compliant-contented-conforming and replace it with a more virtuous cycle providing challenge-courage-consensus-collaboration-choice. Scotland has to free itself from the negative effects of history and start to promote national self-interest and self-belief.

Making these changes reality will challenge the political classes to their limits. Insecurity and the desire to feed a habit (don't break the mould and don't over-reach) are typical of a nation which values dependency over personal independence, solidarity over enterprise, public over private, caution over risk and has difficulty with success. To bridge the aspirational and achievement gaps, we need a 'new Enlightenment'.

CHAPTER FOURTEEN

The Social Aspiration Gap

CARRYING ON AS WE are in Scotland may be 'okay', but will do nothing to bridge the social aspiration gap. On the one hand, there is our enlightened past, our industrial history, our human resource potential, our world-class assets and our aspirations. On the other, our current and more limited achievements and underperformance, our undistinguished international performance relative to many social and economic indicators and our some-what hesitant, negative and uncertain attitude.

Reinforcing this limited world view is a set of seemingly intractable, complex and enduring problems, hardly helped by a growing and profound pessimism of the public in relation to the political process, politicians and governance. The complex constitutional issues now surrounding the future of Scotland's relationship with the United Kingdom and our uneasy rela-tionship with new ideas, new thinking and the issue of change only add to our national dilemma.

The social aspiration gap is defined as the 'future we aspire to and the one we will create if we rely on current modes of thought and behaviour' – a concept created by the Royal Society of Arts (RSA) in London. We accept that in certain specific areas of national life, such as medicine, bio-sciences, education and technology, renewables and financial services, Scotland is a world-class performer. But this book addresses the bigger and wider issue of achieving that status in Scotland as a modern nation reflecting a mood of confidence and self belief (national self worth) as well as being perceived internationally as having a brand which others recognise and respect (global worth). The work of the RSA represents a new way of looking at this com-plex reality and poses the fundamental question: 'what do we need to do to create the future we want?'

The new global challenges are based on the two issues of the population explosion and the new world economy. Bridging the aspiration gap in Scotland holds out the prospect of helping us understand better: what we need to do to anticipate and cope with change; what the results of change would be; and, in the process, outline what Scotland would be like in the future, what specific benefits would be achieved and for whom.

We should not under-estimate the challenge of change. In a complex and competitive world: change is hard, demanding, threatening and challenges our innate conservatism. Change requires inspiration, innovation and enthusiasm. It calls for dramatic time scales and deadlines, especially in a climate of intense and intensifying competitiveness. Change needs leadership, focus and discipline, change needs self-belief, self-confidence and self-esteem. Change in the new world order needs a new world view and a new sense of purpose and role for Scotland. Change is difficult to start and difficult to manage.

It is much easier to be complacent and comfortable. However, we are getting by – but for how much longer? It is one thing to believe and aspire to a new vision for Scotland; it is much more difficult to escape from current modes of thought and behaviour and deliver. For change to happen a certain number of important factors have to be in place and all the evidence from other successful 'change' countries suggests that this 'transformational mix' or 'aspirational elixir' doesn't just happen but has to be carefully created.

Transformation of this order is not just a matter for the political or government class or a ruling elite but has to involve the wider society. This, of course, raises some basic questions about the processes, purpose and potential outcomes for our country. How was Scotland's current outlook shaped over the centuries? We have looked at this journey from the Reformation, the Union of Parliaments and Crowns and the Enlightenment through Industrialisation, Empire, two World Wars to more recent times where our knowledge society builds on some remarkable changes in technology, finance, industry and communications in an increasingly interdependent world.

This is also a world where our survival, security, stability and prosperity are under threat from new global phenomena including terrorism, climate change, poverty and various extremisms and fundamentalisms.

How well placed is Scotland to respond to these new realities? Have we the incentive to change? Are there qualities that set us apart from other Nations? What are our positive traits which are often understated and undersold as we let ill-informed criticism and negative sentiment overwhelm us, dominating our national temperament and psyche and undermining our national mood and morale? What will it take to bridge this aspirational gap in Scotland, acknowledging that we are talking about a diverse society and a complex economy? Are we dealing with 'a civic renaissance' or 'a new Enlightenment' or 'coping with a post-bureaucratic state' or 'social and economic transformation' or all of these?

Francois Rischard in his book *High Noon – 20 Global Problems, 20 Years to Solve Them*, published in 2002, provides some valuable thinking and insights. The book develops outlooks for dealing with the new global order as well as presenting ideas we can use in understanding and interpreting the current challenges facing Scotland.

Rischard seeks to bring clarity to the debate and provide explanations for some of the most difficult issues facing the modern world. He argues that there are two big forces at work, bringing spectacular changes to the planet and which have very significant implications for society at the start of the 21st century. First, the sizeable population increases, already stretching global resources and manifesting themselves in higher oil and commodity prices. Second, there is the new world economy, which is driven by a technological revolution and an economic revolution.

Rischard suggests the new forces affecting human institutions as they try to adapt are: the struggle of the nation-state and the blurring of boundary lines between the public sector, business and civil society.

Existing international, European, UK and Scottish approaches are not delivering solutions to the urgent global issues facing us. Indeed, it is not clear whether we recognise, understand or appreciate their urgency. The problem is that most of the players tend to think along traditional and often obsolete lines, but there is much we can do if only we think differently and imaginatively.

As Rischard argues: 'Never have there been such massive opportunities for improving the human condition. Yet never has there been such uncertainty about our ability to grasp these opportunities'

He suggests that the population increase and the new world economy will bring a long list of stresses besides some striking opportunities.

These stresses promise a sort of crisis of complexity as societal issues become more intricate, the rate of change truly breathtaking, and institutions more and more handicapped by the snail-like pace at which they evolve. In Scotland one of the big issues is raising the game of these institutions and particularly those in charge of governance.

Like the authors of this book, Rischard states that his book is very optimistic but he also says that traditional thinking and behaviour will not do. We agree and this represents one of our central beliefs for our vision of a new Scotland. This reflects the discussion of the social aspiration gap where the RSA states that we cannot rely on 'current modes of thought and behaviour'. The focus has to be on changing Scotland's way of thinking and behaviour if we are to embrace the future, deal with intractable problems, tackle the new challenges and secure a world class standard of living and quality of life.

Like the authors, Rischard states that his book is very optimistic but he also says that traditional thinking and behaviour will not do. In the discussion of the social aspiration gap, the RSA states that we cannot rely on 'current modes of thought and behaviour'. We agree and this is central to our vision of a new Scotland.

TREATMENT: Current thinking is not delivering solutions to urgent issues, neither fast enough nor effectively enough. The focus has to be on changing Scotland's way of thinking and behaviour if we are to embrace the future, deal with intractable problems, tackle the new challenges and secure a world-class standard of living and quality of life.

CHAPTER FIFTEEN

The Power of Ideas

Here I stand at what is called the Cross of Edinburgh, and can,
in a few minutes, take fifty men of genius and learning by the
hand
WILLIAM SMELLIE, editor of the first Encyclopaedia Brittanica

THE POWER OF IDEAS should be a central thread running through the fabric of Scottish society. The Scottish Enlightenment in the 18th century represented the most creative period in the history of our country with an outpouring of ideas and new thinking on a remarkable range of important subjects. We need a new and modern Enlightenment, linking knowledge and imagination and transforming Scotland into a more significant and consistent player in the decades that lie ahead.

Unlike the Enlightenment of the past, where elite discussion and debate took place amongst a brilliant few in Glasgow and Edinburgh, we need to introduce the inquiring spirit, the search for objectivity to every level and every aspect of society especially education.

Utilitarianism has created a curriculum which stifles free-spirited and creative thinking. Learning and confidence go together and Scottish education should be focussed on the thinking citizen not just the doing citizen. There are too many good minds going to waste in Scotland; every child and every adult has to be part of this renaissance.

Our economy and society are becoming more complex and change is likely to pose a threat to institutions. The rate of change required in Scotland will contrast starkly with the slow evolution of human institutions, whether they are nation-states, government departments or other large organisations.

Human institutions are struggling to respond to global forces because many organisations, especially those responsible for public governance, were never designed for the changes that are taking place. The real challenge is to raise the response of the human institutions and this will be hard to do. Institutions, more wedded to custom and practice and convention, are even more resistant to change than individuals. So there are two crises to tackle: a crisis of complexity and a crisis that arises as government struggles to respond to these complexities.

Nation-states are struggling. From as far back as the Peace of Westphalia in 1648 when each country was governed as its ruler desired, nation-states and the concept of national sovereignty have been constantly evolving. Francois Rischards captures the essential tension between Scotland, the Union and the EU when he says, 'The nation-state is a territorial concept defined by a geographical border. In simple terms, inside a physical territory you find a political system, and environmental system and an economic system. When the nation-state is firmly in control of all three, the sovereignty meter is at 100 – although in reality this condition has probably never existed.

'For decades, this has been the basis of the world order. This is now changing. There is a new reality. What is happening now – and what will be happening more in the next twenty years of intense change – is that the two big forces of demography and the new economic order will take the economic system and the environmental system outwith national borders. As this happens the political system decupled from the other two systems ends up weakened. The sovereignty meter falls to 50- again, as a figure of speech.' These forces are operating on a truly global basis but for the United Kingdom and the 'Union' there are two further important and far-reaching factors which have implications for the future of politics and governance in Scotland. First, the European Union is now a supra-national entity with 27 nation-states and a population of 500 million. Second, sub-national government has devolved significant powers and responsibilities from Westminster to Scotland, Wales and Northern Ireland.

Within the 20 issues that can be described as inherently global, but having implications at every level, there are three categories: The first has to do with cross-border effects and the physical confines of our living space, usefully described as the 'global commons' concerned with how we share our planet. The second has to do with social and economic issues of global concern, whose solution requires the critical mass that only global coalitions can achieve. These issues have to do with how we 'share our humanity'. The third deals with the legal and regulatory issues that must be handled globally. These issues are concerned with how we 'share our rule book'.

In the emerging global order, sharing becomes a more important part of the diplomatic language and reflects the interdependency and interconnectedness of both the Nation-State and the different levels of sub-national government. Scotland's current position in the United Kingdom does reflect our history and shared experiences with England, Wales and Ireland in a well defined political space for the last 1,000 years. Increasingly, though, Scotland's future will be shaped by the bigger picture of global and European issues and the changes they will generate. The preoccupation of our country with all things to do with England and the Union will inevitably change and the prospect of being part of a wider and more substantive agenda must be matched by a rise in the political and intellectual level of our constitutional debate.

At present the debate about Scotland's future is depressing and fails to embrace any sense of urgency as the world changes and demands higher levels of national ambition and determination. We have to free ourselves from the real or imaginary shadow of England and the complacent positions we too easily adopt.

A simple test of this would be our ability to see independence and the existing devolution settlement as merely two options amongst many, rather than the battleground for endless and limited exchanges between ideas of the past which fail to measure up to a changing world.

Twenty Global Issues
Twenty Years To Solve Them

Sharing our planet; Issues involving the global commons
Global warming
Biodiversity and ecosystems
Fisheries depletion
Deforestation
Water deficits
Maritime safety and pollution

Sharing our humanity: Issues requiring a global commitment
Massive step-up in the fight against poverty
Peacekeeping, conflict prevention, combating terrorism
Education for all
Global infectious diseases
Digital divide
Natural disaster prevention and mitigation

Sharing our rule book: Issues needing a global regulatory approach
Reinventing taxation for the twenty first century
Biotechnology rules
Global financial architecture
Illegal drugs
Trade, investment, and competition rules
Intellectual property rights
E-commerce rules
International labour and migration rules

European Issues

Adopting the approach of Rischard, we can look at the shape of the agenda facing Scotland in the first half of the 21st century. The scale of the challenge in the different political spaces is dramatic and clearly reinforces the view that a new mindset will be a great asset but not necessarily a guarantee for achieving positive outcomes. Without a doubt, being positive not negative, being global and European in our thinking as well as local and being innovative and adaptable not inward-looking, will be essential qualities in our march towards progress and prosperity.

The 20 European issues highlight the major areas of interest which Scotland will have to navigate and be part of if we are to fulfil our national objectives and understand where the drivers of change are likely to be of most significance. This approach raises some fundamental questions about the extent to which Scotland's involvement in Europe has to be stepped up. Put simply can Scotland just remain dependent on the UK for its European involvement or does it need to secure more concessions from the Union to expand more direct links with the EU and the benefits to be gained from being at the heart of Europe.

Other sub-national governments in the EU have more involvement and this suggests that the new global order will continue to have significant implications for the way we structure our democracy and our governance. Westminster shows little signs of responding to either the demands of an ambitious EU or the social, economic or environmental needs of Scotland, Wales or Northern Ireland. The question is whether Westminster has a plan for a different and bolder future or merely responds in a grudge-and-grievance way when reality catches up with it.

A Europe of 50 nations and with an EU comprising 27 of them will continue to expand its influence in the world and will undoubtedly be hugely significant for the future of Scotland. This is the positive reality we face despite the efforts of much of the press, insular politicians and some political parties who promote a dangerous notion of nationalism bordering on xenophobia. There is no room for any of this in the new era for Scotland. There can be no doubt that the 20 European issues we have identified will have a huge impact on Scotland and will create further pressure for change and soon.

---

20 EUROPEAN ISSUES

The Lisbon Treaty
Migration – free movement of people
Continuing Enlargement
Neighbourhood policy and the Mediterranean Union
Agriculture, Fisheries and Maritime Affairs
Environment – Global warming and climate change
Employment and skills and Industry
Energy, including renewables
Human Rights
Regulatory Instruments
Democracy in Europe – more powers for the parliament
Sub-national government and Scotland's future role in Europe
EU and US relations – where does Britain's future lie – Atlanticism or Europeanism
Regional policy
European legislation and parliamentary scrutiny
Trade and competition
Food safety and consumers
Institutional Affairs
Internal market
Innovation and information

United Kingdom/Union Issues

The United Kingdom is going through a process of change and an inevitable transition that is social, economic and political. Against a background of a banking and financial crisis, recession and record levels of debt, multiple awkward questions are posed for a Government and Parliament that appear at times to be poorly equipped to respond.

Failure to deal with the realities of a multi-cultural society intensified by immigration, Islamic fundamentalism and terrorism, an ambivalence towards the EU exacerbated by migrant workers and growing anti-European sentiment and recent events at Westminster concerning the expenses row, suggest the Union has a personality or identity problem which raises doubt about its ability to change.

The highly centralised nature of the Union; the make-up of its key institutions, Westminster and Whitehall; the London-centric focus and the serious failure to learn the positive lessons of devolution are real problems for a Union that has to adapt quickly to a rapidly changing and at times threatening world. What is beginning to look like a crisis of confidence engulfing our democracy, governance and politics has significant implications for the ability of our political institutions to deal with the issues we have identified.

The Westminster Parliament, recently described as 'a gentleman's club' and 'planet Westminster' has serious institutional problems: preciousness, exceptionalism, a narrow view of sovereignty, an obsession with Britishness in a nation of diversity and a failure to distinguish between nationalism and nationality are likely to prevent speedy progress to a better political place.

---

20 UNITED KINGDOM ISSUES

Constitution
A voice for England and /or devolution for England
Scotland at Westminster
More powers to Holyrood
War on terror and preserving human rights and freedoms
Asylum seekers
Immigration and migrant workers: Home Office and Scottish priorities
Britishness, multiculturalism, Islam and Muslim communities
Energy especially nuclear, oil and renewables
Transport and infrastructure
Regulation
Employment, unemployment and Labour Market policy
Welfare and pensions
Economy
Broadcasting for four nations
Climate change, Carbon and global warming
Devolution settlement and Barnett
Wider constitutional reform
Taxation and public spending
United Kingdom and the European Union

Scotland Issues

The Scotland agenda comprises five distinct themes. First, there are a large number of enduring, deep-seated and seemingly intractable social and health problems. Second, a range of obvious economic problems exist, which despite being well documented, seem impervious to serious and sustained improvement. Third, there are constitutional and political issues still seen in the context of 300 years of history and 10 years of our new parliament: a debate now centred on the future of devolution, the Union and the need for a new politics. Fourth, there are the issues surrounding Scotland's role on the world stage, the idea of Scottishness and our global diaspora. Fifth, the issue of inequality remains high on the agenda and regardless of the language used – social inclusion, poverty, disadvantage, exclusion, distressed communities – this remains one of the most corrosive and divisive issues in Scottish society.

Transformation is not easy but for Scotland to succeed we need a revolution in our approach and thinking. Contradictions, flawed assumptions and fictions, complacency, myth and make-believe, negativity and narrow thinking, culture and character all combine to hold Scotland back or blunt the edge of a nation of talent, aspiration and world class assets. A shared agenda built on shared ambition is the best way to build 'Scotland the brand' at home and overseas.

---

20 SCOTLAND ISSUES

Economy, growth, productivity, innovation and competitiveness

Inequality, social and economic inclusion, deprivation and social mobility, employment, unemployment and the workless

Rights and responsibilities, the family and the individual

Transforming dependency and the role and size of the State

The public sector and enterprise versus solidarity

Constitutional change: Calman – what next?

Scotland on the global stage

The Union and England

Social agenda, comprising some issues that are embarrassing in Global terms

Health

Demography and the challenge of age

Institutions and governance

Learning, literacy, knowledge and reforming education

Democracy and the political process

Intolerance , bigotry, sectarianism and class divisions

Crime and punishment

Alcohol, drugs, substance abuse

Environment, energy and carbon footprints

Communications and information technology

We have to move beyond traditional thinking if we are to achieve in Scotland a shared prosperity, a sustainable future and a more serious effort to tackle inequality. In all of this, our institutions have a central importance in creating the conditions for change.

Yet government institutions are particularly resistant to change and we have a distinct propensity for too many agencies and institutions, scant oversight of performance and outcomes and, once set up, a reluctance to remove or modify. The 21st century will require a different approach.

TREATMENT: Solutions and strategies required to deal with the Scottish agenda need a variety of inputs, including financial investment, institutional change, new thinking and leadership. Are our institutions and political systems up to the new challenges?

More important, though, is the need to be honest with ourselves and recognise that, after our long journey through history, we need to distinguish between what is positive and should be retained and the negative which needs to be dropped. Our desire for Scotland to be a world-class nation will require a scale of effort unprecedented in our post-WW2 history.

CHAPTER SIXTEEN

A New Society

A quality of life unbecoming for 21st-century Scotland.
Joseph Rowntree Foundation report on child poverty in Scotland,
May 2009

FROM THE FIRST PART of the book, it is clear that Scotland has significant social problems which in an absolute sense are deep-rooted and not easy to solve. Equally worrying is that many of our problems provide grim reading as far as global and European comparisons are concerned: we are at the wrong end of international league tables. At the heart of policy making, we again seem to suffer from the confusions that bedevil a great deal of Scottish society.

Social policy requires investment and the extent and availability of finance can make a huge difference to the myriad of problems we face. Scotland, though, suffers from two problems not necessarily found in other countries.

Despite spending large sums of money, we seem to find it hard to base our policy on evidence and often end up doing things that do not result in positive outcomes. We find it hard to turn political rhetoric into practical reforms. And in our adversarial politics we suffer from a dated political tribalism that takes comfort in rhetoric rather than reality, ideology not ideas. The principles and values that drive our political debate are firmly rooted in our culture, character and a bleak view of humanity and human nature.

The list of problem areas is long – health, crime and punishment, prisons, alcohol, teenage pregnancies, young male suicides, domestic violence, violent crime. The way we respond to most of them is out-of-line with modern practice in other Western European countries. If being out-of-line was consistent with better policy outcomes and more enlightened treatment, Scotland would be a utopia! But in Scotland that is not the case as we continue to debate, legislate and spend in ways that beggar belief.

Too often, the views of the public are cited to justify the need for these policies, when in fact all the evidence suggests that the public have more common sense and fairness than some vocal members of the political classes. The more significant player in influencing views on many areas of social policy is the media and, in particular, the red-top tabloids. Always negative, often angry and hysterical headlines scream from the newspapers in a way which is not found in other European countries and certainly not in Scandinavia.

The most obvious example is prisons policy, where being punitive and looking for humiliation of offenders is the mark of a vengeful society. Evidence-based policy is often ignored; in the fevered atmosphere created by populist politics and certain sections of the Press.

This is most evident in the coverage of crime where the language used is primitive, the tone is merciless and there is little or no concession to the underlying causes of much of the offending and little appreciation of alternative policy other than the crude equation crime=punishment=prison. Again, why should this be happening in Scotland and not found anywhere in Europe beyond the UK?

Our culture seems to be content with an approach which demonises offenders, takes a hard and uncompromising approach to punishment and seeks to heap the maximum amount of revenge and humiliation on the offender. This 19th century-style thinking does not work but, more importantly, leads other countries to question whether we are a nation which on the surface is progressive and modern but deep down continues to exhibit the principles and values of a darker side of Scotland's past

What prevents us from learning from our European neighbours? (England has major problems of crime and punishment and are in no position to advise anyone.) This raises the bigger issue of two insular and inward-looking countries, time-warped in their thinking, both unable and unwilling to change failed and embarrassing policies and determined to keep both countries in the lower leagues of sane penal policy.

We have failed to transfer some of the more progressive ideas from the various models in Finland, Sweden, Denmark and Norway. Finland, in particular, with a similar size of population and some tough times behind it after the collapse of the Soviet Union in 1991, has half the prison population we have. Their criminal justice system is based on punishment but with the focus on treatment and rehabilitation and an acknowledgement that people offend but that, in turn, this is often the result of a wide variety of other causes and conditions in society.

When we look at the cause-condition-context continuum of social policy in Scotland, we start to get to grips with the serious issues of poverty, inequality and their concentration in specific areas of urban Scotland. There is a link with between our societal issues and the level of poverty and inequality in modern-day Scotland. Factors such as physical and mental ill-health, poor diet, poor health, crime and offenders, alcohol, drugs, substance abuse, teenage pregnancies are all found in many of our poorest areas.

Social policy in Scotland remains confused and underpinned by inconsistencies and contradictions. We have some of the most progressive and liberal thinking on issues like stem-cell research, abortion, civil unions, embryology and, more recently, gay ministers in the Church of Scotland but in many areas of social policy which cut deep in the psyche of Scots and touch a cord with old values and beliefs we seem like another culture. Often, fear becomes an important part of the mix and this becomes difficult to break down. The brighter and darker sides of Scotland seem to coexist without much difficulty.

We have the eighth highest level of alcohol consumption in the world; it is our drug of choice but we cannot accept that everyone should be part of the solution. We have one of the highest prison populations in Europe but cannot agree that sending most people to prison doesn't work. We have the lowest age of criminal responsibility in Europe but are only now doing something about it. Three-quarters of our prisoners and crime comes from one-quarter of local government wards in Scotland and yet we find it impossible to accept that the conditions of poverty and inequality are responsible. We are rightly angered and upset by horrific child abuse cases and demand the best services and highest standards possible but tend then to publicly abuse, smear and tar all social workers in child-care with the same brush, driving many of them out of the profession.

It is also hard to escape the conclusion that an old Poor Law mentality operates in terms of the 'deserving' and 'undeserving'. Scotland is inclined to make value judgements about people and groups rather than make decisions on objective need.

Much of the way social policy is dealt with by the political parties results in wasted investment, poor returns and outcomes, confusion, mixed messages and global embarrassment. The adversarial nature of the political process is getting in the way of effective decision-making in many areas of public policy. Poverty linked to inequality remains the 'elephant in the room' and, without concerted action across party political lines, improvements will be slow and begrudgingly received. Bi-partisanship is not a feature of politics in Scotland but it is now needed so that important and practical reforms can be achieved across a very wide-ranging agenda.

Approximately 21 per cent of children in Scotland are living in poverty, according to a report published in May 2009 by the Joseph Rowntree Foundation, which said that despite earlier progress over the last decade in reducing child poverty – reductions were greater in Scotland than in other UK regions – levels have stalled since 2004/05: 'Children already living in poverty must be protected and households with child poverty must be enabled to move beyond a quality of life unbecoming for 21st-century Scotland.'

It stated that the Scottish Government could do more to reduce child poverty in Scotland and recommended a wide range of policy measures, from increasing the availability of affordable childcare to encouraging the Scottish Government to look seriously at defining and paying a living wage. Joint author, Stephen Sinclair of the Scottish Poverty Information Unit at Glasgow Caledonian University, said: 'The political opportunities to end child poverty in Scotland are potentially greater than in many other parts of the UK. This places a huge responsibility on the Scottish Government to do all it can to achieve the target of eradicating child poverty by 2020.'

Specific measures suggested for implementation by the Scottish Government included:

encouraging employers to create more flexible jobs which allow parents to combine work and care responsibilities; increasing access to affordable, flexible childcare; providing in-work support and advice to help parents remain in employment.

However, the authors acknowledged that some measures required to reduce child poverty in Scotland are beyond the current devolved powers of the Scottish Government. The UK and Scottish Governments could work more closely together to improve anti-poverty interventions, including reducing the benefits trap by allowing greater overlap between employment and benefit entitlement and exploring opportunities to adapt UK Government welfare reforms to local labour market conditions.

John McKendrick, also from the Scottish Poverty Information Unit at Glasgow Caledonian University, said in the report: 'These are challenging times for everyone. More than ever, there is a need for all levels of government to focus on what must be done to eradicate child poverty in Scotland.'

The politics of Scotland can change but for that to happen we need to focus on: learning from other countries; providing investment; tackling inequality; cross-party debate and co-operation; sensible and responsible media coverage; a modern viewpoint; more adaptable and effective institutions and – the most significant of all – leadership. 'Scotland the brand' can be enhanced by a radical and reforming agenda of social change.

TREATMENT: To achieve social change in Scotland, we need to learn from other countries, provide new investment, make existing interventions more effective and radically readdress inequality. This requires cross-party debate and co-operation; sensible and responsible media coverage; and – the most significant of all – leadership.

CHAPTER SEVENTEEN

The Economy

SCOTLAND'S ECONOMY in its present form represents the outcome of centuries of significant achievements, the ebb and flow of growth and investment, political and constitutional change, the age of Empire and in the 19th and 20th centuries the creation of huge industries in coal, steel, shipbuilding and heavy engineering. Post-WW2, investment was concentrated in manufacturing and electronics, largely based on inward American investment.

More recently, our economy in the final part of the 20th and early 21st centuries has faced new difficulties and setbacks.

The decline of our heavy industries demanded change and Scotland's economy has been transformed in the last three decades. Faced with challenges from the European Union, globalisation and in more recent years devolution, Scotland now seems set to embark on a new era, building on the achievements of recent years and tackling a new agenda of problems and opportunities in what is likely to be a tough, competitive and rapidly-changing world.

It is worth highlighting again that global population growth will put enormous pressure on the world's resources. The new economy created by globalisation, international institutions, international finance, the remarkable changes in information technologies and communications and the rise of China and India will be the demanding backdrop for Scotland's attempt to progress and prosper.

The Scottish economy is presently combining traditional sectors such as financial services, tourism and hospitality, drinks manufacturing, services, transport and energy with new and emerging sectors such as bioscience, medicine and health care, renewable energy, creative industries, education and a whole new green industry based on reducing the carbon footprint, climate change, global warming, energy efficiency and sustainable living.

In terms of the economy and employment, the public sector in Scotland is very significant with positive and negative consequences. The size of the sector, the proportion of GDP it consumes, its cost to the taxpayer, its levels of productivity and employment have become part of the debate about Scotland's future.

Four other issues can be linked to this: the implications for Scotland's growing dependency on government; our ambivalent attitude as a country to enterprise and entrepreneurship; the tension which seems to exist between the public and private sectors; and the debt crisis facing the UK government with the threat of an austerity era looming ahead. All are likely to impact on the future of the public sector and services.

Consistent with the line taken in this book, we must be hard on weaknesses inherent in the economy but it is worth pointing out that in certain areas of the economy we are doing well, by any international standard, and are world-class in areas such as bio-sciences, renewables, medicine and medical research, computer games and technology.

It is also important to remember that we live in interesting times. A global banking and financial crisis, the deepest recession in a generation, high and fast-growing unemployment, a debt crisis occasioned by fiscal stimulus, bank bail-outs and low tax revenues, and now a crisis of political confidence, mean that the next decade will present a trying time for the Scottish economy, in addition to any culture or character problems we have picked up on our journey through centuries of economic and industrial development.

Solidarity or enterprise – or both

Our approach to our economy has understandably been influenced by history and the business and industrial cultures which have emerged as part of our building, trading and exporting experiences over many generations. Certain characteristics are now evident which pose some real anxieties for Scotland. The overall business and enterprise culture is vitally important, both for the success and for the direction of the economy. Aspects of our current approach need to be reformed if we are to emulate best practice in the successful economies of the world.

Enterprise sits uncomfortably with solidarity in the eyes of many Scots. It is hard to understand the issue but if we look at other countries there are different balances achieved between enterprise and solidarity (terms which have become the two poles of overall economic strategy.)

The solidarity of the European Union (in which the UK and Scotland are generally included) is contrasted with the United States which is seen as more enterprising. However some of the Scandinavian countries manage to combine both.

The knock-on scenario looks like this: Scotland has been reluctant to embrace enthusiastically the concepts of enterprise and entrepreneurship, which in turn hits on our propensity to be both risk- and success-averse. This leads to comments about the lack of innovation and ideas and is reflected in on our large public sector, where the state is a large proportion of GDP, a major employer and a focus for dependency.

A consequence is that we need to provide for and service an expanding welfare community with large numbers of able-bodied generational workless. Resulting notions of inefficiency and waste deter private investment, leading to greater dependency on the State and more tension between public and private, suggesting big unions, over-regulation and red tape, throwing up soft and complacent employer organisations too cosy with governments, with young people and students turned off by employment and engagement with private enterprise.

That the prevalence of a solidarity mentality in Scotland is, therefore a defining issue in assessing whether Scotland is indeed up to the economic tests of the future.

Power to do better

Employment becomes a crucial factor in the economy. Much of the increase in employment over the last 15 years has been in the public sector due to an unparalleled boost in public investment from 1999 to present time. This expansion is now likely to be at an end and employment levels may start to fall as the era of spend gives way to an era of austerity. These changes will also impact on the private sector. Another area of contention is the generational workless and the low levels of workforce participation rates in certain areas of our cities.

We have a real conflict between compassion, Calvinism and the notion that the taxpayer should support people in self-enforced idleness when jobs are still available and will be even more so as the recession ends. This contradiction involving Scotland's work ethic highlights the acceptance of welfare and dependency at the heart of our employment policy.

This would not be the case in a truly modern nation which would have a presumption against generational worklessness affecting individuals, families and communities alienated or excluded from paid employment. Welfare dependency is a challenge to our notion of a modern Scotland where the value of work, training and education is key to personal as well as national success.

There are real tests for the government of Scotland as we attempt to repair weaknesses in our economy that have resulted from cultural weaknesses. Strong leadership on the direction and content of our economic strategy is vital.

For efficiencies sake we must clear away the vast number of business development agencies in Scotland.

Other countries like Ireland and Finland do not have this problem. What they have and we do not have is a national consensus on the importance of the economy, organisations that understand the importance of constant change in modern economies and cross party agreement on a national purpose and national direction. For them, long-term thinking is essential. To ensure success they give a higher priority to learning, education and the demands of the knowledge society with its embrace of global communications technology and the use of the internet for learning and confidence building.

The Scottish Government and Parliament need new economic and financial powers.

For example, the Scottish labour market faces different pressures in terms of declining numbers of the working-age population, fewer young people and a need for migrant workers. So for employment and labour market concerns, as well as home office policy as it affects migration and welfare policy, there are compelling reasons why Westminster should see the need for a new look at the Scotland Act.

The Calman Commission ought to be bold about change; Scotland needs more say over its economy and areas of policy that could help boost jobs and prosperity.

The UK is too big an economic entity to be hypersensitive to the multi-national set up that exists within its boundary. As an explicitly multi-national state (indicated in its very name) created in successive unions of England and Wales in 1536, with Scotland in 1707 and with Ireland in 1801, the UK was never a unitary state. Changes that are taking place throughout the world should encourage us to argue cogently for a further restructuring of the Union. In this context, Europe provides some new thinking especially in terms of economic powers. A new strand of thinking in Europe is based on the idea of 'adding value' to existing structure, territorial politics and sub-national government. This allows us to look at the United Kingdom and the process of devolution through the prism of the 'competitive region or nation'.

In the post-war period up until the early 1990s, the economy, industry and unemployment were the main drivers of regional policy. Since then, the nature of the debate has changed but social and economic disparities and inequalities between different parts of the UK remain an important priority for the Westminster government. Its ability to influence events has significantly diminished, however, as a result of international and European economic change, the impact of the global rule-book and the new economic order.

In recent years, a new political dynamic has been evolving which has seen the European Union take more trade, environmental, business and regulatory powers from London to Brussels and at the same time we have seen London cede some limited economic powers to Edinburgh.

Faced with these new challenges and the accelerating pace of change, there is a very positive case for the Union to be more flexible and modern and to look upon the nations and regions of the UK as having more economic potential, if only they could be given more responsibility and powers to lessen their dependency on Westminster and Whitehall.

The UK, in its present form, is too big and too set in its ways to deal with the new economy and we need instead to give parts of the UK the freedom and the powers to set goals and new priorities. The UK one-fix-for-all no longer makes any sense.

This solution sees competition between different parts of the UK but, in turn, these areas would be complementing the economic drive at UK level.

This form of economic federalism also opens up new political solutions as devolution inevitably progresses. There is abundant evidence from other countries that creating competitive regions and cities and different tax approaches based on local economic needs works. The UK remains highly centralised and, outwith Northern Ireland, Wales, and Scotland, there is only administrative devolution to the English regions. If the highly centralised UK adopted a more enlightened economic approach it would not only release the energies of each part of the UK but in turn create this new dynamic – an approach that would not only advance the regions but boost the productive and competitive potential of the UK as a whole.

For this to happen, we need to recognise that globalisation and European integration have forever changed the psychology and practices of economic intervention, subsidies from the centre and top-down initiatives.

The new global order has also transformed the economic landscape and, in a world without borders and barriers, there is no reason why economic power cannot be devolved downwards from the centre as well as being ceded upwards to the EU. This radical reconfiguration of economic power should lead to new economic structures in the UK. Each part of the UK has to take more ownership of its economic destiny, be more competitive and – in partnership with the UK as a whole – make a bigger and more sustained contribution to tackling economic exclusion, poverty and employment growth.

As the UK overcomes the banking and financial crisis and recession of 2008–9 and looks to build forward and learn lessons, this approach could provide the window of opportunity for bold and radical ideas. There is always the danger, though, of becoming trapped in a climate of fear and insecurity about future economic prospects leading to a cap on new thinking: this has to be avoided.

This new thinking is especially relevant to the emerging economic climate, dramatically accelerated by the information and communications technology revolution, in which the development of human capital through learning, education and knowledge becomes the driver of economic success. The potential for this exists in every part of the UK and in many respects Scotland is better placed than most.

Inspired and enthusiastic political and business leadership is required to tap the UK's potential in the emerging economic climate. The unlocking of these untapped reserves of intellectual energy, enterprise and entrepreneurship can only be done by empowering the regions and nations of the Union through new thinking on economic policy. It requires a belief that there is capacity and the leadership for these nations to be full partners in tackling enduring problems and the new challenges, some of which we can only imagine.

This 'competitive' dimension to devolved government is absolutely vital if we are to see any change for the English regions. It is frequently argued that the English regions lack the clear-cut cultural and community identities and historical characteristics that help to define Scotland, Wales and Northern Ireland and entitle them to a special status within the Union.

The English regions do have many distinct characteristics, qualities and differences but, regardless of this, there is undoubtedly a case to be made for more devolved economic powers and responsibilities being part of the solution to the English question, while at the same time helping to reinvigorate the UK economy. After all no-one has ever argued that a lack of specific historical characteristics will actually prevent an area getting better government and a more responsive economic policy!

A wealth of academic work now points the way and there are excellent examples throughout Europe and the USA of progressive approaches to the new economic order and the challenges of the knowledge society. The UK is out-of-step with progressive thinking elsewhere and has so far failed to grasp the essential and fundamental issue that political and economic devolution will strengthen a Union, not weaken it.

Backing the case for change there is overwhelming evidence that, despite a long period of economic growth, stability and high employment levels, the key fundamental of the UK economy lag behind other countries in Europe and the USA. More importantly for this narrative, Scotland lags behind the UK in a manner which has been both consistent and worrying.

At the same time, the gap between the income levels of the rich and poor continues to widen, while real problems of social and economic exclusion remain. Crucial drivers of change such as demographics, migrant workers, public investment, technology, environment and learning are posing urgent challenges for every part of the UK including Scotland.

TREATMENT: Find the balance between enterprise and welfare, recognising that generational worklessness is a waste of a human resource, as well as a social evil. De-clutter the business and industry scene. Above all, more economic powers for Scotland.

CHAPTER EIGHTEEN

It's the Economy *AND* Devo, Stupid!

DEVOLUTION SHOULD BE a way of thinking as well as a way of governing. The devolution debate includes the future of the economy and is about facing up to new challenges, not a fight to retain exclusive status for a Westminster and Whitehall operation which needs reform if it is to be fit for purpose in the 21st century. The culture of big and centralised government always seeking to control and direct and unwilling to let go is deeply embedded in the UK. Devolution is about more effectively realising the potential of all of the UK and providing the best form of governance to achieve that. Devolution is the solution, not the problem – and centralist diehards need to realise this.

Devolution runs with the grain of decentralisation, empowerment and decision-making at the lowest appropriate level. It is about responsibility, confronting people with change and choice and the consequences of action or inaction. Although many at Westminster refuse to accept the obvious, it goes without saying that there are inevitable consequences and requirements for this new way forward.

In order to work well as part of the economy, devolution depends upon the 'new politics' of consensus and must be about more cross-party cooperation on the most pressing issues; bipartisanship and practical policy making for pressing problems. It is a suitable response to the changing nature of political spaces and the constantly shifting distribution of economic and political power and responsibility at global, European, UK and regional levels. Devolution requires every part of the Union has to be engaged in the task of tackling more effectively the strategic issues of productivity, growth, competitiveness, workforce participation rates, business formation and innovation while at the same time building confidence and self-belief.

In a telling and deeply incisive commentary about Scotland Michael Keating says: *'The hesitancy looks like a legacy of Scotland's recent institutional past, in which politics, culture and economic development were for political reasons kept in separate compartments. Scotland is still presented as a place where things might happen rather that a dynamic society giving birth to distinctive forms of social relations and collective action. Labour is still reticent about invoking Scottishness as a mobilising force for fear of giving heart to the Nationalists and jeopardising the Union. The nationalists for their part cling to Scottish independence as the solution to the nation's problems without attending too much to nation building and the challenges of globalisation and European integration.'*

Politicians do not address how a sense of nationality and identity might be mobilised to pursue social, political and economic ends within the nation-state of the United Kingdom or to face the challenges of globalisation beyond it. Gradually, however, an understanding may be emerging about the relationships of culture, economics and politics and the need for a distinctive Scottish synthesis. Seeing the future economy and devolved government as integral to each other gives more credence and relevance to the arguments for further constitutional change. The economy should be a bigger part of our political renaissance in Scotland.

Putting the economy at the heart of further constitutional change will put Scotland in a far stronger position as new challenges emerge. The aftermath of the credit crunch, bailing out the banks and the recession should focus us collectively on the need for a new sense of national purpose and strategic direction which delivers solidarity in terms of shared experiences and a vision for the future alongside an enterprise and entrepreneurial culture free from a dependency culture and the self doubts of the past and with a greater respect for the well-being, spiritual and material, of every Scot.

What needs to change? First, there is no guarantee that the current levels of jobs (with the current security and pensions on offer) in the public sector can be maintained. This looming period of hardship beyond 2011 is likely to pose real challenges to every aspect of public provision, none more so than in Local Government where there are nearly 300,000 employees, one in eight of the working population. We need productive and efficient public services and, for the first time in at least a decade, some soul-searching will have to take place about priorities and the role of public services in key areas of our national life.

There has been a debate in England about reforms but to date there has been little discussion in Scotland post-devolution about the future of public services. Debate is long overdue and requires us to focus on the vital role public services play in a modern society – such as Norway, Sweden and Denmark – and how they can be modernised, renewed and made more cost-efficient. The debt crisis facing the UK government should be seen as an opportunity to think aloud and be more imaginative about the future of public services.

We have to recognise that we are a trading nation that depends on the two-way flow of people, goods and services. Exports are key and more must be done, particularly in the new areas of knowledge, learning, education and skills. No country owes us any form of preferential treatment and, if globalisation means anything, it is fierce and unrelenting competition. In terms of our nation output, the debate must move away from focusing on manufacturing. Our reluctance to see ourselves as a services nation is a real problem. We still have the hang-up of 'real jobs' from our traditional heavy industries and manufacturing history. Scots tend to see service as servility and linked to a range of other negative characteristics. This attitude poses real problems because we are an economy heavily dependent on the service sector for employment and increasingly in terms of our national wealth.

Our national economic culture needs to refocus on the growing base of sectors – traditional manufacturing and the new creative industries – whose products can be traded in world markets.

Scotland must face the harsh truth that our levels of productivity, growth and competitiveness, with certain exceptions, are not world-class or even European class. These are long standing problems in Scotland, probably made worse by a large services sector, both public and private, with low levels of productivity and efficiency and this has reflected badly on Scotland's balance sheet. Raising our levels in these areas will be difficult.

Our reluctance to see ourselves as a services nation is a real problem. We still have the hang-up of 'real jobs' from our traditional heavy industries and manufacturing history. Scots tend to see service as servility and linked to a range of other negative characteristics. This attitude poses real problems because we are an economy heavily dependent on the service sector for employment and increasingly in terms of our national wealth.

To improve our most basic economic indicators we need a quiet revolution throughout the Scottish economy which lays particular emphasis on excellence, higher standards, greater productivity and production, innovation, vastly improved skill levels and greater rewards for workers in contributing to these improvements. This will represent the fusion of individual self interest and national achievement.

World-class standards require long-term commitment not short-term responses but there has to be something in it for all the players. We are not good at providing incentives which will generate positive and sustainable results.

The size of the state and the consequential effect of creating greater dependency on Government for employment and services is a problem. Some of the Scandinavian countries seem to have a better balance in providing extensive levels of high-quality public services, supported by high levels of tax and popular public support, without a growing dependency culture stifling individual freedom, self reliance and concepts of family and community responsibility and initiative. This area of public debate is often seen as political and value-driven from a left or right perspective. But the issue is much more practical and deserves to be at the heart of any debate on the idea of a renewed sense of national purpose in Scotland.

Education and learning remain powerful and positive aspects in our search for a more fulfilling future for our country. In higher education – universities and the college sector – we have real achievement and potential to develop. There are, however artificial and unhelpful attitudes within the sector which reflect again some of our learned behaviour and legacy thinking. A two-tier mentality exists within the university sector and between them and the colleges.

Parity of esteem should prevail but this is effectively blocked by a residual class-based notion at the heart of education. Each college and each university in different ways contributes to society, employment, tolerance and under-standing and the search for truth and objectivity and in the process providing students with inquiring attitudes. Learning for life and the knowledge economy require a much more integrated approach where the two parts of the sector combine more effectively in the national interest. Steps are being made along these lines but progress is slow.

There is also a need to co-operate in Scotland so we can compete more effectively internationally. This is a sector that is vital to Scotland's long-term future and while each of the seventy institutions involved need to be conscious of being more efficient and being able to reorder their back office functions to put more resources in front line delivery, it should continue to be a high priority for increased long-term investment. This is neither helpful for students or for the economy. Sweeping away unnecessary baggage is an important part of building for the future.

In all of these areas, economic and business leadership becomes vitally important. We can 'get by' and our world may not collapse if nothing changes in Scotland: the 'muddle through' approach. There is also the danger that after the seismic shock of the banking and financial crisis, a recession and a political crisis at Westminster, people feel more insecure and fear for the future resulting in an atmosphere in which change becomes less likely and much more difficult to achieve.

But the drive for modernity has to permeate every level of society through a more inclusive approach and ordinary people need a sense that their con-tribution is being valued and their individual efforts will make a difference to national well-being. Leadership is left to the political classes – not always the best guarantee that wisdom and judgement will see us through!

The realities of Scotland in 2009 demand a different approach. The Scottish community and its workers will not think differently, work harder or have a greater sense of national purpose if they have no incentive to greater commitment and enthusiasm. The psychology of this is fundamental; Scotland will not change unless individuals feel that there is something in it for them. That may seem like self-interest but it is nevertheless fundamentally important.

A barrier in the way of this progress is the exclusion and exclusivity that are rampant in Scottish society. We are far more class-based, unequal and income-differentiated than we care to acknowledge. This matters to make 'one nation' inclusive economics and politics a reality. Scotland is brimming with talent but what is important is to acknowledge and celebrate it, to reverse the national tendency to deprecate success.

Massive opportunities lie in dealing with big global issues. A good example of this is the new climate/energy era. The new global order is rightly concerned with energy security, climate change, global warming and reducing our carbon footprint: issues that are complex and inter-related but have the potential to save the planet and create a jobs revolution in a green and sustainable world. We are at the forefront and in a very real sense we can lead the world in protecting our planet while at the same time creating jobs. This idea is both inspiring and transformational – but has yet to capture the imagination of Scotland.

Currently much of this debate is over the heads of people, there is a limited grasp of its potential, politicians argue on the margins and the transformational benefits are in danger of being lost. The future presents incredible opportunities; a sustainable economy, a low carbon footprint and a renewable energy, energy efficient country all create jobs. Do we really lack the imagination, confidence and leadership to get this ethical jobs revolution underway?

Radical reforms can turn rhetoric in to realities. Scots have shown throughout history that we have the qualities and characteristics to transform our country much more that we are currently doing. Enlightened self-interest backed by self-worth and self-belief are key to a new approach. A new politics reinforced by a new social and economic activism is the way forward.

The national 'glass half-empty' mentality will not do. Young people, as yet untainted by this, should be seen as agents of change, optimistic, full of energy and enthusiasm and the potential to have different views of life and the world. They have the potential to be different Scots.

TREATMENT: One of our negative national character traits is to caricature, stereotype, categorise and label sections of society in terms of problems, burdens and dependency. This makes little sense when we need to focus on realising potential and nurturing attributes. Scotland's greatest asset is its people and the future wealth of our nation is in that human capital.

CHAPTER NINETEEN

Scotland and The World

'SCOTLAND IN THE WORLD' is a concept that is vital for our social, economic and political well-being in the 21st century. We are now at the point where being international, interconnected and interdependent is the path to success.

Devolution has given our nation a new status and a new role within the UK. Yet after a decade of devolution, we have still not thought through what we do with the international dimension. We still wrongly regard Scotland's role on the world stage as the property of the UK.

The SNP Government has certainly expanded the level of thinking and activity in relation to our international role but we are still not doing enough to re-examine our attitudes and our approach to the UK, Europe and the rest of the world. To do that, and to take advantage of the exciting opportunities presented to us as a nation, we must first change the national image we present to the world.

In his book *How The Scots Invented The Modern World* Arthur Herman wrote: *'Being Scottish turns out to be more than just a matter of nationality or place or origin or clan or even culture. It is also a state of mind, a way of viewing the world and our place in it.'*

He goes on: *'We often complain that Scotland's place among nations deserves more exposure than it gets – but these complaints have an ironic, rather than a beseeching tone and we seem to take a perverse pride in being so consistently under-estimated! That must change.'*

Scotland's self-image is governed by our levels of self-esteem and self-confidence yet the traditional and often highly sentimental perception of our national identity overseas often becomes a reason for complacency and an excuse for not changing. Inside and outside the Scottish Parliament, there is a collective complacency, a lack of awareness and a lack of urgency in addressing the remarkable changes that are taking place around us.

There is much more that can be done in the Parliament, in Government and in the country that has nothing to do with the Scotland Act, but has a lot to do with aspiration and optimism. Even with foreign affairs being a reserved matter, more can be achieved abroad on Scotland's behalf.

The urgency of the situation must be recognized. While we are drifting into the 21st century the rest of the world is surging forward. We need to anchor the debate on the future of devolution and embrace four important factors: devolved federalism within the UK; the new regionalism of Europe; new models of social and civic development in Scandinavia, states of America and elsewhere; and economic restructuring.

This new regionalism/sub-national government is an issue of increasing importance to Scotland. We should be looking ahead to when there will be a powerful regionalism in Europe and a potentially different United Kingdom with federal devolution. All of this is taking place alongside supra-nationalism, political and economic integration in Europe, the transformation of the nation-state and the revolution in information technologies. This is a powerful dynamic which we need first to understand and then prepare for.

Within nation-states and within Europe. the idea is growing of the competitive region, so that regions like Scotland would compete for economic advantage in the UK, Europe and globally. Subsidies will have to give way to subsidiarity and redistribution will have to give way to competitiveness. These changes will have profound consequences for Scotland. The present danger is that we are not doing that.

Our current position is blinkered to looking no further than the United Kingdom and ignoring what goes on beyond its shores. But we now have the opportunity to build new alliances and relationships elsewhere in Europe and the world. What is needed is a substantive and strategic change in our aspirations, our selling of Scotland world-wide and understanding the challenges and opportunities that exist, especially in the US, Asia and Europe.

That requires us to free ourselves from the fiction that all roads lead to, or through, London. Of course, the UK brings us economic, social and political benefits but we can also have our own direct routes to the wider world.

We will also have to ignore the predictable knee-jerk criticism from ill-informed and short-sighted sections of the media who will attack the Scottish Government for 'hi-jacking' UK responsibilities and powers – as well as those at Westminster, who have always been hostile to devolution and will oppose further powers for Scotland.

For a small nation on the periphery of Europe to become a nation with a leading place in the world requires Scotland to have ambition, confidence and imagination. We cannot be content to sit back, wait for developments and react; we must look ahead, seize the opportunities and put Scotland in pole position to exploit those opportunities in our national interest.

Where does Scotland want to be – in the United Kingdom, in Europe and in the world?

The nation-state of Britain will have to acknowledge and embrace the growing impact of globalisation and the many aspects of the new Europe, supra-nationalism, enlargement and the further integration of the European Union and, in turn, the increasing pressures from the regions and the devolved nations of the UK. We think devolution is exceptional but it is really part of a worldwide process and *we* have to see ourselves as part of a new 21st century order.

Part of the solution is for the UK, one of the late entrants into devolution and regionalism, to make another significant constitutional shift and adopt a form of devolved federalism. It would also have to mean constitutional safeguards for power-sharing within the United Kingdom and competitive status for each British region.

There is an inevitability that the United Kingdom will have a form of devolved federalism sometime in the future. There *will* be regional devolution within England complementing Scotland, Wales and Northern Ireland, giving UK a symmetry which it lacks at the moment.

The United Kingdom remains out-of-step with the emerging Europe and there is an obvious need for a solution to the English dimension. That solution will be about shared power, not devolved power, and the UK government will have to think in terms of the regions and nations of the UK.

There will be pressure on Scotland as we face competition from these regions, with the recognition that economic problems cannot all be solved by government in London. The notion of the competitive region in a globalised world has still to take hold.

In all of that, Scotland will play a much greater part – and it is also inevitable that more powers will be devolved to the Scottish Parliament. Our financial regime will have evolved with more control over and responsibility for tax and spending. The Calman Commission report has given this an impetus which cannot be reversed.

In a truly devolved United Kingdom, there must be freedom for the Scottish Government to handle external affairs in areas vital to Scotland. Any rigid insistence that foreign affairs and Europe are wholly reserved matters must be met with spirited and intelligent resistance from both the Holyrood Parliament and the Scottish Government.

Initial post-devolution attempts to increase Scotland's role abroad (particularly in Europe) met with difficulties at Westminster and Whitehall where it was regarded as 'forbidden territory' for the Scottish Government. It was no surprise that London would seek to protect their responsibility for reserved matters; but, equally, it is the job of Edinburgh to assume responsibilities and powers that apply specifically to Scotland's interests.

Within the United Kingdom, there will be keen competition between regions and nations. That kind of competitive regionalism should be encouraged by the UK government as part of a macro-economic system that each region to develop to its own advantage. In the end, that will also be to the UK's advantage.

However, we may also want to form alliances with some of these English regions, Wales, Northern Ireland (and with the Republic of Ireland) in certain areas of economic activity. We are all on the periphery of Europe and by working together we can compete more effectively with other parts of the world – something which is increasingly commonplace in Europe. Put simply, Scotland must open up its economy and society to the outside world.

After the recent enlargement of the European Union, there are 27 member-states, Bulgaria and Romania have recently joined, accession talks will continue with Turkey, Macedonia and Croatia and, despite recent setbacks and growing concerns about further enlargement, we are likely to see membership of the EU increase over the next decade. There is the prospect of a significant number of other countries seeking to become members of the EU, some more likely than others including Norway, Switzerland, Lichtenstein and Iceland. The countries of the Balkans and countries which are part of the Commonwealth of Independent States formerly part of the Soviet Union, such as Ukraine, may also seek membership.

All of that could mean a European Union of 40 countries, one-fifth of all the countries in the United Nations, representing the largest single market with the highest economic output of any global regional grouping in the world. It will also be a Europe where the development of regionalism and sub-national government will parallel enlargement and further political and economic integration. The identity and nationality of the smaller nations and regions will matter even more and cultural, social and political diversity will be a Europe-wide strength.

Throughout Europe, the new regionalism takes many forms, as in the federal systems in Germany and Austria, the autonomous regions in Spain, and the provinces of Italy. What they have in common is that, while all are working closely with their national governments, they are also in Europe, building new relationships and alliances.

Cross-border co-operation can be directly established by the regions themselves without any involvement from the national or the supra-national authorities. There is a real growth in regional consciousness.

Already, there are serious questions to be asked about the representation of Scotland in the existing European Union. How can Scotland hold its own while Europe is expanding? How should Scotland participate in UK delegations and policy matters where Scotland has a dominant interest? How should our Parliament participate in legislation emanating from Europe? How can

Scotland build closer links with regions, autonomous states and provinces in an increasingly integrated Europe? Issues that were not dealt with by Calman will be the focus of the continuing debate on the future of Scotland and the Union.

An outstanding example of modern federalism working to the benefit of a region and Europe as a whole is 'the Free State of Bavaria'. The Bavarians have a clear idea of their status within the Federal Republic of Germany, while stoutly maintaining their freedom to act on their own behalf. Lest there be any doubt, they have adopted the aphorism of King Ludwig I: 'We want to be Germans and to remain Bavarians.' Could 'We want to be British and to remain Scottish' apply to the new Scotland?

The Bavarians have made a priority of participation in the European policy formulation, especially in relation to preserving Bavarian sovereignty and scope for political action as the bond of integration tightens and an increasing number of decisions directly affecting them are being taken at EU level. They have insisted that in Brussels negotiations, the Federal Government has to consult them and take into account their regional interests.

They have also have built up a network of influence and interest within Europe and aim to gain a place in the prospective markets in America, Asia and Africa through partnerships with California, Quebec, Sao Paulo, the Shandong Province of China and the provinces of Western Cape and Gauteng in South Africa (which includes Pretoria, Johannesburg and Soweto).

In Scotland, we have already embraced the concept of a 'Europe of the regions'. The 'Flanders Agreement' in 2001 opened a new chapter for Scotland in Europe without undermining the United Kingdom because it enabled the regions of Europe to build their own economic, social and cultural links. It illustrates that we can push out the boundaries and since then there have been further projects and partnerships undertaken.

Similarly, in Europe productive alliances can be created with individual regions with which we have much in common, in terms of key manufacturing sectors, financial services, environment, tourism, technology, education, learning and the knowledge industries and creative industries. Scotland has much to contribute...and much to learn.

On another front, 'social' Scotland can benefit from more direct links with Scandinavia and those northern European nations whose histories are similar to ours. These are increasingly sophisticated nations with the highest quality of life, enlightened and effective policies on health, housing, social services, citizenship and civic pride and innovative approaches to alcohol, drugs and social problems – all of special concern to Scotland – and highly advanced environmental policies, especially in renewable energy technology.

Scotland should also have a distinctive role, along with the United Kingdom, in the development of European policy. As enlargement and integration proceeds, there should be opportunities for Scotland to have a more significant say on matters that are presently the preserve of the United Kingdom government.

In Scotland House in Brussels, which promotes Scotland's governmental and non-governmental interests to the European Union, we have a model of Scottish representation abroad. It provides the vital two-way contact, allowing a wide range of Scottish bodies to access and influence the EU and to receive information and early alerts about European developments.

Why constrain ourselves to Brussels? Scotland House should be replicated in other European capitals and in Eastern Europe, where there is great potential for us in offering assistance but also exploiting opportunities in an emerging market.

Above all, Scotland should set an example to the rest of the UK with a much more pro-active embrace of Europe.

Taking our rightful place in the world will lead to rising standards of wellbeing and a better quality of life for our people. But before we take that place, we must have a clear idea of our mission and objectives. The new global and European context means nation-states like the UK can do less and less in terms of influencing the policies that affect its nations and regions. It is up to Scotland to do more.

Scotland has played an important role in the world and the presence of the Scottish 'diaspora' around the globe reminds us of that. This history of world involvement has reflected our traditions of internationalism, humanitarianism and in our passion for education all of which are captured in what can be called 'the Marseillaise of humanity', the Robert Burns song *Is There for Honest Poverty* with its timeless hope 'That man to man the world o'er Shall brithers be for a' that'.

The early 21st century will see the growth of supra-nationalism in which the world will be comprised mainly of large economic and trading blocs – the Europe Union, the recently formed African Union with its Pan-African Parliament, Latin America, the North American Free Trade Alliance and the Asian-Pacific grouping. Against that changing background, Scotland will need a strategic over-view, a more distinctive voice and a much sharper focus for existing international activities and reform in all Government departments and institutions in order to take advantage of international opportunities.

We have to extend our global reach and be prepared to act in countries like India, China, Japan and the United States; the countries which along with the EU will be drivers of the global economy.

An example is Flanders, a 'federated entity of the federal Kingdom of Belgium' with a population of 5.9 million and its own Flemish Parliament and Government with almost identical devolved powers to Scotland's. It has more than 100 different representatives abroad, including a special diplomatic representative to the United Kingdom with an entirely separate London office for a Flemish Government envoy, the Flanders Export Promotion Agency and a Tourist Office.

Scottish representation in the British embassy in Washington was an historic first for the devolved Scotland, now followed up by a First Secretary in our embassy in Beijing. There is no reason why there should not be a First Secretary for Scotland representing our interests at British embassies in other world capitals This can only be done on the basis of a deeper under-standing of Scotland's needs and our financial resources; being progressive should also mean being practical. This global network would complement but not duplicate the work of the United Kingdom; it would sell 'Scotland the brand' more directly abroad.

The 'diaspora' – our world-wide army of millions of Scots and those of Scots descent who are fiercely patriotic and want to be enlisted to help Scotland – is an under-valued asset. In many parts of America and else-where, the Irish community are high-profile, proud of their roots and energetic and active in promoting their ancestral nation's interests.

The Scottish exiles' love of country and pride in their ancestry should be recruited as the Irish have done so successfully in recruiting second- third- and fourth-generation Irish-Americans to present a traditional Irish image, combined with the impression of a modern, progressive and economically successful nation.

Without this radical reappraisal of our outlook on the world, Scotland will simply fall further behind.

A foreign policy journal in the US recently published its annual index of the nations setting the pace, based on four factors: economic integration, technological connectivity, personal contact (communications, travel, tourism, telephones) and political engagement. Before the global banking and financial crisis and the world-wide recession, Ireland ranked as the most global nation in the world for the third year in a row and, with the exceptions of US and Canada, the top ten slots were filled by smaller countries including Finland, Switzerland, Singapore and Denmark. If Ireland with a population of 3.5 million and other countries with smaller populations can be global players, why are we with our five million population not doing better?

In the past, Scots have turned blame and scapegoating into an art-form. The danger is that these become a distraction and create a sterile debate in which we avoid asking that searching question of ourselves: Why are we not better?

With the right answer to that question, Scots can be what they have been throughout the centuries – global citizens of this new world.

TREATMENT: It is all too easy to blame London and the powers reserved to Westminster, when the real fault lies in our lack of ambition to engage internationally. It would also be easy to seek a simplistic solution like Independence. But a simplistic approach will increasingly make little sense in the world we live in. We have the resources, assets and the talent; it is simply a question of attitude and leadership with a bold and confident new world view.

CHAPTER TWENTY

Scotland and the Union

*I ken, when we had a king and a chancellor and parliament-men
o' our ain, we could aye peeble them wi' stanes when they werena
gude bairns – but naebody's nails can reach the length o' Lunnon.*
MRS HOWDEN in Sir Walter Scott's *The Heart of Midlothian*

DEVOLUTION HAS CHANGED forever the constitutional and political face of
the United Kingdom. Since the setting up of the Scottish Parliament in
1999, the politics of Scotland have undergone a transformation and this has
impacted on all the political parties; in particular, the election of an SNP
Government in 2007 has had a profound effect on Labour.

Despite Westminster's lack of interest and, indeed, ambivalence towards
devolution over the past 10 years, the Union is facing enormous challenges
as it comes to terms with a pressing need for radical reform and renewal –
a new multi-national, multi-cultural and multi-ethnic political structure and
the need to have a vision of how the rapidly evolving process of devolution
could make more structural and constitutional sense in the 21st century.
These challenges require some form of political federalism to be at the heart
of the debate, taking on independence as one of the key constitutional
obstacles to be overcome if the Union is to survive.

Since the dramatic developments in Scotland in the wake of the 2007
Holyrood election, Westminster has taken centre stage. The problems facing
Prime Minister Gordon Brown and the Labour Government, the apparent
rise in support for the Conservative Party, the extraordinary fallout from
the Westminster expenses scandal, the banking and financial crisis and the
deepest recession in a generation have created a mood for political change
in an unprecedented climate of public outrage at the state of politics and the
performance of politicians in the United Kingdom.

In this period of political turmoil, Scottish Labour, UK Labour and the
Labour Government face far-reaching challenges to reform and renew their
platforms and policies and reconnect with electors whose social, economic and
democratic characteristics are changing – threats to their political hegemony
and credibility after 12 years of government in the UK; a political situation in
Scotland where Labour continues to be at a competitive political disadvantage
relative to the SNP and still finds difficulty in recovering from their defeat in

2007 and, as a consequence, has failed to provide effective opposition to an SNP Government that has gained in both confidence and popularity.

There are real strains and tensions underpinning politics in the UK and the fevered atmosphere which currently exists is not conducive to either sensible debates on the major issues of the day or developing a long term vision for either the Union or Scotland.

Does sovereignty matter?

This transfer of powers and responsibilities seriously affects the sovereignty of the United Kingdom but in a way which is consistent with other global processes and, in that sense, is both unsurprising and inevitable. The future of politics and governance in Scotland, and the consequences for the economy and the environment, will increasingly be played out on four interdependent platforms – Global, European, United Kingdom and Scotland.

Sovereignty, as we presently understand it will be imperilled and will assume new forms as the realities of change render redundant the increasingly abstract notion of the old nation-state. Scanning this new and complex political landscape will require Scotland to make more informed choices about how it manages its national self-interest and answer some uncomfortable questions about our thinking, our behaviour and the way we govern ourselves in this new political order.

There is a growing sense of malaise about traditional politics and politicians. The expenses crisis at Westminster has only served to highlight this widening gulf between the electors and the elected. The crisis has acted as a tipping point for further consideration and debate about our democracy, our governance and our political classes.

There is now an entrenched lack of trust and confidence in the ability of the political system to deliver for the elector and a growing cynicism about the inability of political and governance institutions to counter the often-perceived negative effects of global issues. This sense of political hopelessness and a belief that there is a growing disconnect between government and the governed mean that, for many, party politics has little relevance or meaning and the public now question whether the political system is fit for purpose.

Traditional politics is being shaken up; voters are more impatient and less tolerant; more prone to change political parties and traditional affiliations, allegiances and loyalties are crumbling. The class basis of political support is being replaced by more self-interest and small 'n' nationalism politics;

and party funding, membership and the narrow base of candidates for elections are increasingly under the spotlight as the relevance of what politicians do is being further undermined by global and European change.

The politics of Scotland may be a better bet at a time when global interests seem remote, complex and impossible to influence and localism appears as a more understandable, immediate and accessible antidote to the public fears. One thing is clear: the UK parliament is likely to be the loser in a situation where the effectiveness of a nation-state in the form of Westminster and Whitehall is increasingly losing out to other political spaces and strong currents of change.

There is a feeling that if existing institutions are unable to influence world events and the impact on people, then voting may become a minority interest and public concerns will find new expression outwith the traditional political process. Politicians and the political system are failing to understand the changes in society and the profound impact the Internet age is having on the volume, speed and intensity of the information and news now available to the public.

Surveys of young people show a great disaffection with the traditional political class. Young people pursue single issues which are more immediate and easily understood and they seek new forms of identity and solidarity, on a global scale, through the Internet using Face Book' and 'You Tube'. New forms of 'community' are being established and new concepts of global citizenship are being developed through new groups and networks using the Internet. Access to global communications is transforming our political systems and reshaping the political awareness of a new generation of young people.

Debates between left and right are losing their significance and are giving way to another form of debate between those who resist changes and those who see them as opportunities. Elements of the political right and left are often united in resisting changes. For them, issues of practical public policy are regarded as a distraction from the traditional political knockabout where ideology and narrow adversarial politics retain their fascination. Much of the political class is becalmed in a bygone age but the public has moved on and their views have changed: ideas not ideology; practical not partisan; cooperation not confrontation; public policies not party politics; solving problems, not settling scores.

Growing challenges to traditional politics are producing a kind of perpetual bad mood in political life. This is not helped by a broadcasting media and printed press which play a significant role in providing information, ideas and opinion to the public. Whether this adds value to the political process or the quality of democracy is an increasingly relevant question.

The debate in Scotland on a new politics will become an important influence on how we respond to change and how we view our relationship with our larger neighbour.

The Calman opportunity

The report of the Calman Commission on Scottish Devolution provides a real opportunity to take this debate forward but much of the initial response to Calman has missed the point. The real significance of Calman was not technical, not fiscal and not about powers. It was about politics. It gave the Unionist parties the opportunity to move forward the debate about Scotland's political and constitutional future: a debate currently dominated by the SNP.

The report's findings on finance and taxation are tentative and complex and the proposals on powers are hesitant and modest but that should not surprise anyone. It should not disguise the fact that Calman has moved the argument on and provided a more developed platform for the Unionist case: a new settlement founded on a new understanding of Britain's unwritten constitution.

For the first time in 10 years, the Unionist Parties in London and Edinburgh, have something to talk about. Calman has breathed new life in to the constitutional debate and, for Labour in particular, this is a 'get out of jail' card. The question is whether Labour, the Conservatives and the Liberal Democrats will seize the opportunity. More importantly will London allow this to happen?

The overwhelming significance of Calman is that it should open a debate that may result in a more relevant and sensible 'third way' alternative to Scotland's constitutional future. Calman has broken the log jam, by proposing partial fiscal responsibility and by proposing the transfer of more powers from Westminster. A form of federalism is now taking shape.

This is just the beginning but for the Labour party the next step could be enormous, breaking the mould of current practice with consequences for both Scotland and the Union. The Unionist parties cannot continue to contract out their political responsibilities to independent commissions, nor be seen to ride in the SNP's slipstream. There can be no decisions about finance and powers until the political parties have come up with a political and consti-tutional structure for the future of Scotland and the Union and Calman accepts this.

But the importance of the report has to be acknowledged in London, where the stakes for the future of the Union are high. Paradoxically, the impetus for the break-up of the Union may be created at the heart of

Unionism itself. Westminster could create the conditions in Scotland that bring about the very outcome they have worked for 300 years to avoid.

The key question is whether the Unionist parties can turn this into a genuine national conversation about Scotland's future and have the confidence to take ownership of the debate. The Prime Minister has embarked upon a programme of democratic and constitutional reform and renewal within the UK and the Calman report offers him a chance to give his full support to this new phase of change.

This new enthusiasm for constitutional reform and renewal, if genuine, is timely. Independence looks tired and dated and increasingly out-of-step with the global agenda and the new world view where interdependence and interconnectedness are key. Some form of federalism is now inevitable and if we move on the Calman recommendations, the doors to fiscal responsibility and new powers will open.

The constitutional debate is not about the SNP. The SNP is only part of the constitutional debate but if the SNP did not exist we would still need a debate on the future of Scotland and its role in the Union. *The SNP tail should not be wagging the constitutional dog!*

So far, the Unionist attitude has not provided an intelligent and enthusiastic advocacy of a new and modern Union, and Scotland's role in it, nor an inspired and forensic assault on the obvious shortcomings of Independence. Westminster's uncompromising refusal to contemplate any serious challenge to the Scotland Act and Scottish Labour's ambivalence towards moving devolution forward have no place in this new debate.

Informed opinion was right to be sceptical when the Calman Commission was set up. It seemed like a token response by the Unionist parties to the SNP Government's so-called 'National Conversation' on the proposal to hold a referendum on the break-up of the Union. The Westminster Government was also lukewarm in its support.

The majority of the Scottish people and the majority of the political parties do not support independence, yet the public still seem to be giving general support to the SNP. All roads do not lead to independence and Scotland's departure from the political Union. But, if the opposition parties and Westminster do not urgently embrace the new debate and new thinking, then all options will remain open. In other European countries, nationalist parties have become the default political position in sub-national level elections.

The 'F' word and other unmentionables

There are great unasked questions, probably because the political class are afraid of the answers: What are the scenarios for change, for both the Union and Scotland? How do we create and sustain an informed and inspired debate which is both attractive and intelligible to voters in Scotland and the rest of the UK?

What does the Union stand for? Is it fit for purpose and what does it mean in this changing world? Can it adapt to cope with a radically different future? Federalism in some form has to be the answer.

Our failure to grasp the bigger picture may be explained by a sentimental attachment to British history. Our British sense of exceptionalism, notions of power and out-dated thinking blind us to the new world of opportunity, where national and regional politics have enormous potential waiting to be tapped.

Other important factors are the 'English question' and devolution for the English regions: when will England and the English start to take themselves seriously and fulfill their need for more effective national expression? This as well as the Barnett Formula and the West Lothian Question, the unresolved reform of the House of Lords, European integration and devolution should all be part of the new agenda for constitutional reform promised by the Brown government.

Unresolved is the question of what the Union actually means in 2009. After 300 years of the Treaty of the Union, there is no reason why it cannot be re-assessed to give it a 21st century meaning, with a view to further radical change in the political, social, economic, monarchical and constitutional make up of the United Kingdom.

1536, 1707, 1801 an' a' that

The issue of the Union is not about whether it has been good for Scotland nor about the unions of 1536, Wales; 1707, Scotland; and 1801, Ireland. It is whether the Union in its present form is fit for purpose in the 21st century existing as it does against a backdrop of significant political change brought about by devolution, global and European influences, the shifting alliances and loyalties of the electorate and, for England, the need to tackle some emerging problems.

There are two fundamental issues: the politics of Scotland and the future of the Union. A Union, of limited devolution for Scotland, Northern Ireland and Wales and a Westminster obsessed with sovereignty and an ethos of power are now being faced with demands for more radical constitutional change, claims for shared sovereignty and for issues of identity, nationality and democracy to be dealt with in new and different ways.

A more flexible and modern Union may help focus public and political opinion on what the Union stands for in a modern society and at the same time put independence for Scotland under forensic examination for the first time. The United Kingdom comprises many unions not one: monarchical, political, economic, social, cultural and constitutional.

The Union, in turn, is part of other unions: UK powers have been transferred over time to global and European institutions. The UK now faces unprecedented tests of its authority in the form of multi-culturalism, multinational devolution and multi-racialism. Our governance structures have become complex and inadequate for the modern era and we live in a world where different levels of political space demand new structures and a different form of politics and democracy.

This is a time of incredible social, economic and political change but as yet we seem to lack the necessary urgency, inspiration or intensity in trying to comprehend its scale or its speed. The new world order and this new era of change also provide a useful prism through which to look at independence.

The SNP First Minister of Scotland has tacitly acknowledged this line of thinking with his comment that he wished to repeal the Treaty of Union but would leave intact the Treaty of the Crowns. This raises, then, questions about the social Union, the economic Union, the cultural Union and constitutional Union – and, in turn, the role of Scotland and the Union in terms of globalization and European integration. It begs the important question of whether the Union in its present form and the independence being promoted by the SNP have relevance for today's world.

Are there genuine alternatives? Recent developments have also highlighted the need of democratic renewal as well as reform of other aspects of our constitution. This represents a formidable agenda of democracy, political structures and politics, governance and constitution. Is Scotland ready for these challenges? Do we have the political will, the leadership and intellectual energy to effect change and help create world class structures and ideas? How do we recast the Union and re-shape the independence aspiration into something more meaningful for Scots?

The Calman Commission has breathed new life into the change process, taking the devolution debate into a new phase and it remains to be seen to what extent the Westminster government will sign up. It is developments in London that will ultimately decide the constitutional fate of the Union.

Political parties underestimate the growing importance of Scottishness and

Scottish interests and the declining importance of concepts of Britishness. Westminster must appreciate the significance of this and the reality that identity, diversity, nationality and some sense of sovereignty cut across or undermine traditional political and class loyalties and allegiances.

We are at the point where political structures for the future of Scotland and the Union have to be part of the political debate. The electors need some form to the political ideas and concepts they are discussing and the SNP benefit from a simple idea which is easily stated but is rarely understood fully. We should be talking about the 'F' word – federalism both as a workable option for the future of the UK, as well as an alternative to Independence.

As never before, politics north of the border is distinctive and volatile. There are grounds for cautious optimism for Calman which should be seen as contributing to the future of the Union – and not criticised through the narrow prism of the SNP and independence.

TREATMENT: We should have the vision and the sense of national purpose to shape our future rather than leave it to the circumstances and expediencies of the moment. The tendency has been to muddle through with the Union and other political issues as they are. We cannot leave it to the politicians; it is for the nation to make the choice by an act of national will.

CHAPTER TWENTY-ONE

Localism and Globalism

A VITAL PART OF OUR political system is local government but is often relegated to a postscript in the debate – but localism is often more important than globalism to the ordinary citizen who depends on councils for a range of cradle-to-grave services. Yet local democracy is clearly at risk in Scotland and there are real dangers that councils may be sleep-walking into more central control and a further erosion of local autonomy and independence.

An important part of Scotland's governance and a key institution in our democracy, local government has experienced a great deal of change as a result of the May 2007 elections. The introduction of proportional representation – intensely disliked by councillors, especially Labour caucuses who had been in long-term power across a broad swathe of Central Scotland – has altered the power structure of local government and the composition of every council in Scotland.

Labour's influence in local government has diminished as a result of PR and the SNP has now the largest number of councillors. There is a certain irony in all of this in that the Conservatives tried to destroy the power of Labour in local government by dismantling the regional councils, with Strathclyde the foremost target, and gerrymandering the boundaries of the 32 newly-created unitary councils. The real aim of destroying the Labour hegemony failed and it was left to proportional representation, a measure spurned by the Tories, to do that job in 2007. Paradoxically, PR has also allowed the Tories to remain a political force in both the Scottish Parliament and the councils.

What is more striking is the degree to which the SNP Government and local government have become so close and, as a result, the limited autonomy and independence of local councils is in danger of being eroded even further. This is more remarkable as there has never been parity of esteem, political warmth or much mutual respect between local government and either Westminster or Holyrood.

Local government is an important part of our social, individual and community provision and it has a role to play in economic development. Local councils deliver an extraordinary range of cradle-to-grave services. They employ over a quarter of a million people – nearly one in nine of the Scottish workforce. And in 2009/10, the SNP Government will be providing to local councils £10.8 billion in revenue funding and £1 billion in support for capital expenditure.

Recent events have highlighted the dilemma facing local councils. On the one hand, concordats and single-outcome agreements seem like a sensible way to deliver national policy outcomes. There are no constitutional safeguards for the powers and responsibilities of local councils. Change should always be viewed against the background of the balance between central control and questions of local democracy and accountability. Currently, over 86 per cent of local council spending comes from central government and there is now only a tenuous link between local budgets and electoral accountability – and no real link between raising finance and spending it. The introduction of a Local Income Tax would have addressed some of these issues but it has now been abandoned for the current parliament, which means nothing will happen on that front until 2011–2015.

What is of more immediate interest is the SNP Government's 'council tax freeze'. On the face of it, this is a measure that will keep local budget increases in check. To achieve this, central government provides a less-than-adequate amount of cash subsidy so councils can maintain the freeze. The costs of this exercise – politically and financially – are potentially significant.

First, councils are cutting services to meet this centrally-imposed freeze. Second, whilst this may have made political sense as a transitional measure in the run-up to the introduction of a local income tax, the fact this has now been shelved raises the question of whether this freeze makes any sense.

If it is to be permanent, who pays for the freeze? If it is scrapped, how will local councils handle the reintroduction of higher council taxes? Third and more significant, how can central government continue to set the budget level of every council in Scotland?

Put simply: why should central government seek to impose more centralised control and attempt to 'tax cap' local councils? Whatever happened to the protests we heard from local councils about 'rate capping'?

Devolution of power from Westminster to Scotland, Wales and Northern Ireland was about acknowledging difference and valuing and enhancing diversity. Local government should have the same freedom. If a council wishes to increase its budget it should be able to make a case to its electors and then be accountable to them at the ballot box for its actions.

At the heart of this debate lies the crucial issue of increasing centralisation versus independence and local accountability. Sameness should be regarded as antithetical to a vibrant democracy and innovative service delivery.

It is a curious fact of political life in Scotland that local councils in every part of the country and of every political colour are all willing, with little if any protest, to help an SNP government achieve a national political objective. This is a political game in which local government can only lose out.

Local government faces many challenges and will, amidst gathering storm clouds, have to make real choices about its future. Faced with the importance of council services, the large sums of public finance involved and the vast numbers of people employed, we need a new, more inspired and informed debate about the future of local government.

Perhaps a new urgency and sense of purpose will be created by the prospect of stand-alone elections in 2012; the cuts in public expenditure which will follow the credit crunch and recession; the efficiency savings to be imposed by the Scottish Government; the salaries and pensions liabilities of local councils; the impact of more and more legislative responsibilities; the dramatic demographic changes, especially the growth in older people and the need for 32 councils to be more enterprising and collaborative in the way services are delivered, priorities are defined and savings realised.

TREATMENT: Local government needs to take itself more seriously, to be more self-confident and open itself up to a more inclusive and comprehensive debate about its future. It needs to decide on whether it retains some degree of real independence or is willing to concede more and more power and influence to central government.

CHAPTER TWENTY-TWO

The Psychology of Independence

Although Scotland is not officially an independent state,
Scottishness is a recognised state of mind: sometimes an inde-
pendent state of mind, occasionally a theocratic state of mind,
frequently a confused state of mind –
ALAN BOLD, Scottish poet, author and artist (1943–1998).

IN THE CONTEXT OF THIS BOOK, the psychology of independence is important in terms of providing a 'shock to the system' provoking Scots into
taking ownership of their own destiny and being able to tackle deep-seated
problems, without being dependent on anyone else nor blaming anyone else
for shortcomings.

The question for Scotland is whether, without some dramatic event, a
new level of economic and social performance can be achieved. Could that
event be a collective decision of the Scottish people to become independent,
regardless of the financial and economic conditions of Scotland? Could that
really be what it takes to become world-class and confident?

Another important consideration is whether it is possible that a future
Westminster government might be willing to cede independence before they
will cede sovereignty or share sovereignty with Scotland.

Sovereignty has become so deeply embedded in the DNA of Westminster
that a growing impatience with Scotland and the different political culture
which is emerging could, with the ascendancy of right-wing thinking and anti-
Scottish sentiment within the Westminster bubble and the media, create a
mood in which sacrificing Scotland or ceding independence would be preferable to ceding sovereignty.

This may be dismissed as a scare-mongering scenario, impossible to
imagine with Gordon Brown and a UK Labour Government; but it could be
conceivable under future administrations and a new Prime Minister, particularly with Scotland contributing nothing to a Tory majority and English MPs
representing the interests of four-fifths of the people of the United Kingdom.

In such a situation, it might not be Alex Salmond and the SNP who take
Scotland out of the Union; the break-up of Britain could happen at
Westminster. This is thinking the unthinkable...but it is sometimes as well
to do so.

Thus, the role of the Union and Unionist thinking remains a powerful factor in the politics of Scotland. It is why we have to widen out the debate in Scotland, Wales and Northern Ireland to the whole of the United Kingdom.

In working out the implications of all of this, we also have to factor in developments in Europe, where the sharing of power and sovereignty are more common and the issues of multiple identities, diversity and plural nationalities are fully understood. They are accepted aspects of the way new configurations of regions, nations and nation-states are being reordered in new political structures.

It is not now a question of whether the constitutional programme evolves; it is a question of how, when and to what extent. There are real and substantial choices for Scotland between the established positions of the Union or Independence.

Political leaders in Scotland also have a choice to make in terms of either taking ownership of the debate or continuing to be dragged along in the slipstream of the SNP, who currently drive the agenda. There is a 'third way' scenario that sees Scotland move radically forward in a completely transformed union but stopping short of independence.

For that to happen, Westminster has to abandon its obsession with sover-eignty and find other ways of handling power and authority. But in Scotland we have to build some real consensus for change which is based on a well-informed dialogue with the Scottish people, a well-reasoned alternative to independence. This will have to be sold to the electors as an important part of changing the way we do politics and reconnecting with their needs and aspirations.

For far too long, devolution and the whole question of constitutional change has been looked upon by the media and Unionist politicians as a dis-traction from the 'real' issues. It should now be centre-stage and linked with other social and economic issues.

In their first two years in power, the SNP managed to establish a degree of competence and authority as well as giving enhanced stature to the office of First Minister. Setting aside the novelty factor, the reasonable nature of the Scottish people made them willing to give the SNP a fair wind, whilst the Unionist majority in the parliament who form the opposition were con-strained and, in fact, are still in denial two years after their defeat. Thus, the impact of the SNP has been considerable both in tone and style but also in terms of creating a new excitement in Scottish politics by apparently and paradoxically making devolution work.

But what is remarkable is the fact that much of the SNP's success is based on some simple concepts: Scottishness, an uncompromising defence of Scotland's interests and the ability to capitalize on contentious issues.

They do not continually have to look over their shoulders to Westminster and, by giving a bigger and louder voice to self-government within the Union, devolution has been given a real boost.

First Minister Alex Salmond has listed his reasons why Scots have warmed to further constitutional change: the demise of the British Empire; the loosening of deference in the 60s; globalisation eating away at the bigger nations but boosting smaller ones and the change in Scotland's self-image wrought by Margaret Thatcher and her policies, which finally politicised the cause of a Scottish Parliament.

Thirty or 40 years ago, much of the SNP's public image was bound up with the preservation of the Gaelic language and other cultural totems and an association with the Presbyterian church that found them bumping up against west Scotland's often bitter sectarianism. Salmond's SNP is more inclusive and makes a point of keeping Catholic opinion on side (he advocated the repeal of the anti-Catholic Act of Settlement) and has established a similar bond with Scotland's Asian community.

A Guardian article on his first six months as First Minister described him as 'sweetly reasonable' in putting his case for independence and 'a disarming Braveheart' – terms which previously would never have been applied to the abrasive Alex Salmond!

Thus, a crucial part of Salmond's biggest achievement has been to turn his party from being unfit to govern into a successful contender for power. As he said: 'I have to reach out ... to project the cause of independence in the inclusive way, as a civic, democratic, liberating movement that everybody can buy into.'

And, whereas Labour talks about 'Scottish answers to Scottish problems', the SNP Government now offers the more positive 'Scottish answers for Scottish aspirations'.

The reaction to this has been illuminating. Opinion polls show a significant bounce in the polls for the SNP yet an equally significant reduction in support for independence. The lessons for the other parties are obvious. The distinctive nature of Scottish politics is taking shape in that Scottish voters may want to see an avowedly Scottish party like the SNP govern Scotland but simultaneously continue to support Labour to govern the United Kingdom. In doing this, the electors will also paradoxically continue to reject independence and see their future within the Union.

This could change but what is currently happening in Scotland is also happening elsewhere in Europe and could therefore be a long-term reality. This is another indication that the constitutional road is dividing.

As they adjust to these new realities, the opposition parties north of the border may also wish to ponder the question of whether an SNP administration at Holyrood is a bigger short-term threat than full independence. If both issues are left unchecked, they may come together in the medium- to long-term to change Scottish politics forever.

Two years out from the next Holyrood elections and one year from a UK general election, there are signs that the Unionist parties in Scotland and the Labour Government at Westminster are beginning to understand the distinctive politics in Scotland and the need to engage in a more radical approach to devolution, the findings of the Calman Commission being the most visible sign of this rethink.

The opposition parties have to re-engage with the constitutional process and feel comfortable in doing so and accept that radical constitutional policies are not the preserve of one party and will not inevitably lead to independence. They should be confident of their own ideas about Scotland's future and be undeterred by the hesitancy of United Kingdom political parties and Westminster.

For the first time, instead of seeing them as existing on separate levels, we have to link up the constitutional and political debate with the public policy agenda where the debate on new powers is rooted in the long term needs of Scotland.

The Calman approach makes sense as it seeks to build change on perceived weaknesses of the current settlement. The case for new powers should be based on whether the current distribution of devolved and reserved powers is preventing or inhibiting the government of Scotland and the Parliament from achieving the aims and aspirations of the people. Calman has recommended some modest but nevertheless relevant changes. Similarly, the ideas on tax-and-spend powers are complex and tentative but make sense as the first step towards a federal solution.

Equally important is the question of what needs to be done to tackle issues and solve problems that have stubbornly endured and are deep-seated. This is where a more radical transfer of powers may be needed in reserved areas where it is felt that Westminster-based solutions have not worked and a new approach is required. Or it may simply mean that Scotland simply wants to move quicker or do more than Westminster does. This could be the next step for a follow-up to Calman.

There are three areas of significance:

- The economy, taxation and borrowing, where the strengths and weaknesses of the Scottish economy should dictate any new powers. There is a compelling case for more significant levers of economic power to be transferred to the Scottish Parliament and the Scottish Government. General taxation is a limited power in relation to the economy especially if there is no control over corporation tax and other economic tools.

- Social security and employment powers where they interface with workforce participation rates, employment and skill training, education and the issues surrounding economic migrants from Central and Eastern Europe. Labour market and immigration powers increasingly impact on the economy and will be of crucial importance if the Scottish Government seeks to intervene in the economy.

- Europe, where there are examples that could usefully be looked at as the EU increasingly impacts on our future. Views on Europe are more positive in Scotland. On the issues of the Euro, the Lisbon Treaty and our attitude towards inward economic migration, divergent views and experiences may demand different responses. Europe remains an important consideration where more powers for Scotland would make sense in some form of federalism.

Any review would also have to look at the new global challenges such as energy, our carbon footprint, the environment and global warming and the increased expectations of a population with more lifestyle choices.

Embroiled with the question of powers is the question of the Sovereignty of the Westminster Parliament; in the absence of a written constitution and checks on the power of the executive, the writ of Parliament is questionable but unassailable. Westminster could abolish the Scottish Parliament with a one-line Bill as there are no safeguards written into the Scotland Act to prevent this or other changes to reserved and devolved matters. The issue of sovereignty is a major stumbling-block to shared power instead of devolved power. While it lasts the stability of the Scotland Act will always be at risk. There is a powerful case to be made for sovereignty in different sites and in relation to different powers and responsibilities. There is no reason why Westminster should have exclusive responsibility over sovereignty.

Labour's dilemma

For Labour in particular, never completely at ease as a party with the devolution or the constitutional debate, their basic attitude has to change radically and urgently. It is Labour that has the most to gain from the new way forward. Why has the SNP been allowed to hijack the status of being the only party prepared to be uncompromising in the defence of Scottish interests? Why is the SNP driving the constitutional agenda? Why is the SNP able to make great political capital of its embrace of Scottishness and the Saltire, over which it actually has no monopoly?

Is the explanation the not-so-invisible hand of UK Labour, MPs and the Westminster Parliament and Government, as Scottish Labour fails to establish its own identity and therefore appears ambivalent about the need to re-visit the settlement? The relationship or *modus operandi* between Scottish Labour and UK Labour/Westminster has to be reviewed and re-written to reflect the realities of Scottish politics and the changes that are taking place in Scottish society. A substantial part of Labour's support has moved on but the party has not moved with it.

Labour's base in local government, the trades unions and within the electorate is shifting and elector/party alliances, allegiances and loyalties are loosening as new and different constituencies of interest are being created and as social and economics aspirations change.

The Labour Party needs to renew and refresh its approach to Scotland's political future and resolve the tensions and conflicts between London and Edinburgh. There is after all no reason why Labour should not be leading the debate on Scotland's political future.

The preconditions for this to happen seem to be: a confident and ambitious approach to change; a new look for the Union at Westminster; more independence for Scottish Labour and their MSPs; and the development of a 'third way' loosening the present constraints of the Union and the current settlement with the aim of providing greater autonomy with more extensive powers and a shared sovereignty for the Scottish Parliament.

It is always worth remembering that current opinion polls suggest there is no great enthusiasm for independence and that should give Labour the confidence that it is running with the grain of constitutional and political thinking in Scotland. But this requires courage, leadership and a new vision for Scotland. Again. Calman may have broken the mould. Once again, there is a compelling case for this to happen but so far little change is evident.

There is a substantial body of public opinion that wants an intelligible alternative to Independence that will capture the imagination of the electors, guarantee stable-state politics and meet the aspirations of individuals, families and the nation, while convincing the Scottish people that the political and constitutional future of their country is safe in Labour's hands. Labour's task could become more difficult as recent events continue to erode public trust and confidence in our democracy and politics. Anger and fear of the future do not inspire progressive politics.

That would be the point where the SNP could be tested on what Independence actually means. Labour could extol the virtues of a radical blueprint that achieves all the stated benefits of independence within the Union but without the uncertainty, instability and anxiety that repealing the Treaty of Union would bring.

But the case will have to be made and Labour will be aware of an alternative scenario where the debate remains deadlocked and the SNP remain in power for much longer than anticipated as a minority government or in coalition. Popular support will spill over from being support for the nationalists and Scottishness to being support for Independence.

It is reasonable to say that while they ran the country for eight years (as the leading partner in coalition with the Lib Dems) the political and constitutional agenda in Scotland was not the main focus for Labour. Developing devolution from 1997 to 1999 and delivering the outcome between 1999–2007 may have resulted in not enough thought being given to the bigger picture.

As a result, the constitutional debate has largely been closed down within the Labour Party so that for nearly a decade it seemed as if the business had been completed. The period of SNP government from 2007 to 2009 has certainly changed all of that!

The lack of real interest about a next phase of devolution has reflected the somewhat schizophrenic approach to devolution throughout Labour's history from the early part of the last century. Some may have thought that the Scotland Act would kill off the SNP and others hoped devolution was an event, not a process.

Whatever the reason, Labour has demonstrably lost ground and needs to engage and re-establish its hard-won credibility as the party that delivered devolution in government and can now be trusted to drive the agenda forward.

Bannockburn is history

A complete rethink is required of the drift towards independence and of the failure of the Unionist parties to embrace a post-devolution strategy. It makes no sense to deal with independence by trying to turn every aspect of Labour/SNP or Holyrood/Westminster politics into a modern-day Bannockburn.

Hysterical and outdated attacks and painting the SNP as either dangerous extremists or hopeless romantics ignores the facts that they won the last Scottish election and are now the Government of Scotland and have more MSPs and councilors. To believe this is an aberration, a mistake and the public just got it wrong in the elections is to remain in a pointless state of denial.

This approach by the Unionist parties is ineffective and, in the long term, counter-productive. Equally it fails to recognise the fact that the modern SNP comes with Scottishness, sentiment, emotion, national pride and a sense of identity which all Scots share and embrace to differing degrees.

These are issues in a post-devolution period that the Unionist parties ignore at their peril if they are to get to grips with modern Scotland in this new political era. Throughout Europe, sub-national politics has absorbed all of this and political parties have had to adapt. Labour in particular has failed to understand that being pro-home rule is entirely consistent with being pro a modern Union.

In addition to the limitations of the attack strategy on the SNP and independence, the Unionist parties need to develop a coherent, intelligent and marketable alternative to independence. This is even more pressing in the aftermath of the MPs' expenses crisis which has triggered a wider-ranging debate about the future of our democracy, constitution and politics.

This alternative would allow a more mature and politically robust critique of independence to emerge, arguing that this vision for Scotland is outdated, unnecessary and inadequate to deal with the problems facing a modern Scotland. The critique would emphasise the nature of the world we live in, a world without borders and boundaries, where the global agenda does not respect blinkered concepts of the nation-state and narrow nationalism, a globalised world where we are interdependent, interconnected and international. This is an issue of growing importance to younger Scots, who have little difficulty in seeing themselves as citizens of not only Scotland but as also having global, European and UK connections.

For Unionists, there is a compelling case for this logical approach to be adopted as a strategy with four elements: a new political approach, a radical and relevant critique of independence, a new campaign setting forth an alternative (which has to be some form of Federalism), and a start on the reform of the Union.

Failure to do so will result in two consequences. Firstly the SNP will quickly become the default position in elections to Holyrood and, as we have seen in other European countries, the nationalist party becomes the insurance policy against the hostility or excesses of nation-state Governments. Secondly, the absence of a clear and well-understood alternative could result in the idea of independence gaining more popular support in the longer term. The perceived benefits of nationalist governments or coalitions could block out in the public thinking the more unattractive aspects of independence as the once inconceivable becomes more acceptable.

A cursory read of the SNP Government's White paper on the Referendum illustrates how independence could be cloaked in softer, more nuanced and attractive terms!

There is an intriguing psychology underpinning this constitutional debate. For the Unionist parties the stakes are high. The past decade and in particular the last two years have revealed a failure to understand the reality of post-devolution Scotland which has led to a widening credibility gap between a renewed SNP and a confused Labour Party.

The changing dynamic in Scottish politics means the electors are now 'boxing clever' as they get to grips with proportional representation, list systems, second votes, coalitions and tactical voting. A politically-aware electorate, exercising more political judgement than politicians and media commentators give them credit for, have created in Scotland a very distinctive situation which may continue to diverge sharply from election results for Westminster. When shifting party loyalties, changing expectations, an embrace of single issues, and changing economic, social, employment and education considerations are thrown into the mix, then no-one should be in any doubt that Scotland is on the move. While its destination is still unknown the constitution and political future of Scotland must and will remain a live issue.

This reality has to be recognised in London where the stakes for the future of the Union are high. If the UK refuses to be flexible in the face of demands for further progress to be made on the devolution settlement, every Scottish election will become a battlefield fought over by the opposing forces of Unionism and separatism.

If, however, it is accepted that the case for change and more devolved powers is compelling and based on substantial consensus, Westminster could loosen up and progress be made within a more flexible Union. This would mark a degree of maturity being achieved in relation to the importance of devolution.

The UK parliament could go further and see the merit in tackling some of the outstanding English questions, taking seriously the wider future of the Union in the new circumstances of post-devolution Britain. An even more radical reform of the Union is possible, where concepts such as sovereignty, identity, nationality, diversity, pluralism, respect, culture and democracy are given new weight.

At the heart of any future debate, the concepts of independence and Unionism should be put under the microscope and subjected to a thorough and detailed examination of what they mean in 2009 and whether they still have relevance to the problems and challenges faced by Scotland and the

United Kingdom – or whether there are better and more effective ways of achieving social and economic outcomes in the future.

Serious consideration must be given to the philosophy and purpose of the Union in the 21st century. The mere existence of the Union in its current form is not in itself a rationale for its continued unreformed existence, nor an explanation of its relevance and importance. If the Prime Minister is serious about his desire to have radical constitutional reform, then a written constitution and a Bill of Rights would go a long way to enshrine the ideas of shared power and shared sovereignty alongside proper constitutional safeguards for the emerging shape and political structure of the new and modern Union.

The Union has now to become the focus of a far more critical review and the idea that the constitutional issue is essentially 'Scottish business' has to be dropped.

The Holyrood parliament now has a maturity which it could not have had in 1999. This allows the real prospect of a new political culture and will generate a fresh understanding of the real potential of devolved government. It will also provide a more credible base for arguing for further changes and more powers.

Calman has provided a get-out-of-jail card or a get-off-the-hook opportunity to the Unionist opposition in Scotland. As such, the detailed findings of the report are less important than the fact that it marks a new phase of devolution and a statement of real intent about tax, spend and powers. The experiences of Wales and Northern Ireland only serve to illustrate the real potential of breaking the Westminster mould. There is more that unites the parties at Holyrood than divides them.

TREATMENT: The post-devolution debate is a mess. The Unionist parties need a new clear narrative which takes them beyond devolution; a new political structure for the future of Scotland and the Union; to connect with the people; to embrace new concepts of sovereignty, identity, nationality and diversity; to provide a response which resonates with the electors sense of country, Scottishness, aspiration and commonsense.

Scotland should be presented with an alternative to independence which stops short of leaving the Union but provides Scots with full fiscal responsibility, significantly more powers and a new renewed relationship with the United Kingdom. In one form or another. we are talking about FEDERALISM and the challenge is to bring this alive for the electorate and connect with their day-to-day concerns and aspirations.

CHAPTER TWENTY-THREE

The Politics of the Future

Politics are too serious a matter to be left to the politicians.

PRESIDENT CHARLES DE GAULLE

Most people are just scunnered by politicians who argue for the sake of argument at a time when we are fighting an economic crisis.

SCOTTISH SECRETARY JIM MURPHY, Scottish TV interview on 25 June 2009.

PREDICTION: The results of the 2010 UK General Election and 2011 Scottish Parliament election will result in a political realignment – of parties, of ideas, of policies, of coalitions around issues and interests.

If that is the case, Scotland has a head-start. Thanks to devolution and the advent of new institutions and systems, new ways of working, new alignments and coalitions, and new thinking (although it has to be said this is woefully limited so far), we should be more adaptable and readier to accept still more change.

In the New Scotland, the debate is already about a more accountable Parliament and a new kind of politics. But it must go further – instead of leaving the crucial decisions to politicians, institutions, government and parties, what are we as citizens doing about it?

Our allegedly democratic system is dominated by factional and polarised politics with parties influenced by big companies, big unions and powerful lobbies. Politics has become the province of the elite and the anoraks.

We need to have more direct influence on what is being done on our account. We should be more questioning and articulate about our own country. In effect, as a nation and as an electorate, we have to take ownership of our country again.

That will require more education, more knowledge and more than just an 'X' on a piece of paper every couple of years. The media are not doing the job – too much personality and not enough policy. A quality democracy requires an informed citizenry. To be fair, they are in a fight for their own survival and have to sell newspapers, make on-line earnings and achieve viewer ratings, all of which, it seems, are being achieved at the expense of information and thoughtful analysis.

In the decade from 1999 to the time of writing, we have seen unprecedented developments on three fronts – political and constitutional change, the fragility of our democracy and the way we do our politics. Particularly in 2007–9, developments have been momentous:

The end of ten years of the Blair government and the election of Gordon Brown as Prime Minister.

A new SNP First Minister in Scotland.

The first minority SNP government; Unionism and Republicanism in government in Northern Ireland; Labour and Plaid Cymru in government in Wales.

Commemoration of 300 years of the Treaty of Union.

The SNP's White Paper on Independence and the 'national conversation' in Scotland

The Brown government's Green Paper on reform of the governance of Britain.

Polls in Scotland showing rising support for the snp but declining support for independence.

New constitutional treaty for the European Union, The Lisbon Treaty, agreed by heads of Government but rejected by Irish voters in referendum

A global banking and financial crisis and the worst recession in a generation

The Brown premiership under severe pressure

An expenses crisis at Westminster having a deep and dramatic impact on politics and the electors

Catastrophic European election results for Labour and the election of two British National Party candidates to the European Parliament

Moves to 'clean up Westminster', and embark on an ambitious agenda of democratic renewal and constitutional reform

Calman Commission reports and recommends more powers for Scottish Parliament and changes to tax and spend powers

For not the first time in recent history, the public are questioning the value of our politics and appear to be losing faith and confidence in our politicians and our institutions.

Underpinning these serious concerns may be other factors which are less easily defined but may pose even deeper and more serious challenges to the role of politics in a modern society. There is a real disconnect between the public and the political process. This is partly due to the tired and outdated nature of much of our politics and the complacency that blights our representative system of democracy.

What is not so obvious is the failure of the Party political system to understand the nature of the electorate and society in this modern era. Political parties have evolved based on membership and rigid procedures; fixed ideologies or a corpus of beliefs and ideas; social and economic class; generational loyalties; community and territorial identity; dependency on demographics; workplace allegiances; trade union affiliations; and narrow candidate bases for elections.

Society, however, is changing and perhaps the structure of political parties is no longer relevant nor credible to the public who see things through a much more complex prism of needs and ambitions: less collective, more personal; less ideology, more ideas; more single issues, less about manifestos; more problem-solving, less about policies; more about consensus, less about conflict; more bi-partisanship, less political infighting.

Put simply, are political parties fit for purpose in the 21st century? Do the global agenda and the challenges of a modern era require new thinking and a radical transformation of how we do politics? Are the political parties being left behind by modern society?

In *Culture, Institutions and Economic Development – A Study of Eight European Regions* the authors outlined this new world:

'*The communications revolution: The internet; instant links across the planet; the creation of an information society not limited by space and time; emergence of virtual communities and social and political movements divided by space but united in so many ways; no regulation by national-states, empowering groups and individuals; diversity but also uniformity and individualism; emergence of a global culture and lifestyle, especially among the young in a world of text, e-mail, mobile phones, the internet; all of this emerging with the dissolution of old territorial communities. Political Dimension: The rise of global social movements dedicated to special causes, such as the environment and globalisation; new political spaces configured in different ways. People are operating in a global space, not just a Scottish space; their perceptions are changing and they do not see the world through the prism of Unionism.*

'*In contrast, their Scottishness may be something they hold on to in a time of dramatic change; for many, territory, borders and boundaries have less significance as their understanding is limited and these do not affect their lifestyles.*'

The realignment predicted at the start of this chapter will offer the opportunity to create people- and not party-based politics; not political infighting, but issues and the best solutions. People have problems – parties have procedures and dogmas.

This does not mean the end of ideology but the re-emergence of principles and a new egalitarianism. Structures and doctrines created 100 years ago should not be reaffirmed out of blind loyalty, but reformed and modernised while retaining the basic ideals.

Bursting the Westminster bubble

A powerful catalyst for change will be the expenses crisis which has rocked the Palace of Westminster. For the first time in modern politics, a single issue has exposed the scale of the alienation and disillusionment of the British electorate. Trust and confidence lie at the heart of our democracy. Government and legislature can only operate when there is a balance between the expectation and aspirations of the electorate and the achievements of those elected.

There is a growing demand for a new politics and serious questions are being asked about whether Westminster and Whitehall are fit for purpose in the 21st century. The Prime Minister has described Westminster as 'a gentleman's club' and said it 'can no longer operate as a 19th century institution'; 'Planet Westminster' opined *The Guardian*, while other newspapers were more vitriolic and less generous to the Mother of Parliaments.

It is hard to believe that one issue, however dramatic the scale and detail of the revelations, could have unleashed such a response. The more likely explanation is that the expense issue mined a deep and enduring seam of discontent, mistrust and dissatisfaction about the politics of Britain, a level of resentment that could have serious consequences if not met with an inspired and modern approach to the way we do our politics.

The expenses issue will be resolved and the Commons now has a new Speaker. This should be the beginning, not the end, of the renewal of our democracy and the radical shake-up required to reform all of British politics. It should provide the catalyst for the changes that have been talked about for decades but which have been opposed and dismissed by the political classes on the grounds that these are not 'real' issues of interest to 'real' people. Hopefully, they have learned the lesson of their arrogance.

Let us not underestimate how difficult change will be for the London institutions and their politicians. The political class have been insulated from public opinion inside the Westminster bubble and an institutional culture has been shaped over many centuries resulting in a *modus operandi* steeped in conventions, archaic procedures and a remarkably strong sense of preciousness and exceptionalism.

Being on the same site for 1,000 years gives Westminster a very powerful sense of place, an unchallenged aura of conservatism and an inbuilt resistance to change. Evidence of this comes in the form of Devolution when after 10 years of progress and achievement, Westminster barely acknowledges any of its effects. It remains ambivalent about learning the hard lessons of political renewal and a more inclusive politics and refuses to accept that the 'sovereignty of Westminster' argument is tired and outdated.

So how does this institution and also Whitehall handle this deeper malaise and re-focus on a radical modern agenda? The Prime Minister after taking office in 2007 started a debate about constitutional and political change in Britain. This had potential but unfortunately the banking crisis, the recession, an obsession with Britishness coupled with a narrow focus on the relationship between Parliament and the Executive have ensured that this initiative has stalled.

It could be given a new lease of life in the form of a Constitutional Convention – much talked about in Cabinet – but, for Scots, probably lacking originality! The Prime Minister also promises to provide the 'big idea' for the constitutional and political renaissance of the UK, an agenda of bold reforms which could take more than one parliament to achieve and requires intellectual leadership to drive it forward.

The idea of popular sovereignty, not parliamentary sovereignty, should be uppermost with the genuine notion of shared power, not devolved power, in the nations and regions of the UK. Diversity, nationality and identity should be looked upon as strengths for a modern Britain.

The agenda should be wide-ranging and inclusive: extensive review of the procedures of Westminster; electoral reform for Westminster where some form of PR will bring them into line with every other election in the UK; reform of political parties including party funding, membership and widening the base of political candidates for elections; House of Lords reform where the second chamber could be elected and where members could come from the nations and regions of the UK. If Westminster is interested in a stronger Union; a draft constitution and a bill of rights and responsibilities; more powers for the devolved countries, a voice for England and progress on devolving power to the English regions; more positive support for an informed debate about working with the EU and tackling the emerging Global challenges are all needed.

The agenda must be designed to modernise the Union, its Institutions and politics, and make it fit for purpose. It may take a generation to achieve but the work should start now.

Political realignment has to be seen in terms of ideas, issues and coalitions of common interest and not dated, hidebound and unattractive adversarial tribalism. Manifestos should be examined for their relevance in a fast-changing world; they can, of course, be statement of principles but giving the electorate a shopping list of promises, most of which are unachievable, does not constitute politics with a purpose.

To take the Labour Party as an example: having undergone the convulsions of the 1990s to become 'New Labour', the party requires another revolutionary rethink to renew its ideas and its standing with the electorate. The decline of the membership base and party machine and the loss of domination in the unions and local government combine to create a 're-reform or die situation.

Under proportional representation, attitudes and thinking matter much more than traditional stances and entrenched policies. Modern thinking is needed, especially about the 'party' approach – people are looking for solutions to problems, not for affiliations, loyalties, allegiances and discipline. Voters have their individual concerns – and, more and more, are prepared to look at candidates as individuals, rather than party representatives.

In this setting, is it preferable to have US-style primaries in the choice of candidates for elected office in councils and parliaments? Why should a couple of dozen (if that many) people sitting in the proverbial room (no longer smoke-filled) in any part of Scotland select your candidate? A hustings of registered party supporters, even if not paid-up members ensures that the largest possible number of like-minded people make the choice of who will represent their shared views and basic political principles.

The result must be a higher quality of elected representatives, not in terms of university degrees, trade union sloggers or apparatchiks who have no work experience outside political machine-minding but a wider range of candidates with diverse qualifications and life experiences.

Proportional representation (PR) in Scotland has also meant that shared attitudes and aspirations matter much more than traditional allegiances and rigid policies. There is a significant fluidity in our politics which is often ignored in the more dramatic adversarial politics beloved of the media. In this new dynamic, realignment is possible and indeed likely over the issue of the constitution.

There may be new political party formations where deep divisions within parties and agreements between members of different parties require break-up and re-merging in new forms of political expression. For example, is there scope for a new Social Democratic Party in Scotland or some looser party structure around a federal solution to the nation's political future?

It is doubtful whether the changes to renew our democracy and reform our constitution within the present rigid party political system. Our political structures, institutions and elections will have to be more relevant and attractive to the electors.

Scotland has four sets of elections in the political cycle and the numbers of people voting continues to decline. The strength of our democracy should have some link, however tenuous, with the level of interest of the electors. Nor can trust and confidence in the political process be rebuilt without addressing the political implications of our demographics where, by 2020, one in three electors will be over 60/65 years of age. Connection with young people and single-issue politics has to be established amidst a revolution in communications, the Internet and the 24-hour news cycle where mobile phones and social networking are changing how people engage with politics or find other ways of protesting, campaigning, outwith the traditional party political system. There is a danger that, in the future, those voting will be protesting rather than positively supporting policies for the future.

Unless we can make elections more attractive and engaging and the institutions to which we elect representatives more relevant and necessary, then we run the risk of widening the gap between the electors and the elected.

This raises the issues of too many elections; too many MPs, MSPs, MEPs and too much government; too much dependency; and too little knowledge, information and education as citizens to understand and better inform our democracy. There is a shockingly low level of political awareness and education in our society – yet politics deals with cradle-to-grave policies, decisions at different levels from the global to the local and spending billions of the peoples' pounds.

The public are given the impression that leaving them ill-informed between elections is a natural part of the political process. This, in turn, suggests to them that an 'x' on a ballot paper is all their contribution to the democratic process need be.

A confident, modern and forward-looking Scotland would give a high priority to ensuring the people are both informed consumers and citizens. The European Union is probably the best example of this elector neglect; setting aside the background political noise which drowned out any debate on the importance of the EU, the level of debate during the 2007 European election campaign was nothing less than a scandal.

Certain sections of the right-wing press, much of the Conservative Party, plus political misfits, Euro-sceptics and extreme parties such as the British National Party and UKIP all combined in an anti-European campaign and completely distorted the truth about the benefits of membership of the EU. Their success was boosted by the failure of mainstream political parties to promote Europe and the failure of the Labour party, in particular, to promote over the last decade a positive case for Europe that could have confronted misinformation and promoted an informed debate.

The Scotland-UK fault line

There is now a significant divide between the politics of the United Kingdom and those of Scotland. The fault-line is not yet seismic but certainly perceptible, running through the party system, our political process and government. Devolution has changed the political landscape and created new, previously unthinkable alliances and many political traditions have been discarded along with many of the attitudes and ideas that ought to underpin the Unionist model.

Labour in Scotland need to adapt and change to win political success in Scotland and develop a convincing constitutional alternative to independence for Scotland. This has not happened and there are now serious strains and tensions between UK Labour and Scottish Labour over the future of devolution.

Devolution should have created a new relationship between Scottish and UK Labour but that has been stifled by central control, Westminster dominance and acquiescence by the Scottish leadership

The UK government has been lukewarm, even hostile, to any further progress on devolution and this has allowed the SNP Government to dominate Scottish politics. The opposition parties to the SNP government at Holyrood now find themselves in an impossible position.

For Scottish Labour, the prospects are grim unless they can become more distinctively Scottish, stop looking over their shoulder to Westminster, develop a political way forward on devolution, which embraces some form of federal structure, and persuade the Union to reform as part of Gordon Brown's renewal of democracy agenda.

The Unionist parties, who now find themselves in opposition in Scotland, have been slow to adapt to a very different Scotland. The SNP remains a party with a plan for government but also with a political plan for the country – in contrast to Labour who were too absorbed by governing to give any real consideration to the changing nature of public opinion and the mood of the nation. Perhaps for understandable reasons, Labour failed to appreciate the country was moving on.

The SNP and their policy of independence have a gut 'Braveheart' appeal but cannot withstand intellectual investigation – and they are only one part of the debate. Labour should forensically expose independence and at the

same time promote a logical, easily understood and viable long-term feder-
alist alternative for Scotland's future. The Scottish majority do not support
Independence but, in the absence of a distinctive Scottish alternative which
is both pro-home rule and pro a new and modern Union, the electoral
prospects look bleak.

This should not be a hard concept for Scottish Labour and the other
Unionist parties to grasp; but their failure to do so merely reflects the iron
grip of Westminster and UK Labour on developments north of the Border –
and feeds the nationalist 'them and us' mentality. Since the future of
Scotland depends on this issue being resolved, the political benefits of a
more independent Scottish Labour party and a distinctive political regime
north of the border are obvious.

Voters, consumers, citizens

Some would argue that in this post-devolution politics a wider set of considerations should be influencing our future and the way we order our politics and our democracy. The excesses of materialism, greed, risk-taking and
selfishness in our society have been exposed by the banking and financial
crisis. We are an indulgent society and as people reflect on the nature of our
democracy, there is a growing debate about whether the political process
should be concerned with a much wider set of social, moral and human
considerations rather than just hard economic issues such as economic
growth, productivity levels and competitiveness.

Inevitably people are beginning to question 'the rat race mentality' and
in turn are looking for a deeper and more significant meaning to the lives
they lead. As the Scottish political and cultural icon Jimmy Reid, leader of
the historic Clyde shipyard work-in, said in his remarkable Glasgow
University rectorial address: 'The rat race is for the rats.'

It would be wrong to exaggerate the significance of this change in public
attitudes, but there are clear signs that people are not only disillusioned
with the outcomes of our politics and the remoteness of our political classes
but are beginning to question the narrow basis of our current debates and
the lack of vision about the future of the UK and Scotland in a world of
change and globalization.

As consumers, they can see the benefits of global economics but as citizens
they are increasingly fearful of how much control or influence they now
have in their communities, in their councils and in their Parliaments. Also
impacting on their consciousness are climate change, global warming and

the search for secure energy, all of which lead people to consider their wider responsibilities for the future of the planet. Despite the material prosperity of the majority of people there is now more emphasis on quality of life issues, personal life-style and well-being and what could best be described as spirituality.

It is worth remembering, however, that one in five Scots live on or below the official poverty level. They do not necessarily have the luxury of reflecting on their spirituality or their well-being as they struggle to survive from one day to the next. A one-nation Scotland should be concerned about the challenge posed by this level of inequality and the poverty, disadvantage and distress which accompanies it. The comfortable mainstream in Scotland tend to categorise the victims of inequality in terms of character defects, geography, family history and fecklessness, without much regard to individual qualities of intrinsic worth, talent and ambition.

There exists in the national psyche a complex of emotions: some people are angry, some fear the future, some struggle to get by, some are disillusioned with politics, some are bewildered by change, some are overwhelmed by the complexity and uncertainty of globalization and technology. Most, however, want to make sense of the world they live in and make the most of their role in it. Leadership – political, civic, business and religious – becomes vital as we deal with change and seek new solutions to old problems and at the same time elevate the idea of individual self-worth and personal well-being much higher up the political agenda.

Professor Michael Sandel, Harvard Professor of Government, giving his 2009 Reith lecture on 'A New Citizenship' outlined the prospects of a new politics of the common good and a more morally engaged public life:

'We live in a world of financial crisis and economic hardship – everybody knows that – but we also live in a time of great hope for moral and civic renewal. We saw this hope in the election of Barack Obama as President of the United States. In many democracies around the world, there's a similar hope, a restless impatience with politics as it is.

In Britain, the public have been outraged by revelations that Members of Parliament have claimed reimbursement for inappropriate housing expenses. Whatever reforms may emerge, one thing is clear: the better kind of politics we need is a politics oriented less to the pursuit of individual self interest and more to the pursuit of the common good.

A new politics of the common good isn't only about finding

more scrupulous politicians. It also requires a more demanding idea of what it means to be a citizen, and it requires a more robust public discourse – one that engages more directly with moral and even spiritual questions.'

TREATMENT: Whether we have reached a real watershed in our political life, a once-in-a-lifetime tipping point, remains to be seen but returning to the politics of the past is not an option.

CHAPTER TWENTY-FOUR

The Change Agenda

THE NEW GLOBAL ORDER and the electronic revolution are rapidly altering the nature of every nation on earth as well as forcing change, regardless of whether it is welcome or not. In this tough and challenging world how does a country like Scotland survive and scale new heights of success and achievement in which the whole nation plays its part and in turn shares the benefits?

We need to look at a number of factors which in themselves do not provide clear-cut answers but do start to create and shape a new way of looking at Scotland in this new era.

Understanding the future requires us to look at the drivers of change. The accelerated pace of change is gripping every aspect of modern life and in Scotland this requires us to acknowledge and understand what is happening and also to manage the opportunities and threats. A debate about futures has to be ongoing in a way that becomes both an intellectual asset as well as boosting Scotland the brand.

Future thinking has to be an integral part of every institution as drivers of change start to recast our society, our economy and our politics. More specifically, we need to ask: What are we doing now that we could do better? Efficiency, effectiveness and enhancing every aspect our reputation, status and brand are key considerations.

What are we doing now that we should not be doing? Relevance and modernity combined with overcoming institutional inertia and the courage needed to grasp new thinking and ideas are essential parts of a new approach.

What should we be doing now that we are not doing? New solutions to old, enduring and seemingly intractable problems figure prominently in this. The process of dealing with futures requires an approach conceived in the context of overall objectives – understanding and adapting more effectively to change; putting a higher premium on ideas, innovation and creativity in everything we do; raising awareness about what is happening internationally on social progress, political developments and economic success; embracing and contributing to the cutting edge of thinking around the knowledge economy, learning and communications technology because these are the tools of tomorrow's world.

The world is dominated by thinking and adaptive institutions, creative communities and knowledge networks: the speed at which the transfer, application and absorption of new thinking and knowledge takes place is breathtaking. Ideas, innovation, adaptability and creativity are the currency of success in any new Scotland.

Scotland, like many other countries, has traditionally focussed on the past and present. In challenging times, we need to extend our national psyche to more easily embrace the future. The future is the only time-frame we can influence, so integrating a futures dimension into our thinking will help all of us deal more effectively with long term issues and will provide a framework to assess the wide range of moral, ethical and social issues which accompany change.

An important spin-off from a futures mentality is that it could develop an increased sense of individual and institutional responsibility toward the future and future generations. Our look at the condition of Scotland has revealed a country that – while rightly proud of its internationalism, active diaspora and a global embrace of science and medical achievements – still has an insular and at times narrow embrace of our place on the world stage. Our preoccupation with our southern neighbour may have distorted our world view but that will have to change if our global and European footprint is to increase.

Scotland needs an attitude and an ethos which more comprehensively respects a future in which change is ever-present and seeks to be ahead of its implications and consequences. Our national narrative must be forward-looking in the sense that it is based on a futures strategy and reflects the ambitions we want to build into everything we do.

We should recognise Scotland is not just a location but a concept; not just an idea but an inspiration; not just individual assets but part of a Scotland-wide world-class resource. And as part of that vision we need to appreciate the importance of learning and education.

These are the main building blocks for transforming our country and vital for a productive economy, a civilised society, cohesive communities, global understanding and tolerance and the development of individual self-worth and self-realisation. In promoting new ideas learning should be the heartbeat of our society and our nation.

To quote UNESCO, '*Education should contribute to every person's complete development, mind/body, intelligence, sensitivities, aesthetic appreciation and spirituality, developing critical ways of thinking ... learning to KNOW, learning to DO, Learning to live TOGETHER and learning to BE*' and '*We should accept the tensions of the 21st century and their potential to distort and influence our outcomes; global and local; universal and individual;*

traditional and modern; long-term and short-term; competition and equality of opportunity; extraordinary expansion of knowledge and the capacity of human beings to assimilate; certainty and uncertainty; insecurity and security; and spiritual and material.'

Drivers of change

For all of this to work for a Scotland with a renewed sense of national purpose, we have to develop a sharper idea of the environment within which we operate and an understanding of what the 'drivers of change are likely to be. At the end of the first decade these seem to be shaping up as:

- Globalisation, Europeanisation and the reshaping of the UK; the political, legislative, financial and regulatory change from different levels of government and institutions.
- Inequality and social and economic inclusion
- Devolution and the future of the Union as the constitutional journey continues to move forward.
- The challenge of Scotland's demographics over the next 25 years and in particular the dramatic increase in the older population.
- A social agenda where certain indicators demonstrate Scotland occupying the worst positions in Western European league tables
- EU enlargement, the role of immigration and migrant workers.
- The economy, including productivity levels, growth rates, competitiveness, new business growth, innovation and research, and workforce participation rates linked to generational worklessness
- Quality of life, life style changes from the practical to the spiritual
- Welfare reform and the Labour market
- Education and learning and the need for reforms
- Employment, patterns and workplace changes, the diversity and equality agenda, the demands of knowledge and technology and the nature of work
- The greening of Scotland, global warming, climate change and the sustainable agenda
- A more confident, ambitious, less dependent, more entrepreneurial, innovative, risk taking, success driven and competitive Scotland
- Developments in communications and information technology, especially the internet.

- Shifts in the levels of public expenditure post the banking and financial crisis and the recession and a serious debate about the size of the State and our dependency on the public sector.
- Renewal of our democracy, governance, legislature and the electoral system as the public become more questioning of politics and politicians.

Incentives to change

The most important idea driving our thoughts on Scotland's future is the notion of a country striving for world-class status. We are a nation trying to balance a past dogged by self doubt, enduring social and economic problems, negativity and a lack of confidence, with a future where we have much to offer in terms of our undoubted talent, world-class resources and a patchy but positive global perception.

We have argued that Scotland should adopt a futures mentality which recognises internationalism and the importance of global reach as well as understanding the importance of the 'drivers of change'. Bridging the aspiration gap and the confidence and achievement gaps remain the overall mission for a new Scotland.

Much of the debate about Scotland's future is inextricably linked to the constitutional debate and the various alternatives for the future governance of both Scotland and the United Kingdom. In *Scotland: the Road Divides* published in 2007, we drew attention to the fact that radical change in various countries at particular times in the recent past have been occasioned by 'shocks' to the system.

In that context the psychology of independence is worthy of consideration. Could such a shock to the system provoke Scots into taking ownership of their own destiny and into becoming able to tackle their deep-seated problems for themselves?

Independence for Scotland as a way forward as international aspects of globalisation and interdependence of trade and finance have become more important. An interesting body of literature exists that links the external or internal shocks a country experiences with the success and achievements it ultimately wins, with a number of examples – such as Finland, Ireland, Japan and Germany – where change or some kind of stimulus brought about a radical transformation in the prospects of a country.

Obviously, some of the shocks were one-offs but these examples show how effective political and economic change can take place and how a nation responds to the conditions in which it finds itself. The question for Scotland is whether, without some dramatic event, new levels of economic and social performance can be achieved, and whether such an event could be a collective decision of the Scottish people to radically change their political and constitutional status within the UK, regardless of the economic and social conditions the country inherits.

There is some is some evidence to suggest that significant periods of change in Scotland were occasioned by events, although it is difficult to identify actual cause-and-effect relationships. Does Scotland need a major shock to the system before change can take place or are there less dramatic ways? The mood, morale and momentum of the country are key considerations. The desire for change will occur when we reach a point where we overcome our fear, our innate conservatism and our complacency.

There will be a need for our political classes to build consensus and move away from the simplistic adversarial politics that blights much of the debate on serious social and economic issues. The role of the media will be crucial: press, broadcasting and the new electronic platforms influence the mood and morale of the public as citizens as well as consumers. Without a more positive approach from the 'fourth estate', it is difficult to see a change mentality evolve across society, government and our institutions.

The media have different roles to perform in a democracy but it is surely evident that their overall negativity and often superficial treatment of politics makes them under-perform in relation to 'Scotland the brand' and the idea of a world-class country. A country often lacking self-confidence and self-worth is not helped by being constantly reminded of its shortcomings!

TREATMENT: It may well be that, based on the lessons of history, we just patch up and move on – muddling through is our default position. But the global banking and financial crisis, the deepest recession for a generation and the expenses scandal at Westminster could be the shock to the system and the catalyst for change.

CHAPTER TWENTY-FIVE

Changing Scotland's Mindset

THE POTENTIAL INHERENT IN new ways of doing things will not be realised unless other factors are part of the mix. Leadership is essential in all parties and they need to have a strong belief in the benefits that devolved government and a more flexible Union can provide. They need a vision for our democracy and our country and to embrace big ideas in order to encourage people to engage with politics. In short, we need an all-party determination to move Scotland in a new direction with a renewed sense of national purpose and self confidence.

We need to be intellectuals as well as pragmatists. Although we live with hard practical realities and tough day-to-day decisions these should constantly be seen in the context of a broader understanding of on-going change and future needs.

One hindrance that must be overcome is the rigid attitude to nationality, sovereignty and identity and the doggedly traditional ways of expressing these in political terms. There has to be a better way, a way which looks at individuals and their needs in Scottish society and loses the obsession with geography and endless talk about differences and divisions. Change in the wider world is making much of this talk redundant.

What does independence mean in the 21st century? If the ongoing debate is to make any sense, it has to acknowledge the fact that there may be other futures for Scotland which embrace different ideas and structures and require new ways of seeing the world and our role in it.

It also requires our political, business, media and civic leaders to work more closely together to change attitudes and project a more positive, consensual and ambitious vision for the nation. There is no other way forward if we are to tap into our talent and potential and make Scotland an internationally-recognised learning and knowledge capital. The country's constitutional and political future within the Union is inextricably linked with its practical performance in a rapidly changing world.

It is essential that the Scottish psyche should also change; the success of Ireland, Denmark, Norway, Finland, Singapore, Bavaria, and US states like Virginia was achieved by being confident and determined in the pursuit of economic and social objectives. Scots have these qualities but as yet do not apply them in any sustainable form.

Also lacking is the unity of national purpose which is so important and this can only be attained by defining identity and aspirations – not by the anachronistic comparison with England or any other country. Nothing need constrain Scotland but the uttermost limits of the imagination and ambition.

At present, Scots seem uncomfortable with the language of global success, with the emphasis on competitiveness, productivity, growth and aggressiveness where necessary. There is uncertainty about how Scots can shake themselves free from the complacency and apparent lack of drive which is holding the nation back.

Most successful countries have needed some kind of crisis to create the conditions for change. In the absence of anything as dramatic, Scotland must reach that tipping-point that creates radical change. Can this come about within the existing Union or is independence or some other drastic alteration in thinking and structures of government required?

Whatever the choice, taking more responsibility for successes and failures has to be the Scottish way forward. There is a pressing need to learn from the experiences of other countries and the sub-national structures that exist throughout the world in various forms of devolution. It is important to think beyond the UK and acknowledge that devolved government with significant power is commonplace elsewhere. It is difficult to transfer a complete model from overseas but there are ideas and experiences which could provide lessons and which could enrich the efforts to obtain improvements in the governance of Scotland.

Perversely, the nation imposes unnecessary handicaps on itself while at the same time aspiring to be world-class, with a high-performing and productive economy and an enviable learning and knowledge infrastructure. Scots do not like to acknowledge their self-imposed restraints: a surprising diffidence about self-promotion; suspicion of success and achievement; failure to admit to or address weaknesses in innovation, entrepreneurship and enterprise; lack of self-esteem and embarrassment about talking the language of competition.

TREATMENT: Scotland's mood is a key factor in adapting for the future. We have to start to embrace both the actions and language of a nation liberated from the past.

CHAPTER TWENTY-SIX

Conclusion

HAVING SCRUTINISED SCOTLAND'S NATIONAL faults and failings as 'symptoms' the question is: Are Scotland's ailments capable of cure – or are they characteristics which are too deeply ingrained to be changed?

The need for treatment is obvious; at the start of the 21st century, with the UK and Scotland in political and constitutional ferment and the world engulfed in financial crisis, only a healthy, clear-sighted and strong-willed nation will survive and prosper.

We make no apology that this has become a continuing theme with us. In our previous book on the new post-devolution politics *Scotland: The Road Divides* we wrote: 'It is essential that the Scottish state of mind should change ... the nation's mood is a key factor in adapting for the future.'

The more sensitive Scots (and who can deny that touchiness is one of our most obvious traits?) will feel that, especially in Part One where we describe the nation's flaws, we are ourselves being all-too-typically Scottish: downbeat, negative and self-denigrating. We have had fun at the expense of our national stereotypes and the sometimes comical image we present to the world as well as drawing attention to some truly disturbing and discreditable aspects of modern Scottish society.

But we cannot correct our faults until we confront them. Optimism leads us to believe that Scotland can change and, in fact, has little choice. The key problems are self-evident and, having understood the nature of the condition, the debate is about how change can be started.

Our agenda is ambitious:

- A more dynamic and successful social, economic and political Scotland.
- Closing the social aspirational and achievement gaps.
- Rethinking inequality and addressing the '80/20 society' in which 80 per cent of the working-age population keep the economy going and the other 20 per cent live on some form of welfare.
- Democratic renewal, constitutional reform and a new politics.
- Building confidence by removing negativity and developing a positive culture.
- Dealing with our deep seated and enduring problems and becoming a world class nation.

Scotland will change by:

- Creating the capacity and building inspired leadership in Scotland.
- Developing a new narrative for the Nation with simple and consistent messages.
- Having less dependency and more responsibility.
- Bi-partisan politics and a strong sense of national purpose.
- Insisting on a new and positive media culture, old and new
- Reforming our institutions.
- Becoming more informed and enthused citizens as an antidote to consumerism and materialism.
- Becoming global citizens in a 21st century world that is interdependent and interconnected.

National objectives

The national objectives should be: creating a Scotland with a deeper and more positive sense of national and individual purpose; finding a new approach to societal problems; revisiting inequalities and bridging gaps, especially the social aspiration gap; tackling the dependency culture which has become a way of life for a large and marginalised sector of the population; talking up the importance of well-being, the common good and quality of life; re-interpreting strategic concepts such as enterprise, innovation, dependency, competition, risk, success, solidarity, self-belief and self-worth.

The capacity for change has to be built into our institutions. Politically and constitutionally the tasks are: renewing our democracy, reforming our constitution and rebuilding confidence and trust in our politics; modernising and reforming the Union and Scotland's role in it while being less obsessed with our southern neighbours; inaugurating genuine 'national conversations' (in which people talk to people, not exclusively politicians to politicians) using modern media and the new communications; and being global citizens with a new view of the world order, with an acceptance of the different levels of agenda – global, European, UK and Scotland.

In fact, we have to become a confident people in a confident country. This requires new and more vigourous leadership and changing the way we think with optimism and self belief to the forefront in our a new lexicon of national traits and qualities.

In an audit of the good and the bad in the Scottish character, the positives outweigh the features which are holding us back. We Scots do have a propensity for what an Irish writer has called 'begrudgery', a resentment of individual success, an unwillingness to bestow praise and a pessimistic delight in the misfortunes of those who try something new but fail. There is a 'know-your place' mentality and, for some, 'competitive' is a derogatory term. It is confused with capitalism and confidence is confused with arrogance. This is reinforced by media, whose influence is far-reaching but often strikes a carping and cynical chord.

We need more emphasis on our well-known positives:

The Scots are admired for being: Serious. Responsible/canny and cautious. Reliable. Educated. Substantial. Hard working. Honest. Moral. Charitable. Financially astute (despite recent events!) Trustworthy. International. Inventive (The Enlightenment and the Industrial Revolution). Proud and passionate about their history, culture, their spectacularly beautiful country and their icons – tartan, whisky, bagpipes, castles and customs.

But we need less of the negatives that tarnish the brand:

Contradictory, dour, down beat, pessimistic, punitive, quick to anger, bigoted, sectarian, anti-English, macho, addictive, dismissive, defensive, judgemental, intolerant, dependent, scapegoating, underselling, ambivalent, lacking self belief, risk-averse, success-averse, knowing your place, accepting of mediocre standards and low expectations, fear of failure, inward-looking, adopting 'the Scottish cringe', grudge-bearing.

It is a misrepresentation (and an insult) to say these are all national characteristics that apply uniformly across Scottish society. But they are common enough and pervasive enough, especially at official levels, to be a handicap in creating the upbeat mood that will drive change; they undermine our national purpose and place unnecessary constraint on our ability to be world class.

A region or a nation?

The nation can decide whether it wants a personality make-over, but a political and constitutional reformation is inevitable. It will be forced on us by circumstances and developments, at world, European, UK and Scottish levels. Ten years on, we are now at a stage where devolution must develop further and the United Kingdom has to adjust and renew itself to avoid crumbling under the pressures of narrow nationalism and a wider frustration. Scotland has a greater sense of nationhood than at any time since, arguably, the start of the 20th century. Sovereignty, identity, nationality and diversity are all current topics but they are difficult to define and we need to know what they stand for if we are to have a meaningful debate.

Is Scotland a region, a separate country or an idea of a nation? The 1707 Union of the Parliaments was, in theory, a political union between two powers: Scotland and England (including Wales). It is worth noting that under the so-called Act of Union of 1536, Henry VIII made clear that Wales 'shall stand and continue forever from henceforth incorporated, united and annexed to and with his Realm of England'.

The 1707 Acts of Union joined the Kingdom of England and the Kingdom of Scotland, previously separate states, with separate legislatures, into a single United Kingdom of Great Britain. Whatever the intention, annexation was not mentioned but Scotland was absorbed and effectively regionalised – although it was never described as a region of the UK until World War II when, in the mood of united British resistance to a common enemy, the word slipped into official use. The revival of the separate Scottish Parliament has created an uneasiness about the difference between 'region' and 'nation' and politicians, especially, began to talk about devolution in terms of 'the nations and regions'.

But this is all history now. The question for today is: why should we be obsessed by a narrow concept of nationality if we are to be citizens at so many different levels – Scottish, UK, European and global?

On the constitutional front, again, change is inevitable. Whether the future is devolution-plus or independence will be decided by the people, not necessarily in a referendum but at future general elections, but that must be matched by a change in the Scottish attitude to the hitherto dominant next-door nation. Contrary to the extreme nationalist myth, we do not live under the 'shadow of England' and under the forthcoming settlement, which is likely to be more federal, we can regard them in a new way as productive partners, not just as neighbours with whom we rub along but do not really like.

'Tartanry, Kailyardism, and Clydesideism'

It has been persuasively argued that without certainty in politics and con-stitutional affairs, the distinctive national identity from the past is too easily converted into stereotypes and caricatures. Ten years ago, just before the opening of the Scottish Parliament, the New York-based academic and media and communications authority Douglas Bicket warned that as long as an ambiguous state persisted it would be difficult to break away from the 'pernicious discourses: Tartanry, Kailyardism, and Clydesideism'.

Bicket said: 'They are the basis of such well-known stereotypes as the kilted buffoon; the drunken hard-bitten Scotsman and the canny, tight fisted Scotsman on the make. The central and abiding myths are those of the Kailyard – a nostalgic and overly sentimental parochialism: Tartanry – heavily romanticised depictions of heroic deeds of yesteryear against spectacular highland backdrops: Clydesideism – the Glasgow-centred 'dark and dangerous city' stereotype where urban squalor, religious strife and bigotry and social breakdown provide fast-moving thrillers or social realism pieces.'

Other images invoked by Bicket are – 'Glasgow hard men, prim Edinburgh lawyers, Clyde shipbuilders and rural very proper Presbyterian villagers, plucky Gaels and ruddy cheeked whisky swilling Highlanders in ridiculous plaid dress'.

Unfortunately, these images are still recognised as 'Scottish' although they have nothing to do with reality and the true Scottish identity. While they may provide 'typical' characters for film and TV writers and 'couthy' memories for exiles and are useful in promoting history-tourism, the overriding international image should be one of Scotland as a modern country.

Equally unfortunately, too many of our representatives at home and abroad play up to these stereotypes. A recent example would be the Scottish Nationalist MSP who called for stores to label and sell their goods 'according to the most commonly used Scots phrases north of the border', so that potatoes would be sold as 'tatties', swedes as 'neeps', turnips as 'tumshies' and Spring onions as 'syboes'. He was being serious – if it is possible to be serious and silly at the same time!

The Politics of Common Good

Cynics dismiss the discussion about the nation's happiness as mere psychobabble but that is too facile. It is a genuine attempt to address the problem of mood and morale affecting large sections of our population and reflects an international acceptance that the basic point of politics is to bring about the well-being of individuals and society as a whole.

In Scotland, the necessity for a crash course in confidence and wellbeing is clear in the description of the Scottish people by Professor Ed Diener quoted at the very beginning of this book: 'They said too much happiness might not be such a good thing. They like being dour, and didn't appreciate being told they should be happier.'

Happiness will not be achieved by political stability, economic improvement and material improvement, even if these conditions could be achieved. The realization is dawning that such things as optimism and self-esteem are more important, with the satisfaction that, as a nation, we are doing the right things for the right reasons – not out of selfishness and gratification.

Whether they like it or not, the political parties will be compelled to renew themselves and re-align. Instead of being dogmatic and thirled (to use a fine Scottish word) to confrontational squabbling, they will have to take account of the public mood which is more fluid and wants politics based on solutions to society's problems and not on knee-jerk traditionalism.

Both UK and Scottish parties have yet to take account of the new 'politics of the Common Good'. It may have to be long-term but we have to make a start now.

The 'You've never had it so good' catch-phrase was a politician's crude formula for the feel-good society and the late 20th century was typified by the desperate pursuit of economic growth, higher spending and better material conditions for the average family. But the luxury life-style of the few contrasts with the poverty of a significant but forgotten many; in Scotland the '80/20 society' continues to cast a shadow over our egalitarianism. This disparity of income and life style is worsening and the gap between the rich and poor is widening in the US and the UK, including Scotland.

However, the global economic crisis and the revulsion at the revelations of naked greed in the financial, corporate and political classes have caused people to re-examine their values and to question the true meaning of 'happiness' and 'success', both of self and society.

This has led to a new emphasis on 'the politics of the common good' or its other guises: the politics of fairness, the politics of connectedness, the politics of the citizen, the politics of reality, the politics of soul.

The electors and the wider public have to be taken seriously as mature and discerning partners in our democracy. In turn, disillusion must not blind them to the fact that democracy is not a once-every-couple-of-years visit to the polling station (and, for some, even this is too much of an effort). Parties must realise that pushing leaflets through letter-boxes, or, increasingly, cold-calling and e-mailing, for a few weeks prior to the election or political broadcasts more concerned with slickness than substance or presentation of issues in the most superficial ways using media too often cynical and negative is not enough and does little to inform, educate or inspire the electors during or between elections.

Professor Michael Sandel of Harvard University used his 2009 BBC Reith lectures to make the case for richer political debate underpinned by the need to put morality back into politics. He highlighted the need to refashion the political debate in an era where the end of market triumphalism is in sight and said we should now challenge the doctrine of the idea of public services being run to emulate the competitive market. The credit crunch has demonstrated how the market can get things so badly wrong.

In a thoughtful leader, *The Guardian* newspaper said there are things that 'we all bear moral responsibility for' and 'we should not put too much faith in technical brilliance'. The paper further argued we should be concerned about 'a strategy for replacing uncomfortable ethical choices with a seemingly technical argument'. These big issues need to be more openly and honestly debated and in doing so the political classes have to acknowledge there are tough choices to be made and priorities to be thrashed out but in a way which engages and informs the public and reframes the discourse between parties and politicians.

The 'Politics of the Common Good' based on fairness, equal opportunity, releasing potential, compassion, caring services, and inclusion is actually a combination of traditional Scottish values. The party which re-connects with these values (and it may have to be a new coalition of shared interests) will win the confidence of the Scottish people.

In Scotland, we have become a much less questioning and inquiring society and tend to accept given situations without critical response. This has not always been the case but the example of the period of the Enlightenment has all but been lost. Our society seems less concerned with searching for the truth and more willing to endure a diet of myth and spin masquerading as objective truth. What happened to the questing, questioning and democratic intellect that was once such a feature of the Scottish character and the hallmark of the Enlightenment?

As well as a more critically discerning citizenry, we need to develop sustainable politics in Scotland to meet higher public expectations. Becoming an aspirational society requires us to be less tolerant of words like 'average' or 'standard' or 'norm'; our ambitions should be set against our undoubted potential. Creating a positive culture in Scotland requires inspiring leadership and simple, strong messages that communicate with individuals and groups.

We all want to live in the Good Society, and Scotland can be that society. Utopian? That is not the Scottish way, we are practical and we do what we can, but change IS possible, if the will exists.

This final chapter was drafted in an idyllic setting that encapsulated Scotland's history: the terrace of a fine restaurant overlooking the beach at the ancient village of South Queensferry, between the iconic railway bridge and modern road bridge, with World War gun emplacements and an oil terminal offshore and a ferry from the Continent nearing its harbour. There was even a scorching summer sun! The authors could not but sit there and think: 'What a wonderful country and a wonderful nation!' It was in that spirit this book was written.

In moments of national fervour, some of our more maudlin compatriots beat their chests and chant *The Flower of Scotland*, the reiteration of 700-year-old grievance that masquerades as an unofficial national anthem: 'We can still rise now And be the nation again ...'

The question for modern Scots is: 'What kind of nation?'

Bibliography

Journal of Happiness Studies , Ed Diener. Joseph R. Smiley Distinguished
   Professor of Psychology, University of Illinois and *Newsweek* article
   Feb. 11, 2008.

*How the Scots Invented the Modern World: The True Story of How
   Western Europe's Poorest Nation Created Our World & Everything in
   It.* Arthur Herman. Sept. 2002.

Wee Book of Calvin Bill Duncan Penguin Books Nov 2004.

Scottish Left Review Identity Issue No. 43 Nov/Dec 2007.

Anglo-Scottish Stereotypes 2000 and *The Uses and Abuses of National
   Stereotypes* 1997 Isobel Lindsay Strathclyde University and Tubingen
   University.

The Lithuanians in Scotland John Millar 1998.

*Part of the Scottish Way of Life? Attitudes towards Drinking and Smoking
   in Scotland* – Social Attitudes Survey 2005.

Drug and alcohol services in Scotland Audit Scotland 2009.

How much are people in Scotland really drinking? NHS Scotland 2009;
   and Scottish Health Survey 2003.

Safer Scotland ACPOS and the national Violence Reduction Unit 2007,

European Crime and Safety Comparative Study, UN Interregional Crime
   and Justice Research Institute. 2005.

CCTV *Cities,* Channel Five. Nov 2008

Our nation laid bare – and it's a shameful sight. Lesley Riddoch,
   Scotsman, May 2008.

English People in Scotland: An Invisible Minority. Stirling University
   Department of Applied Social Science, 2008

Nation Speaking Unto Nation Douglas Fraser, IPPR North 'Future of the
   Union', 2008.

Confidence in Scotland Scottish government discussion paper 2004.

Towards a Confident Scotland and *The Scots' Crisis of Confidence,* Dr
   Carol Craig, Centre For Wellbeing And Confidence.

Being Young in Scotland Scottish government survey, 2003.

Scotland – the official gateway. www.scotland.org

Scottish Census 2001.

The Culture of Contentment, J.K. Galbraith 1998.

The Tipping Point. Malcolm Gladwell 2002

High Noon – 20 Global Problems, 20 Years to Solve Them, Francois Rischard 2002

Child poverty in Scotland: taking the next steps, Stephen Sinclair and John McKendrick, Joseph Rowntree. 2009

Culture, Institutions and Economic Development: a Study of Eight European Regions and *The Regional Challenge in Central and Eastern Europe* Michael Keating, Professor of Regional Studies at the European University Institute, Florence, and Aberdeen University.

A New Citizenship Professor Michael Sandel, Harvard Professor of Government, 2009 Reith Lecture, BBC.

Fictional Scotland in Film Drama and Literature Douglas Bicket Scottish Film and Literature, 1998.

Scotland: The Road Divides

Tom Brown and Henry McLeish
ISBN 1 906307 24 5 PBK £8.99

The Brown government must engage with the Scottish question while at the same time, ceding yet more British sovereignty to the European Union... it is here that the interests of the English and the other nationalities of the UK divide.
FRANK FIELD, MP

[This paper] is the first step in a national conversation
UK GOVERNMENT GREEN PAPER 2007
'THE GOVERNANCE OF BRITAIN'

This paper is the first step in a wide-ranging national conversation about the future of Scotland
SCOTTISH GOVERNMENT WHITE PAPER 2007 'CHOOSING SCOTLAND'S FUTURE'

This book aims to take these conversations forward, to engage in the key issues facing Scotland and the UK.

A hard-hitting, incisive and informed look at where the devolution journey has taken us – from the heady days of the new Blair government in 1997 to the dramatic events of 2007 – and where we go from here.

Global Scots: Making it in the Modern World

Kenny MacAskill and Henry McLeish
ISBN 1 905222 37 8 PBK £9.99

Why leave Scotland? What has Scotland provided? What has Scotland failed to provide? What does it mean to be Scottish elsewhere in the world?

Global Scots is a series of over 30 interviews with highly successful expatriate Scots around the world. The interviewees, all of whom grew up in Scotland – including iconic photographer Harry Benson; Chairman of Walt Disney Consumer Products, Andy Mooney; and comedian/presenter Craig Ferguson – reflect on issues such as identity, sectarianism and dour Scottish Sundays.

Although the interviewees vary in age, background and profession, certain values and feelings are universal. They all remain committed to the land they were brought up in, remaining distinctively Scottish no matter where they are in the world, be it Toronto or Tallinn. These voices from afar provide valuable insights into Scotland's role in the modern world. Reflective and often hard-hitting, the perspectives they offer on their native country are enlightening, entertaining and potentially beneficial to a new devolved Scotland.

Wherever the Saltire Flies

Kenny MacAskill and Henry McLeish
ISBN 1 905222 68 8 PBK £8.99

There's much more to Scottish societies than the stereotypical ceilidh club image. Over the years, societies all over the world have provided support and welfare to emigrant Scots, as well as providing social opportunities and business networking. They are also playing a major part in the preservation of Scottish culture and worldwide promotion of Scotland.

Scotlands of the Future: sustainability in a small nation

Edited by Eurig Scandrett
ISBN 1 84282 035 4 PBK £7.99

What sort of future is possible for Scotland?

How can citizens of a small nation at the periphery of the global economy make a difference?

Can Scotland's economy be sustainable?

How do we build a good quality of life without damaging others'?

Scotlands of the Future: sustainability in a small nation looks at where we've got to, where we can go next, and where we want to get to. Essential reading for those who think about and want to take action for a sustainable Scotland, and anyone else who cares about the future.

This book is a contribution to building a sustainable economy in Scotland, a change that will only come about through action throughout civil society. The contributors are all working for a sustainable economy at the front line: through trade unions, business organisations, the women's movement and environmental groups, and at Scotland's parliament. They bring their experiences of transforming the real world to their vision of a transformed Scotland.

EURIG SCANDRETT, Editor

Agenda for a New Scotland: Visions of Scotland 2020

ed. Kenny MacAskill

ISBN 1 905222 00 9   PBK   £9.99

The campaign for a Scottish Parliament was ongoing for centuries. Lamented in prose and championed in print. Petitioned for, marched in support of and voted upon. Dear to the hearts of many and whose absence broke the hearts of a few.

From Kenny MacAskill's Introduction to *Agenda for a New Scotland*

It has now reconvened after nearly 300 years. A Devolved Legislature but a Parliament all the same. Unable to address all issues but able to make a difference in many areas. It is for the Scottish Parliament to shape and mould the future of Scotland. But, what should that future be?

This is a series of contributed articles from politicians, academics and Civic Scotland. They outline opportunities and future directions for Scotland across a range of areas socially, economically and politically. This is an *Agenda for a New Scotland*. Visions of what Scotland can be by 2020.

Some Assembly Required: Scottish Parliament

David Shepherd

ISBN 1 946487 84 7   PBK   £7.99

Will the Scottish people make home rule work?

Will the Parliament building be ready in time?

Will the joiners ever finish their fag break?

It is perhaps a little-known fact that while Scotland's politicians were engaged in a fierce contest to secure seats in Scotland's first parliament for nearly 300 years, the local delivery men were busy trying to figure out how to get the plush blue seats into the Parliament in the first place. Covering the six month period leading up to the opening of the Parliament, this at times tongue-in-cheek account focuses on the intrigues, petty rivalries and humorous incidents which resulted when the Scottish Office and their army of building contractors invaded the normally peaceful Theological College and Church Hall on the Mound.
The story documents not only the gradual transformation of the work-site in preparation for the arrival of the politicians, but also the often frank opinions of the builders on both the job at hand and the future of Scotland and its new parliament.

Getting it Together: Scottish Parliament

Bob McLean

ISBN 1 905222 02 5 PBK £12.99

On 29 March 1999 the Campaign for a Scottish Parliament, which had been established as the Campaign for a Scottish Assembly on 1 March 1980, met for the last time. At that dissolution Bob McLean, the Campaign's Vice Convenor, was asked to undertake a history of the organisation. This is it.

There are several books on the often rocky road to Scottish home rule. The purpose of this particular account is a detailed record of one of the organisations campaigning for Scottish democracy. Drawn largely from primary sources it is essential reading for students of Scottish home rule and pressure group politics.

'Getting It Together' was a favourite catch phrase coined by the late Jim Boyack. As convenor, Jim held the organisation together during difficult and frustrating times. This book is dedicated to his memory, and to the efforts of all of those campaigned for a Scottish Assembly, or Parliament, with such powers as desired by the people of Scotland.

Eurovision or American Dream? Britain, Euro, Future of Europe

David Purdy

ISBN 1 84282 036 2 PBK £3.99

Should Britain join the euro?

Where is the European Union going?

Must America rule the world?

Eurovision or American Dream? assesses New Labour's prevarications over the euro and the EU's deliberations about its future against the background of transatlantic discord. Highlighting the contrasts between European social capitalism and American free market individualism, David Purdy shows how Old Europe's welfare states can be renewed in the age of the global market. This, he argues, is essential if European governments are to reconnect with their citizens and revive enthusiasm for the European project. It would also enable the EU to challenge US hegemony, not by transforming itself into a rival superpower, but by championing an alternative model of social development and changing the rules of the global game.

Scotland: Land and Power – agenda for land reform

Andy Wightman
ISBN 0 946487 70 7 PBK £5.00

Land reform campaigner Andy Wightman delivers a hard-hitting critique of the oppressive absurdities of Scotland's antiquated land laws. His is by no means a purely negative analysis – here are thought-through proposals for reforms which he argues would free both country and urban Scots from the shackles of land laws that are feudal and oppressive.

Andy Wightman's views are controversial, but he doesn't mind a good argument. He is an influential figure in Scottish political life these days. Those who don't agree with his views do pay attention to them, and his contribution to one of the hottest debates of the new millennium is well respected.

Writers like Andy Wightman are determined to make sure the hurt of the last century is not compounded by a rushed solution in the next. This accessible, comprehensive but passionately argued book is quite simply essential reading and perfectly timed – here's hoping Scotland's legislators agree.
LESLEY RIDDOCH

Reportage Scotland: History in the Making

Louise Yeoman
Foreword by Professor David Stevenson
ISBN 1 84282 051 6 PBK £6.99

Events – both major and minor – as seen and recorded by Scots throughout history.

Which king was murdered in a sewer? What was Dr Fian's love magic?

Who was the half-roasted abbot?

Which cardinal was salted and put in a barrel?

Why did Lord Kitchener's niece try to blow up Burns's cottage?

The answers can all be found in the eclectic mix covering nearly 2,000 years of Scottish history. Historian Louise Yeoman's rummage through the manuscript, book and newspapers archives of the National Library of Scotland has yielded an astonishing amount of material. Ranging from a letter to the King of the Picts to Mary Queen of Scots' own account of the murder of David Riccio; from the execution of William Wallace to accounts of anti-poll tax actions and the opening of the new Scottish Parliament. The book takes pieces from the original French, Latin, Gaelic and Scots and makes them accessible to the general reader, often for the first time.

Details of these and other books published by Luath Press can be found at: **www.luath.co.uk**

Luath Press Limited

committed to publishing well written books worth reading

LUATH PRESS takes its name from Robert Burns, whose little collie Luath (*Gael.*, swift or nimble) tripped up Jean Armour at a wedding and gave him the chance to speak to the woman who was to be his wife and the abiding love of his life. Burns called one of 'The Twa Dogs' Luath after Cuchullin's hunting dog in *Ossian's Fingal*. Luath Press was established in 1981 in the heart of Burns country, and is now based a few steps up the road from Burns' first lodgings on Edinburgh's Royal Mile. Luath offers you distinctive writing with a hint of unexpected pleasures.

Most bookshops in the UK, the US, Canada, Australia, New Zealand and parts of Europe either carry our books in stock or can order them for you. To order direct from us, please send a £sterling cheque, postal order, international money order or your credit card details (number, address of cardholder and expiry date) to us at the address below. Please add post and packing as follows: UK – £1.00 per delivery address; overseas surface mail – £2.50 per delivery address; overseas airmail – £3.50 for the first book to each delivery address, plus £1.00 for each additional book by airmail to the same address. If your order is a gift, we will happily enclose your card or message at no extra charge.

Luath Press Limited
543/2 Castlehill
The Royal Mile
Edinburgh EH1 2ND
Scotland

Telephone: 0131 225 4326 (24 hours)
Fax: 0131 225 4324
email: sales@luath.co.uk
Website: www.luath.co.uk